Tastefully Simple.
Simply Delicious.

How hot is *your* fire?

Hold your hand about 4" over the coals. Count the number of seconds you can hold your hand in place before it gets too hot to keep there.

Count, "1 Mississippi, 2 Mississippi, OUCH" = hot (about **500°**)

    3 seconds = medium-hot (about **400°**)

    4 seconds = medium (about **350°**)

    5 seconds = low (about **300°**)

*To create **"indirect heat,"** move coals or briquettes so they are not directly below the food.*

Printed in China

Distributed By:

507 Industrial Street
Waverly, IA 50677

ISBN 978-1-56383-492-9
Item #2910

Camping *Insanity* Busters

🏠 Create a camping checklist that works for you and refer to it before every camping trip. Include the basics *(pillows)*, things that are easy to overlook *(chip clips and twisty ties)*, and special items *(stuffed animals or medications)*.

🏠 Have well-stocked totes, boxes, or bags that you'll take with you on every camping trip. You might keep one loaded with cooking/eating basics like plates, utensils, and pots & pans and the other with camping essentials such as flashlights, rain gear, and sunscreen. Restock after every trip.

🏠 Plan your food in advance and shop for everything you'll need ahead of time.

🏠 Prep as much food beforehand as possible.

🏠 Chill your drinks before packing them in your cooler to make sure they're ice cold as soon as you get to your destination.

🔺 If you're camping with pets, keep their needs in mind, too. Keep Fido on a leash, make sure he has plenty of food and water, and a toy or two might be a good idea.

🔺 Keep charcoal in a large lidded plastic container so it won't get wet.

🔺 Lay a tarp on your tent floor so dirt can be easily removed.

Anything you can do to make your camp time more relaxing, will be well worth the advance planning.

Now, go out and have some fun!

🏠 = to do at home   🔺 = to consider while camping

This is a great one to share with your camping neighbors.

Cheesy Jalapeño Loaf

1 (8 oz.) pkg. shredded sharp Cheddar cheese

¼ C. chopped pickled jalapeños, drained

½ C. chopped green onions

¼ C. butter, melted and cooled slightly

1 loaf unsliced round crusty bread, such as ciabatta

Sea salt and dried oregano to taste

take along

foil

cooking spray

sharp knife

large foil pan

cooking rack

tongs

hot pads

4

Stir together cheese, jalapeños, onions, and butter (you can do this right in the cheese bag, if you'd like).

Coat a large piece of foil with cooking spray and set the bread in the center. Slice bread lengthwise and crosswise without cutting through the bottom; stuff cheese mixture evenly into cuts. Sprinkle with salt and oregano. Wrap foil around bread and seal edges.

Place in a foil pan and set the whole thing on a cooking rack over hot coals. Heat until cheese is melted, rotating occasionally.

More to Share

Phyllo Bites: Fill mini phyllo shells with your favorite ready-to-eat filling (pudding, pie filling, cheesecake filling). Garnish if you'd like.

Trail Mix: Peanuts, almonds, cashews, sunflower nuts, chocolate and white chips, dried blueberries and cherries, flaked coconut...

Foil Pack

Make the chicken salad at home; then at camp, stuff the pitas and set in hot coals.

Hot Chicken Salad Pitas

2 C. cubed, cooked chicken

1 C. diced celery

½ C. slivered almonds

1 C. mayonnaise

2 T. fresh lemon juice

1 C. shredded sharp Cheddar cheese

Salt and black pepper to taste

∧ Pita breads

∧ Cherry tomatoes, optional

∧ = for use at camp

take along

foil

tongs

hot pads

Chilling gives the flavors a chance to blend. And you end up with a creamy-crunchy filling that's just right. Go on – stuff 'em full.

at Home 🏠

In a lidded storage container, stir together chicken, celery, almonds, mayonnaise, cheese, salt, and pepper. Chill.

at Camp ⛺

Stuff chicken mixture into pitas and wrap in foil. Set in hot coals until heated through. Open 'em up and add tomatoes if you'd like.

Try this

By cutting your chicken, celery, and almonds into small pieces, you can store the chicken salad in a zippered plastic bag. Then at camp, you can simply cut off one corner of the bag and squeeze the chicken mixture into pitas. Throw away the bag and there are no dirty dishes to deal with. Neat, huh?

Mix up these drink concentrates at home. Then turn them into thirst-quenching beverages at the campground.

Iced Coffee

At home, place ½ C. ground coffee in a 1-qt. mason jar and fill with water. Cover and let set at room temperature for 8 hours. Pour liquid through a coffee filter-lined strainer; repeat with a fresh filter. Discard solids and pour liquid into a clean 1-qt. jar. Add water to fill jar. Cover and chill.

At camp, fill a 1-pt. mason jar with ice and fill ⅔ full with coffee concentrate. Add a generous splash of half & half and 2 to 3 T. sweetened condensed milk; stir well, sip and say "Ahhhhh." Keep remaining concentrate chilled until needed.

8

"Daiquiri" Delight

At home, combine 3 C. sliced strawberries and 6 T. apple juice in a blender; process until smooth and pour into a 1-quart mason jar. Repeat with an additional 3 C. berries and 6 T. juice. Stir in 6 oz. frozen limeade concentrate (thawed); cover and chill.

At camp, divide strawberry concentrate evenly among four 1-pt. mason jars. Add lime slices, ice, and ¼ to ½ C. lemon-lime soda to each jar; stir. Garnish with sliced strawberries before serving, if desired.

Mason Sippers

You'll need rubber grommets with a hole at least ⅜" in diameter to hold a straw. Drill an off-center hole in a metal mason jar lid, ¹⁄₁₆" larger than hole in grommet (set lid on scrap wood to drill the hole). Fit grommet into hole. Fill jar with your favorite beverage and attach lid with ring. Add straw and sip.

Tropi-Cooler

At home, combine 1½ C. each orange and pineapple juices, ¾ C. lemon juice, and ½ C. sugar; stir to dissolve. Pour mixture into a 1-qt. mason jar; cover and chill.

At camp, divide citrus concentrate among four 1-pt. mason jars. Add ice and about ¼ C. plain or lemon-flavored soda water to each jar; stir. Garnish with sliced oranges or lemons before serving.

9

Pie Iron Breakfasts

Nothing beats breakfast by the campfire. Try these pie iron versions – quick and easy, but oh-so delish!

Stuffed Toast

Mix an egg with a little milk and dip both sides of a slice of cinnamon bread into it. Fit into one side of a greased pie iron. Add a few pats of cream cheese, some chopped nuts and chopped peaches, and a sprinkle of sugar. Dip another bread slice in egg and set on top. Close iron; cook over hot coals until both sides are brown.

Cheesy Bacon Buns

Beat an egg with a bit of milk. Cut each biscuit from an 8-count can of jumbo refrigerated flaky biscuits into eight pieces; add to egg mixture. Stir in chopped precooked bacon, shredded Cheddar cheese, and chopped green onion. Fill one side of a greased pie iron with mixture, close iron, and cook over warm coals until done, turning only once near the end of cooking. *YUM!*

Blueberry Pancakes

Place a frozen pancake (thawed) on one side of a greased pie iron. Add some cream cheese and blueberry pie filling. Top with another pancake, close iron, and cook over hot coals, turning to brown both sides. **Delicious!**

Veggie Frittata

Line one side of a greased pie iron with bacon pieces. Add a few thin potato slices and some broccoli slaw. Beat an egg with a bit of milk; pour over slaw until iron is nearly full. Sprinkle with Italian seasoning. Close iron; cook over warm coals, without turning, until egg is done.

Monte Cristo

Mix an egg with a little milk. Between two halves of an English muffin, layer Swiss and Cheddar cheeses, deli ham, and smoked turkey; add mayo and mustard. Dip into egg mixture; cook in a greased pie iron in hot coals until brown on both sides.

Nachos over the fire? Yes, indeed, and they are hot and delightfully cheesy!

Cast Iron Nachos

Tortilla chips, any variety

Chili con queso cheese sauce

Chopped green onion, tomato, and bell pepper

Taco meat

Sliced black olives

Your favorite shredded cheese

▲ Sour cream

▲ Salsa

▲ Guacamole

▲ = for use at camp

take along

cast iron skillet

cooking rack

hot pads

*Layer upon layer of
goodness goes into the skillet.*

In a large cast iron skillet, layer chips, cheese sauce, green onion, tomato, bell pepper, meat, olives, and shredded cheese. Repeat layers. Set on a cooking rack over warm coals until cheese melts, covering with foil to help melt cheese, if needed.

*That pan will get hot –
use your hot pads!*

Serve with

*sour cream, salsa,
guacamole, and any
other favorites.*

Mix & marinate at home and tuck into your cooler for easy transport to the campground.

Mediterranean Kabobs

¼ C. fresh lemon juice

1 tsp. salt

1 tsp. black pepper

2 tsp. whole-grain mustard

2 T. finely chopped fresh rosemary

¼ C. olive oil

2 lb. boneless chicken breast, cubed

2 red onions, quartered and separated

Cherry tomatoes

Kalamata olives

▲ Cucumber ranch salad dressing

▲ = for use at camp

take along

skewers

cooking spray

cooking rack

tongs

hot pads

at Home 🏠

In a large zippered plastic bag, combine all ingredients except dressing; squeeze to mix. Chill.

at Camp ⛺

Thread meat and veggies onto skewers; discard marinade. Cook kabobs on a greased cooking rack over hot coals until meat is cooked through, rotating skewers now and then to brown. Serve with dressing.

Using wooden skewers? Soak them in cool water for 15 to 30 minutes before using.

Tip

To prevent accidental pokes, push a foam ball over tines of roasting sticks.

Tool Tote

Cut a leg from blue jeans at least 5" longer than your roasting sticks. Hot glue lower edges together. Fold about 1¾" of cut edge to the inside and hot glue edge in place for casing. Cut a short slit through outside of casing near each seam. Insert a 32" cord into one slit, through casing, and out the same hole. Repeat with a second cord through other hole. Knot each cord end. Decorate bag and fill with roasting sticks. Cinch closed to transport.

Cut into pieces and let everyone have a bite. Or eat the whole thing yourself if it's too good to share.

Shrimp Puffs

Mix a 4.5 oz. can tiny shrimp (drained) with 2 chopped green onions, a beaten egg, 1 T. cornstarch, and 2 tsp. water. Cut thawed puff pastry to fit in pie iron. Place some shrimp mixture between two pastry pieces; set in greased iron, close, and toast in warm coals.

Cheesy Italian

Split a Pepperidge Farms Deli Flats thin roll and set half in a greased pie iron. Add a slice of tomato, chunks of goat cheese or fresh mozzarella, and your favorite herbs and spices (anything goes). Cover with remaining roll half, close iron, and cook over hot coals to melt cheese.

Deli Surprise

Press a refrigerated "Grands" biscuit into each half of a greased pie iron. On one half, layer diced ham, cheese curds, and dill pickle slices. Close iron and cook over warm coals until biscuits are done.

Party Rye-Wiches

Mix ½ lb. browned and drained ground sausage, ¼ lb. cubed Velveeta, ¼ tsp. oregano, ⅛ tsp. garlic salt, and a dash of Worcestershire. Butter rye bread slices and put one in each half of pie iron, butter side out. Add some meat mixture, close iron, trim, and toast in hot coals.

Crab Bites

Mix a 6 oz. can crab meat (drained), 3 oz. soft cream cheese, 2 T. chopped green onion, and ½ tsp. garlic salt; put a little on a refrigerated crescent roll. Roll up, pinching ends. Set side-by-side in a greased pie iron, close, and heat slowly over warm coals until cooked.

17

Cheesy, spicy, and grilled. Simple, quick, and M-M good! Gotta love 'em!

Buffalo Chicken Hand Pies

2 boneless chicken breast
   halves, cubed and cooked

½ C. wing sauce

8 oz. shredded Pepper Jack
   cheese

4 oz. shredded Cheddar cheese

⅓ C. ranch dressing

Salt and black pepper to taste

1 (14.1 oz.) pkg. refrigerated
   pie crusts

▲ Extra ranch dressing

take along

grill
foil pie plate
shallow foil pan
tongs
hot pads

▲ = for use at camp

18

*Both sides are
nice and toasty.*

at Home 🏠

Stir together chicken, wing sauce, both cheeses, ⅓ cup dressing,
salt, and pepper. Cut each pie crust into three 5½" to 6" circles.
Put a little of the chicken mixture over each circle, leaving ¼"
along edge. Dampen edges of dough with water, fold circle in half,
and crimp with a fork. Wrap in foil; chill or freeze.

at Camp ⛰

Thaw packs, if frozen. Set a foil pie plate upside down on grill rack
and place a shallow foil pan on top of it. Remove pies from foil
and set in top pan; close grill. Cook over medium-high heat for
15 minutes or until nicely browned on both sides.

Variation

*Instead of pie crust, use two 8-count packages refrigerated crescent
roll dough. Press sets of two triangles together to make eight
rectangles. Fill, fold, chill or freeze, and cook as directed.*

19

Muffin tins make fantastic little "ovens" for all sorts of foods. Try these ideas.

Muffin Tin Meals

Biscuit baking mix, any flavor*

Chunks of fresh corn on the cob

Crumbled pork sausage

For convenience, try one that mixes with water only. We used a Cheddar & garlic mix.

Eggs & Bacon

Place two half-strips of cooked bacon in the bottom and up the side of each muffin cup; add a spinach leaf. Crack an egg into each cup (or scramble first).

Line each cup of one muffin tin with a foil liner. Make biscuit batter according to package directions; fill two compartments half full with batter, fill two with corn, and two with sausage. Place second muffin tin upside down over first tin and hook together with metal clips. Set on a cooking rack over hot coals and add a few hot coals on top. Cook for 15 minutes or until food is cooked through.

Cover with second muffin tin and clip together.

Note

Adding coals on top helps your meal cook from the top and makes those biscuits toasty brown.

Cook until done.

21

Foil Pack Tidbits

These quick-pack recipes are a cinch to put together and they cook perfectly in foil.

Spicy Shrimp

Toss frozen peeled and deveined shrimp with olive oil; add minced garlic, red pepper flakes, a lemon wedge, and fresh herbs (try rosemary, thyme, dill, or others) to taste. Wrap in foil; cook in hot coals for 10 to 15 minutes, turning occasionally.

Roasted Nuts

Stir together 2 C. salted mixed nuts, 1 tsp. chili powder, ¼ tsp. cumin, and ¼ tsp. black pepper; add a few pats of butter. Wrap in foil; cook in warm coals until heated, turning often.

Jerk'd Wings

Coat chicken wing sections with oil and jerk seasoning to taste. Wrap in foil; cook in hot coals for 25 minutes or until done, turning once. Serve with lime.

Mixed 'Shrooms

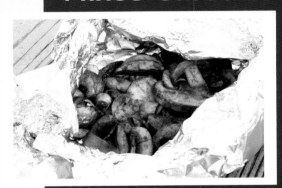

Toss a combination of mushrooms (try cremini, shiitake, Portobello or others) with oil and add garlic, dill weed, salt, and pepper to taste. Wrap in foil; cook in warm coals until hot, turning once.

Mexi-Corn

Brush melted butter over shucked sweet corn. Drizzle with lime juice and sprinkle with Mexican cheese and cayenne pepper to taste. Wrap individually in foil; cook in hot coals until done, turning occasionally.

A great way to have breakfast waiting for you the first morning at the campground!

Overnight Oatmeal

1 C. old-fashioned rolled oats

1 C. milk

1 C. Greek yogurt (flavored or plain)

2¼ tsp. ground cinnamon

2 to 3 T. flax seed

¾ C. chopped fresh fruit

▲ Extra fresh fruit

▲ *= for use at camp*

at Home 🏠

Stir together oats, milk, yogurt, cinnamon, flax seed, and ¾ cup fruit. Spoon into lidded half-pint fruit jars, tighten lids, and chill overnight.

at Camp ⛺

In the morning, simply open jars, add extra fruit, and dig in! (These will stay fresh for days if kept chilled.)

Why not

Make a variety so everybody gets their favorite! Set out brown sugar, sugar, syrup, and honey.

Repurpose

Cut a circle from sandpaper and thin cardboard to fit inside a jelly jar ring; punch a hole through both with a paper punch. Fill jar with strike-anywhere matches; add lid. Shake out matches; light on sandpaper.

Cut a circle around the pour spout of an empty round cardboard salt box to fit inside a jelly jar ring. Fill jars and top with the new spouted lid.

Comfort food while you camp?
This recipe makes it easy!

Individual Chicken Casseroles

2 C. cooked white rice, cooled

4 boneless chicken breast halves, cut into small pieces

4 C. chopped fresh broccoli

1 (10.7 oz.) can cream of chicken soup

½ C. ranch dressing

1 (12 oz.) pkg. Cheddar cheese curds

Salt, pepper, and garlic powder to taste

take along

tongs

hot pads

at Home 🏠

Stir together rice, chicken, broccoli, soup, dressing, cheese curds, salt, pepper, and garlic powder. Coat six large pieces of foil with cooking spray and divide chicken mixture evenly among them. Seal edges of foil. Chill or freeze.

at Camp ⛺

Thaw pack, if frozen. Cook in hot coals for 25 minutes or until chicken is done. As with all foil packs, open carefully; the steam inside is very hot.

For the best pizzas, cook over indirect heat by moving hot coals to one side of cooking area so they're not directly below pizzas.

End-of-Trip Pie

Pat a roll of refrigerated pizza dough onto greased foil. Set on a rack over medium-hot coals and cook until bottom of crust is golden brown. Spray top with cooking spray and flip crust over on foil. Spread with sauce of your choice and add leftover veggies, meat, cheese, and herbs. Cook until crust is done and cheese is melted.

BLT Blowout

Cut a refrigerated crescent roll sheet in half lengthwise. Set on a rack over indirect heat to brown bottom. Flip crusts onto a cutting board; spread with mayonnaise. Add Parmesan and Cheddar cheeses and cooked bacon. Return to heat. Cook until cheese melts, adding tomatoes, black pepper, and arugula near end of cooking.

Tip

Cover pizzas with foil, if needed, so cheese melts.

Garden Goodness

Set a corn tortilla on a rack over indirect heat for a minute or two until slightly brown. Remove from rack and add a thin layer of tomato sauce, salt, red pepper flakes, mozzarella cheese, cooked sweet corn, halved cherry tomatoes, and feta cheese. Return to heat until hot.

Sausage & Bells

Spray both sides of a purchased thin and crispy pizza crust with cooking spray. Spread with seasoned tomato sauce, sprinkle with shredded mozzarella cheese, and add cooked Italian sausage and grilled bell peppers. Set on a rack over indirect heat until cheese melts.

Chicken Alfredo

Brush a purchased gourmet pizza crust with olive oil. Top with Alfredo sauce, grilled chicken, salt, black pepper, baby spinach, cherry tomato halves, and shredded mozzarella cheese. Set on a rack over indirect heat until cheese melts.

29

*Green bean casserole over the fire?
You betcha!*

Bean & Fry Delight

2 (16 oz.) pkgs. frozen cut
   green beans

1 (28 oz.) pkg. frozen
   steak fries

1 (10.7 oz.) can cream
   of mushroom soup

1 (8 oz.) pkg. sliced fresh
   mushrooms

1 tsp. salt

1 tsp. pepper

½ tsp. paprika

2 T. butter

take along

tongs

hot pads

foil pan, optional

Adding butter in a foil pack helps keep everything juicy and delicious during cooking.

at Home 🏠

Break frozen fries in half crosswise. Stir together fries, beans, mushrooms, soup, salt, pepper, and paprika. Coat two large pieces of foil with cooking spray. Divide bean mixture evenly among foil pieces; dot with butter. Wrap foil around mixture, sealing edges. Refrigerate.

at Camp ⛺

Set foil packs in a foil pan and set the whole thing in hot coals (or set foil pack directly in warm coals). Cook until potatoes are hot and beans are tender.

Delicious side dish, or a meal on its own.

Lemon Cookies

For each, cut 2 (1") slices from refrigerated sugar cookie dough and pat one into each side of a pie iron. Spread one with some lemon curd. Close iron and heat slowly over warm coals until cookie is baked, turning often. Let stand in iron a few minutes before removing.

Stuffed PB Cookies

For each, cut 2 (1") slices from refrigerated peanut butter cookie dough and pat one into each side of a pie iron. Place ½ of a Nestle Crunch bar on one side. Close iron and heat slowly on both sides over warm coals until cookie is baked and luscious. Let stand in iron a few minutes before removing.

PB Brownies

Press a brownie into each side of a greased pie iron. Spread each with peanut butter. Add some Reese's Pieces and chocolate chips; close iron. Heat over warm coals, turning occasionally, until hot and melty.

Berry Pies

For each, cut a pie crust into four even wedges. Place one wedge in a greased pie iron and top with fresh fruit. Place another wedge over fruit. Close iron; trim off excess. Heat over warm coals until nicely browned on both sides. Icing is optional.

Cinnamon Bites

Press a refrigerated cinnamon roll into each side of a greased pie iron. Add a little cream cheese and sugar; close iron. Heat over warm coals until golden brown and cooked through, turning often. Frost if you'd like.

Cooking in foil makes clean-up a breeze, plus the smoky flavor tastes great.

Foiled Pesto Pasta

Cooked spaghetti, drained

Chopped tomato

Your favorite pesto

Minced garlic, salt, and black pepper to taste

Goat cheese (try one of the flavored varieties)

Olive oil

Fresh lemon

Chopped fresh basil, optional

take along

tongs

hot pads

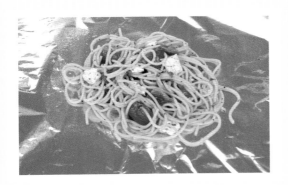

at Home 🏠

Stir together spaghetti, tomato, pesto, garlic, salt, and pepper; place on a large piece of foil that has been coated with cooking spray. Add bits of cheese; drizzle with a little oil and lemon juice. Toss a lemon wedge on top and sprinkle with basil. Wrap foil around mixture, sealing edges. Refrigerate.

at Camp ⛺

Heat in warm coals until everything is nice and hot. Add a little more basil before serving, if you'd like.

Foiled Again...

Following package directions, set a Jiffy Pop popper on a camp stove or over a fire until corn pops.

Yummy fun!

Nothing says family time like popcorn!

Jazz up traditional S'mores with new fillings & flavors. They're S'mores... have fun with 'em!

Zesty Orange

chocolate graham crackers, milk chocolate, orange zest, and a toasted marshmallow

Strawberry Cream

cinnamon graham crackers, softened cream cheese, sliced fresh strawberries, and a toasted marshmallow

Lemon-Coconut

graham crackers,
lemon curd, toasted
coconut, and a
toasted marshmallow

Choco-Raspberry

graham crackers,
raspberry jam, dark
chocolate, and a
toasted marshmallow

Cashew-Brownie

graham crackers,
brownie pieces, chopped
cashews, and a
toasted marshmallow

Anytime is taco time. Corn tortillas make fun shells for your pie iron.

Taco Time

- 1 lb. ground beef, browned, crumbled, and drained
- 1 (1 oz.) pkg. taco seasoning
- ∧ 12 small corn tortillas
- ∧ Chopped onion

- ∧ Shredded Cheddar or Monterey Jack cheese
- ∧ Diced tomato
- ∧ Salsa
- ∧ Sour cream

∧ = for use at camp

take along

pie iron
cooking spray

Keep it simple. Prep as much as you can at home for any camping meal to save steps when you're at the campsite.

at Home 🏠

Mix ground beef, taco seasoning, and water as directed on taco seasoning packet. Cool and pack into a lidded plastic container; chill.

at Camp ⚠

Spray a pie iron with cooking spray and set a tortilla on one side. Place some taco meat, onion, and cheese on tortilla. Set another tortilla on top, close iron, and cut off excess.

Cook over hot coals until tortillas have browned and filling is hot. Serve with tomato, salsa, and sour cream.

Corn tortillas can take the heat and come out crisp and delicious.

Make breakfast, lunch, and dinner in just a few minutes with an insulated travel mug.

Nutty Apricot Cream

In a travel mug, combine 1 (1 oz.) pkg. instant original flavored cream of wheat, 2 T. instant nonfat dry milk, a few ground walnuts, 2 tsp. maple syrup, 1 T. brown sugar, 1 T. toasted coconut, a pinch of salt, and ¾ C. boiling water. Stir well. Cover with lid and foil; let set for 3 minutes. Stir in 1 chopped apricot. Cover and let set again about 7 minutes or until thick.

Veggie Noodle Soup

In each of two travel mugs, combine ¼ C. shredded carrot, a handful of sugar snap peas, and 1 slice finely chopped salami. Divide a 1.6 oz. pkg. instant rice noodle soup (such as Thai Kitchen's Garlic & Vegetable) plus its flavor packet(s) between the two mugs. Fill each with boiling water. Cover with lid and foil; let set about 4 minutes or until noodles are tender.

Curried Shrimp & Rice

In each of two travel mugs, combine ½ C. instant rice, 1 T. raisins, 1 T. chopped dried apple, 1½ tsp. dried minced onion, ½ tsp. curry powder, 1½ tsp. olive oil, and a pinch each of ground allspice, ground cinnamon, and sea salt. Drain a 4 oz. can tiny shrimp and divide between mugs. Stir ½ C. boiling water into each. Cover with lid and foil; let set for 15 to 18 minutes or until rice is tender. Add chopped cashews and seafood sauce, if desired.

Tip

Cover travel mugs tightly so the heat stays inside.

Chili & cornbread make a great combo. Cook them together for an all-in-one meal.

Stuffed Cornbread

1 (8.5 oz.) pkg. corn muffin mix

Other ingredients listed on muffin mix package

▲ Prepared chili

▲ Shredded Pepper Jack cheese

▲ Sour cream, optional

▲ = for use at camp

take along

pie iron
cooking spray

at Home 🏠

Prepare muffin batter as directed on package, but spread in a greased 9 x 13" baking pan (so baked cornbread is thin). Bake for 7 minutes or until done; cool. Cover pan.

at Camp ⛺

Grease your pie iron and cut cornbread to fit. For each, layer one cornbread piece, some chili, a little cheese, and another cornbread piece. Close iron and cook until nicely toasted on both sides. Serve with sour cream.

Open the iron and peek inside occasionally to see how it's doing in there.

Don't worry

If your cornbread pieces crumble, just push them together to fit in your pie iron.

This is a great breakfast to serve the gang.
Dump. Cook. Eat. Yum.

Breakfast Skillet

¼ lb. bacon

½ (12 oz.) pkg. pork sausage

1 C. chopped bell peppers,
any color

⅔ C. chopped green onions

½ (8 oz.) pkg. sliced fresh
mushrooms

4½ C. frozen Southern style
hash browns

Ʌ = *for use at camp*

Ʌ Vegetable oil

Ʌ 5 or 6 eggs

Ʌ Salt and black pepper
to taste

take along

large cast iron
skillet

cooking rack

hot pads

at Home 🏠

Cook bacon and sausage until nearly done. During the last 5 minutes, add bell peppers and green onions. During last minute or two, add mushrooms. When meat is done, drain grease and transfer to a large bowl. Stir in frozen hash browns. Pile it all into a 1-gallon zippered plastic bag and toss in the fridge.

at Camp ⛺

Heat a bit of oil in a large cast iron skillet on a cooking rack over hot coals. Dump meat mixture into skillet. Add eggs, stirring to mix. Cook until everything is hot and eggs are cooked, stirring occasionally. Sprinkle with salt and black pepper.

FYI

This recipe fits nicely in a 10" skillet.

More Skillet Fun

Peppered Eggs: Cook ½"-thick bell pepper rings in an oiled skillet over hot coals about 1 minute. Break an egg in the center of each; season and cook until set.

Pineapple Cakes: Dip drained pineapple rings into pancake batter. Cook in an oiled skillet over hot coals. Serve with maple syrup and cinnamon.

45

Eat right out of the same pan you cook in and you won't even have to wash the dishes.

Pasta Boats

At home, mix cooked pasta, sauce, and Parmesan cheese. Refrigerate in a lidded plastic container.

At camp, hollow out French rolls; spread with butter, sprinkle with garlic salt, and fill with pasta mixture. Set in a single layer in a foil pan. Cover with foil and set in warm coals until heated through.

Stuffed Peppers

At home, stir together ½ C. whipped cream cheese, ½ C. feta cheese, black pepper, and diced tomato, green onion, and green olives. Transfer to a zippered plastic bag; refrigerate.

At camp, remove stem end and seeds from banana peppers. Cut corner from bag; squeeze to fill peppers. Set in foil pan, propping up filled ends with foil; cover with foil and set in warm coals until peppers have softened.

Citrus Salmon

Line a foil pan with lemon slices. Add a salmon fillet, shredded carrot, and broccoli florets. Top with a few butter pats, salt, lemon pepper, and dill weed. Cover with foil and set in hot coals until salmon flakes easily.

Swiss Steak

Arrange onion slices in a foil pan to cover bottom; set minute steaks on top and sprinkle with seasoned salt and paprika. Add green bell pepper rings and pour canned diced tomatoes over all. Cover with foil; set on hot coals until meat is cooked.

Spuds & Burgers

Place onion slices in a foil pan to cover bottom; add potato and sweet potato slices, butter, salt, and pepper. Set sausage patties on top; sprinkle with parsley. Cover with foil and set in warm coals until meat is done, setting several hot coals on top toward end of cooking.

Perfect for camping! They stack, are ready when you are, and let's face it – they're fun!

Layered Veggie Salad

⅓ C. apple cider vinegar

⅓ C. sugar

¼ C. olive oil

1½ tsp. salt

¼ tsp. black pepper

½ red onion, finely chopped

2 celery stalks, finely chopped

1 (15 oz.) can cannellini beans, rinsed and drained

1 C. chopped fresh parsley

1 (15 oz.) can kidney beans, rinsed and drained

1 yellow bell pepper, chopped

1 (15 oz.) can black beans, rinsed and drained

1 T. finely chopped fresh rosemary

at Home 🏠

Whisk together vinegar, sugar, oil, salt, and pepper; divide evenly among eight half-pint fruit jars. In each jar, layer remaining ingredients. Tighten lids and pack in cooler.

at Camp ⛺

Shake jars to distribute dressing. Grab a fork and eat right out of the jars. These will keep for several days.

Just for you

Personalize these salads any way you'd like by using different veggies (frozen corn kernels, green beans, or cucumbers) or changing the dressing (try olive oil with a little lemon juice and seasonings or even a simple bottled Italian dressing). It's all good.

Layered Lettuce

Put salad dressing on the bottom followed by a hearty vegetable that won't get soggy in the dressing (think pea pods or cherry tomatoes). Then add all your favorites, leaving room for leafy greens on top.

Add a lid, chill, & enjoy.

Stays fresh for days.

More S'mores

S'mores by any other name are still just as sweet. Whether made at home or at the campground, you just have to have your s'mores.

S'more Pie

Pour chocolate chips into a mini graham cracker crust. Put a jumbo or regular marshmallow on top. Set the whole thing onto a strip of foil and lower it down into the coals. When toasted, lift out using the foil. Add a candy bar square to the top.

S'more Squares

Beat ⅔ C. sugar, ½ C. softened butter, ½ tsp. vanilla, and 1 egg. Stir in 2⅓ C. graham cracker crumbs, ⅓ C. flour, and ⅛ tsp. salt. Reserve 2 C. mixture; press remainder into a greased 9 x 13" baking pan. Sprinkle with 2 C. chocolate chips; use a wet spoon to spread 7 oz. marshmallow creme over the top. Sprinkle with 1 C. mini marshmallows and remaining crumb mixture. Bake for 20 minutes at 350°.

S'more Chow

Melt together 1 C. chocolate chips and ½ C. creamy peanut butter; stir in ¾ C. mini marshmallows to melt slightly. Add 6 C. Golden Grahams cereal and ¾ C. mini marshmallows; stir to coat. Add to a large bag with 1½ C. powdered sugar; shake, shake shake.

S'more Corn

Boil 1 C. brown sugar, ½ C. butter, and ½ C. corn syrup for 5 minutes. Remove from heat. Stir in ½ tsp. baking soda and pour over a combo of 10 C. popped popcorn, 1 pkg. mini marshmallows, 2 C. Teddy Grahams, and 1 C. chocolate chips; stir to coat. Shape into balls.

S'more Dips

Dip untoasted marshmallows into melted chocolate and roll in graham cracker crumbs.

This cooks to delicious perfection over the fire. Who knew?

Fruity Bread Pudding

3 large baked croissants

1 egg

½ C. milk

¼ C. sugar

1 tsp. vanilla extract

½ tsp. ground cinnamon

Fresh berries, such as strawberries, raspberries, and/or blueberries

take along

foil pie plate

foil

tongs

hot pads

You can use any of your favorite fruits in this recipe. Do you love peaches? Cherries? Toss 'em in there.

Tear croissants into bite-size pieces and place in a greased foil pie plate. Stir together egg, milk, sugar, vanilla, and cinnamon; pour over the bread and stir. Sprinkle berries on top. Set on a large piece of foil; bring foil up and over pie plate and seal edges.

Set in warm coals for 20 to 30 minutes or until bread is slightly crisp and all liquid has evaporated, rotating occasionally.

Note

Put a few hot coals on top of the foil toward the end of cooking to help crisp the top, if you'd like.

53

Cherries, chocolate, cream cheese, and cookies? This dessert pizza has it all.

Grilled Cherry Chocolate Pizza

½ (8 oz.) tub whipped cream cheese

5 T. sugar

1 sheet puff pastry, thawed

Cherry pie filling

Mini semi-sweet chocolate chips

Chopped butter cookies or oatmeal cookies

take along

grill

foil

cooking spray

tongs

hot pads

Preheat grill to medium-high heat. Stir together cream cheese and sugar. Coat a large piece of foil with cooking spray and set on grill rack; unfold pastry on foil. Close grill and cook until bottom is golden brown. Flip crust; spread with cream cheese mixture. Top with pie filling and chocolate chips. Close grill; cook until bottom of crust is golden. Remove from grill and top with cookies.

Variation

Replace puff pastry with pizza dough; omit cream cheese and sugar. After flipping, sprinkle with chocolate chips; spread when soft. Top with pie filling; cook until bottom is brown. Remove from grill; top with granola and icing.

Grilled Sweets

Cut a glazed donut in half crosswise; spray with cooking spray. Grill on foil over medium heat, flipping to toast both sides. Toss in cinnamon/sugar.

Yum-yum!

Flatten balls of cookie dough; grill on foil – low and slow until done.

55

Kabobs are perfect camping fare, and the possibilities are practically endless.

Meatball Sub

Cut flatbread into 1" strips and thread one onto a skewer, followed by partially cooked bacon, a large cheese curd, cherry tomato, fully cooked frozen meatball (thawed), and a chunk of banana pepper. Thread another bread strip on the end. Hold over warm coals until meatballs are hot. Stir together equal parts mayo and BBQ sauce to serve alongside.

Chick 'n Spuds

Push a skewer through frozen chicken nuggets (thawed), gherkin pickles, and frozen steak fries (thawed). Brush with olive oil. Set on a rack over warm coals until everything is heated through and starts to brown. During the last couple of minutes, slide a large cheese curd on the end of the stick until softened. Dunk pieces into your favorite sauce.

Breakfast Anytime

Push a skewer through chunks of fresh peaches, cooked breakfast sausages (thawed), and frozen French toast sticks (thawed). Sprinkle with cinnamon/sugar. Set on a rack over warm coals until toasty. Serve with maple syrup.

Taste of Italy

Thread fully cooked frozen shrimp (thawed), cherry tomatoes, black olives, fresh mushrooms, and Italian bread chunks onto skewers. Brush with Italian dressing; sprinkle with red pepper flakes and garlic salt. Set on a greased rack over hot coals until shrimp is opaque. Serve with extra dressing.

Sweet & Sour

Thread fully cooked frozen meatballs (thawed), mini bell peppers, green onions, and pineapple chunks on a skewer. Brush with olive oil and sprinkle with black pepper. Set on a rack over hot coals until meatballs are hot. Serve with sweet & sour sauce.

Got electricity? Take along your trusty slow cooker for yummy home-style meals.

Simple Taco Soup

1 onion, chopped

1 (16 oz.) can chili beans

1 (15 oz.) can black beans, drained

1 (15 oz.) can whole kernel corn, drained

1 (8 oz.) can tomato sauce

2 (10 oz.) cans diced tomatoes with green chilies

1 (1.25 oz.) pkg. taco seasoning

1 (12 oz.) can beer

2 (12.5 oz.) cans chunk chicken, drained

Salt, black pepper, and cumin to taste

Dump all ingredients into your slow cooker; stir. Cover.
Low: 8 hours

Serve with cheese, sour cream and tortilla chips.

58

Breakfast Scramble

Whisk together 12 eggs and 1 C. milk. Stir in 2 lbs. frozen O'Brien potatoes (thawed), 2 C. chopped cooked meat (bacon, sausage, ham), 2 chopped green onions, 1 diced tomato, 2 C. shredded Cheddar cheese, and salt and black pepper to taste; cover. **Low: 7 to 8 hours**

Pepperoni Dip

Mix 16 oz. softened cream cheese with 2 (10.7 oz.) cans cream of celery soup. Stir in 2 (4 oz.) pkgs. mini pepperoni, some chopped red bell pepper, and crushed red pepper and garlic salt to taste. Spread in greased slow cooker; cover.
Low: 1 hour until hot

Dump Cake

Rub a stick of butter in cooker to grease; cut the rest into pieces and blend with a 16.5 oz. yellow cake mix. Spread a 21 oz. can fruit pie filling in cooker. Sprinkle with cake mixture and ½ C. nuts; cover.
Low: 2 to 3 hours

By adding a padded lid, plastic milk crates go from useful to indispensable.

Crate & Carry
Chair & Table

Cushy Chair

Cut a board a little smaller than inside crate opening so it rests on the lip inside crate. Stain or paint one side of board, if you'd like. Cut a piece of 1″ foam to fit one side of board. Cover foam and edges of board with fabric; staple in place with a staple gun. Easy to make, and you can use them anywhere.

Oooh, comfy!

60

Table Top

Flip the seat over and use the flat side as a night stand, desk, or game table. **Super handy!**

Slap Jack anyone? ⟶

Storage

Stack several crates together without the lid to store cooking gear, clothing, and other essentials. Slide a dowel through two holes in a crate to hold a roll of paper towels. **Nifty!**

Carry-All

When it's time to go, fill the crate, pop the lid on, and you're on your way. Great for use at home, too!

61

Comfy Digs

With a few homey touches, your home away from home can feel first-rate.

Glow stick globes hung from the ceiling are fun and funky. Jars with flameless tea lights make great bedside night lights. Crate chair outside and a rug inside are functional and homey.

Tent Sweet Tent. Make your "front door" inviting. Pull up a few stumps and gather some cute items to have on display (instructions for Luminary Jars on next page).

Breakfast in bed? Fill a tray with yummy Stuffed Toast (recipe on page 10), Tropi-Cooler (recipe and instructions for jar on page 9), and fresh fruit. Deliver some fun-lovin' to someone you love.

Luminary Jars

Wrap a strip of tissue paper around various glass jars and tape in place; tie with jute. Put a little sand in the bottom of each and top with a votive candle or flameless tea light. Light the candles and enjoy.

For each, put glass rocks in a mason jar. Remove the stake from a small outdoor solar light and fit the solar portion into jar ring so solar panel faces the top of the ring; attach to jar. Set in sun to "charge," and set around your campsite at night for pretty illumination.

Put together mason jar lids and rings and set a flameless tea light on each. Invert a mason jar over each light and tighten onto rings. When turned on, these give off a cool glow, giving quiet ambiance to any table or campsite.

Index

Teacher's Edition Level 8

BASIC GOALS IN SPELLING

fifth edition   William Kottmeyer & Audrey Claus

About the Levels: To avoid the problems associated with grade-labeled materials in a multilevel setting, level numerals have been omitted from the covers of all books in the fifth edition. Levels may be determined by referring to the title pages of the teachers' editions or by checking the second-to-last digit in the code number on the back covers of the pupils' books.

About the Covers: The fifth edition emphasizes the concept of symbolization by presenting linguistic sound symbols in all levels and international visual symbols in the first four levels. The covers of the books in the series reflect this feature. The cover symbols are reproduced here, along with level designations, symbol identifications, and code numbers.

Level 1
Airport
Terminal
0-07-034321-7

Level 2
Parking
Garage
0-07-034302-0

Level 3
Picnic
Area
0-07-034303-9

Level 4
Elevator
0-07-034304-7

Level 5
Film-
making
0-07-034305-5

Level 6
Elevated
Train
0-07-034306-3

Level 7
Sailing
0-07-034307-1

Level 8
Hockey
0-07-034308-X

Webster Division, McGraw-Hill Book Company

New York   St. Louis   San Francisco   Dallas   Atlanta

William Kottmeyer has served in the St. Louis Public Schools as teacher, principal, reading specialist, and superintendent. A nationally recognized educational innovator, Dr. Kottmeyer has created a wide variety of basic language-skills materials. Currently author-in-residence in the Webster Division, his publications include *Basic Goals in Spelling,* the *+4 Reading Booster, Decoding and Meaning,* the *+10 Vocabulary Booster,* the *Classroom Reading Clinic, Dr. Spello,* and the *Everyreader Series.*

Audrey Claus has served in the St. Louis Public Schools as teacher, consultant, elementary principal, and curriculum coordinator. Presently author-in-residence in the Webster Division, Miss Claus is co-author of *Basic Goals in Spelling* and the *+10 Vocabulary Booster.*

Sponsoring Editor: Philip LeFaivre
Editing Supervisor: Justine Maier
Designer: George Ibera
Production Supervisor: Gail Paubel

ISBN 0-07-034318-7

TABLE OF CONTENTS

THE BASIC GOALS IN SPELLING PROGRAM

The Fifth Edition of BASIC GOALS IN SPELLING is a flexible spelling program designed both for conventional classes and for classes using small-group individualization. Like its widely used predecessors, this completely new edition takes a pioneering direction in the teaching of spelling and provides a unique and thoroughly researched learning progression through all the spelling patterns of the language.

In Levels 2 through 6, each study unit is organized around either a major high-frequency speech sound or a syllabic pattern and presents one or more spellings of that sound or syllabic pattern. In addition, most units in Levels 2 through 6 feature a Read and Spell word list that coordinates the encoding and decoding skills of spelling and reading and extends the learning objectives of the basic unit list. Each basic text for Levels 1 through 6 is supplemented by Webstermasters that provide correlated enrichment activities for Levels 1 through 3 and end-of-unit mastery tests for Levels 4 through 6.

In Levels 7 and 8, the spelling patterns presented in previous levels of BASIC GOALS IN SPELLING are reviewed and extended into the more sophisticated aspects of American-English vocabulary. Because pupils working at these levels frequently exhibit a wide range of spelling ability, Levels 7 and 8 are organized into more broadly based chapters and sections. Each section within a chapter presents one or several closely related spelling patterns, affixes, or roots, illustrates their occurrence in words appropriate for that level, and provides a generous number of exercises called *skill drills,* which pupils can check for themselves.

This chapter organization combines a sequence of spelling generalizations with exercises that can be checked by pupils. As a result, pupils can work through Levels 7 and 8 at their own rate, or the teacher can present all or part of the material to a group of pupils in a more conventional manner. Except for the final review chapter in each book, each chapter in Levels 7 and 8 concludes with a mastery test covering all the elements presented in the chapter.

The cumulative learning goal of the series is a thorough mastery of every basic spelling pattern and a competence in handling inflectional endings, prefixes and suffixes, multisyllabic words, and all the other related language processes which enable pupils to expand the basic word list into a virtually unlimited personal spelling vocabulary. To enable pupils to achieve this goal, the series is structured according to precise linguistic principles and makes selective use of the following learning strategies.

1   Presentation of words in the order of their frequency of use, grouped by their most important linguistic characteristics, to emphasize the basic relationship between the sounds and the written symbols of American-English words.

2   Introduction of a simple, easily mastered system of linguistic symbols for the forty-odd speech sounds of the language to enable pupils to identify these sounds rapidly and precisely and to analyze them more accurately within the context of words.

3   Sequential development of all the regular, or expected, spelling options for each of the speech sounds in American-English words.

4   Systematic attention in each appropriate study unit to the relatively small number of high-frequency irregular words that violate the expected spelling options.

5   Continuous comparison of similar and dissimilar vowel sounds through activities focused upon the interrelationship of short, long, and other vowel sounds and the shifting spelling patterns by which these sounds are represented in words.

6   Expansion of the spelling vocabulary introduced at each level to demonstrate a natural skills correlation with the much broader reading vocabularies of current basal readers.

7   Synchronization of the complementary skills of encoding and decoding by first introducing sound-symbol and structural generalizations as an encoding concept and then immediately reversing the application of these generalizations in corresponding decoding activities.

8   Integration of a comprehensive program of instruction in dictionary skills with proofreading, the study of word meanings, the mechanics of writing, and other related language arts skills.

9   Implementation of an innovative, individualized testing program that incorporates a continually reinforcing and precisely paced review as well as a criterion-referenced diagnosis of spelling errors.

10   Emphasis of the concept of symbolization by correlating linguistic symbols with a broad variety of internationally standardized symbols and by developing an appreciation of how visual symbols can transmit ideas, as well as speech sounds, instantaneously.

OVERVIEW OF LEVELS 7 AND 8

The principal objective of the texts for Levels 7 and 8 of the Fifth Edition of BASIC GOALS IN SPELLING is to provide a comprehensive study of the elements of spelling American-English words. In using these texts, pupils review the spelling options for sounds and syllables and apply them to multisyllabic words. Pupils are taught to look at words discriminatingly and to note agreement with or deviation from an expected phonetic or structural spelling pattern.

To enable pupils to apply their knowledge of sound-symbol relationships to multisyllabic words, there is a comprehensive program of instruction in the analysis of syllables, the deciphering of a sound-spelling alphabet, and the recognition of roots and affixes. These activities dealing with syllables and pronunciations are intended to provide pupils with a set of skills that will allow them to analyze and master multisyllabic words in the same way that they analyze and master monosyllabic words.

Related language skills are also presented when they are appropriate. For example, by studying suffixes, plural endings, and other inflectional endings, pupils are reviewing the parts of speech and other grammatical elements. In addition, by combining roots and affixes, pupils enlarge their vocabulary. Application and evaluation of these related language skills are provided in the skill drills, the end-of-chapter mastery tests, and the proofreading chapter.

Each text includes a Spelling Dictionary as a source of correct spellings and word meanings and also as a useful reference for identifying parts of speech, irregular plurals, inflectional endings, and word origins. Many activities require pupils to use this Spelling Dictionary, located at the back of the book.

Also included, at the beginning of each book, is the Spelling Alphabet, a set of handwriting models. These cursive models are to be used as a guide to legibility for pupils to follow in their written work.

Since there is likely to be a wide range of spelling competence among pupils using these upper levels, and since classroom organization for these pupils is less likely to include a specific block of spelling instruction time, the format and instructional strategy used in these books are different from those in previous levels of this series. Levels 7 and 8 include seven and six chapters respectively, whereas Levels 1 through 6 have thirty-six units each. Because the range of spelling achievement within a class broadens each year, many pupils in seventh- and eighth-year programs need spelling instruction at levels more than two years below their grade levels. Remedial, or review, material for these students must include more study of the sound-symbol relationships and other rudiments of American-English spelling. This must be followed by an analysis of the components of multisyllabic words, word origins, meanings of root words and affixes, and their effect on spellings. Levels 7 and 8 of BASIC GOALS IN SPELLING provide the review necessary for students needing instruction below their actual grade level. For students who have satisfactory spelling skills, these books also supplement previously learned spelling skills and assist pupils in applying them to more sophisticated vocabulary.

Chapter Format

Since Levels 7 and 8 review the entire sequence of spelling skills, the books are divided into chapters instead of the traditional thirty-six units. This more broadly based chapter format provides the comprehensive, flexible program needed by most pupils working at these levels. There are seven chapters in Level 7 and six chapters in Level 8.

Organization into chapters facilitates the presentation of spelling concepts to more mature students. Because chapters are more inclusive than units, many closely related spelling generalizations, affixes, or roots can be taught together as a single comprehensive study. For example, one of the basic concepts is that the spelling options for spelling monosyllabic words also apply to the parts of multisyllabic words. The first chapter of Level 7 therefore reviews the regular spelling options for monosyllabic words. Subsequent chapters of Level 7 present other patterns in monosyllabic words and discuss compounds made up of monosyllabic word parts. This forms a logical transition to multisyllabic words. The later chapters show how multisyllabic words can be studied in segments to which previously learned principles can be applied.

Another basic concept, explored in depth in Level 8, is that some words can be grouped according to common prefixes. Isolating these prefixes makes spelling easier and meaning clearer. The first chapter of Level 8 covers prefixes and roots. This is followed by a study of roots and suffixes in Chapter 2.

The chapter organization in Levels 7 and 8 allows greater flexibility and independence. Individual learning segments need not be confined to a definite number of pages. The chapters are divided into sections which vary in number and in length. The amount of study of specific spelling concepts in Levels 7 and 8 relates to the importance and usefulness of the concept rather than to a weekly lesson plan. Pupils may cover as many or as few sections or subsections in a spelling class period as is appropriate. This flexible plan also allows students to proceed through the book independently.

Skill Drills

In order for pupils to apply their spelling ability and their knowledge of spelling concepts, there are numerous skill drills in each chapter. In completing the various skill drills, students both practice newly acquired skills and reinforce previously taught skills.

Skill drills appear frequently so that pupils are actively involved in learning. They generate a variety of activities to accommodate different learning styles. In some cases, pupils write missing words to complete sentences. In others, pupils read sound-spellings and write words or sentences for them. In still other instances, they write words to describe illustrations.

Answer Keys

An answer key for the students use appears at the end of every chapter. After completing a skill drill or a group of skill drills, students should take the responsibility of checking their answers with those at the end of the chapter. In some cases, the answers will be guides for checking alternatives rather than restrictive answers. Some skill drills call for students to show the division of multisyllabic words into eye-syllables (the best visual groupings of letters within a word to help one remember the spelling). The answer key for this type of skill drill includes the most plausible divisions according to the clues in that section of the text.

Besides facilitating individualization and independence, the answer key is a valuable teaching tool. Students should develop the habit of thinking of the skill drills not as test material but as practice material that should be checked conscientiously with the answer key to determine whether they have understood and applied the concepts of the lessons. Although this independent pupil use of the answer key is suggested, you should monitor the performance so that assistance may be provided when necessary.

Students take a chapter mastery test after studying the chapter and completing the skill drills. Each mastery test has two parts, labeled A and B. The two parts of the mastery test can be taken in one or two sessions. The two parts cover different aspects of the spelling concepts of that chapter and should be considered together as one test for the chapter.

Answers to the mastery tests appear only in the Teacher's Editions on the pages where the tests occur. The tests should not be checked by the pupils since it is imperative that you know their mastery of the chapter's concepts in order to plan the instruction to follow.

Because the last chapter in each book reviews the year's work in a proofreading context, it does not have a mastery test. If you wish to test this chapter, you might use selected skill drills or selected sentences from various skill drills for a final test of the skills taught in the book.

In order to provide remedial instruction for pupils who do not demonstrate mastery of the concepts, refer to the Skills Outline on pages T-12–T-19 of this text. The outline lists spelling generalizations and identifies the chapter and section in which each is taught. The Skills Outline in this Teacher's Edition covers both Levels 7 and 8.

Additional Skill Drills in Level 7

A special feature of the Level 7 text is the section called *Additional Skill Drills*. Each of the mastery tests is followed by three to six additional skill drills that provide reinforcement of the concepts of the chapter. Often there is an additional skill drill to correspond to each section of the chapter so that students may practice the specific kinds of words they found difficult on the mastery test.

The additional skill drills provide the added stimulus of visual clues to recall the words. While many of the skill drills in the chapters present words in sound-spelling, these additional skill drills include pictures with sound-spellings under them. Students who may not have been entirely successful with the sound-spelling exercises in the chapters may find this added dimension of illustration to be helpful.

It is suggested that after pupils review appropriate sections and complete the additional skill drills, they should be encouraged to repeat the mastery test to try to improve their scores.

Eye-Syllables and Ear-Syllables

In order to help pupils utilize the sound-symbol relationships in multisyllabic words, we have developed two important devices for dealing with the basic concepts of written and spoken language. The learning device that relates to the written concept of our multisyllabic vocabulary we call the *eye-syllable.* The device relating to the pronunciation concept of multisyllabic words we call the *ear-syllable.*

Eye-syllables are visual groupings of letters into those word parts that make multisyllabic words easiest to spell. We signal eye-syllables in words by using brackets in this fashion: ⌊sig⌊nal⌋. As pupils analyze the parts called out by the brackets, they learn to break long letter sequences into smaller visual segments to which they can readily apply sound-symbol generalizations. The eye-syllable breaks are, of course, somewhat arbitrary. They represent our judgment concerning logical visual segments for each multisyllabic word.

Ear-syllables are the word parts we hear when a multisyllabic word is spoken. The pronunciations that lexicographers show for entry words are their attempts to represent the ear-syllables of spoken words. In this series, ear-syllables are shown by sound symbols between slant lines in this fashion: /sig′ nəl/.

The sound symbols between slant lines represent our effort to identify the most common pronunciations of the spelling vocabulary. There may be variations between the symbols we use and those used in some dictionaries. And there will undoubtedly be regional differences in pronunciations. Some of these regional differences are noted in the Spelling Dictionary at the back of each text. Pupils should be encouraged to note other differences between the pronunciations in these texts and the pronunciations of their own dialect. Such linguistic comparisons are a valuable learning experience, and they will further increase the usefulness of the system of pronunciation symbols used in these texts.

In a continuing effort to help pupils master the various spelling options for the sounds they hear, the texts for Levels 7 and 8 rely heavily on the use of ear-syllable representation. We refer to this representation as *sound-spelling* in the pupil texts. In order to assist pupils in interpreting sound-spelling, a Sound-Spelling Alphabet immediately precedes Chapter 1 in both the pupils' text and the Teacher's Edition. Throughout the course of study, this chart will serve as a useful reference for translating sound-spellings and for understanding the sounds for the various symbols.

Irregular Spellings

There are a number of words that are not spelled according to a regular, or expected, spelling pattern. The Fifth Edition of BASIC GOALS IN SPELLING offers pupils a systematic and concentrated study of these irregular spellings.

We have identified 115 violators of the sound-symbol generalizations among the one thousand most frequently used words of English. Levels 1 through 3 of this series introduce these words. Levels 4 through 8 continue to alert pupils to the problems of irregular spellings.

In order to highlight our concern for and our treatment of the study of spelling violators, we refer to them as *snurks*. We define a snurk as follows:

- **snurk** /snėrk/ *n.* A violator of an expected spelling pattern. [A coined word made up of parts of *sneak* and *lurk*.] — *adj.* **snurky.**

Proofreading

It has been repeatedly demonstrated that proofreading practice is productive in reducing spelling errors. The BASIC GOALS IN SPELLING series has therefore included in all levels a substantial program of proofreading activities. If this proofreading habit is developed early, written work will surely improve significantly.

The last chapter in Levels 7 and 8 is a special proofreading chapter. It reviews each of the previous chapters in order. The sections of the last chapter might be used to supplement each of the other chapters and be used in conjunction with them. The chapter can also be used at the end of the year as a review of all the spelling principles of the text.

Sequence of Skills

The Level 7 text contains a complete analysis of American-English spelling. As can be seen in the Table of Contents, all the basic spelling elements are included — spellings for regularly spelled monosyllabic words, for the irregularly spelled words, for homonyms, for compounds, and for longer words that have unstressed syllables.

In this text the spellings of regularly spelled monosyllables are the basis for the spellings of all of the other kinds of words. Generally, the spelling of monosyllabic words is considered easier than the spelling of multisyllabic words. Not only are the letter sequences shorter, but also the vowel sounds are clear because they are stressed. Stressed syllables are easier to spell than unstressed syllables because the clearer vowel sounds make the sound-symbol relationships easier to discern.

The study of monosyllables, then, opens Level 7 partly because these words seem much easier than longer words. Students gradually learn special techniques for spelling multisyllabic words by building on their knowledge of monosyllabic spelling.

While studying monosyllabic spellings, students learn that these words fall into four major vowel groups: the short-vowel, the long-vowel, the digraphic-vowel, and the vowel-r spellings. These vowel sounds have standard sound-spelling options, which are reviewed in conjunction with their sound-spellings.

Immediately following the chapter on the regularly spelled monosyllabic words, there is a chapter dealing with two kinds of monosyllabic words with troublesome spellings. One group of words in this chapter have "silent" consonants. These words contain consonant spellings for sounds that have long since disappeared from spoken English. The second group are those monosyllables that do not have the expected vowel spelling options just studied.

The next group of words presented in Level 7 are the homonyms. The homonyms are arranged according to the same four categories of vowel sounds and include snurks. After studying homonyms, the pupils study compounds, also according to the vowel sounds. At this point, the text introduces the device of the eye-syllable to give students a visual aid to learning the spellings of parts of words. Compounds provide a useful transition between monosyllabic and multisyllabic words because the eye-syllabication is simplest in compounds. Eye-syllabication becomes a very helpful device also with the next group of words, those with soft syllable endings.

Other multisyllabic words are studied in the sixth chapter, which focuses on syllabication. Pupils study various patterns by which they might divide words into eye-syllables in order to study their spellings. After they divide words into syllables, pupils apply their knowledge of sound-symbol relationships. The problems of spelling multisyllabic words thus can be solved with a sensible, sequential application of spelling skills related to the compounds; the soft syllable endings with their spelling options; and other multisyllabic words, presented according to the various syllabication patterns. Six of the chapters into which the text is organized follow this developmental sequence. The last chapter presents opportunities for proofreading for errors in spelling words taken from the first six chapters. Thus the text presents information for spelling, studying, and proofreading words in all the basic English spelling patterns.

The sequence of spelling skills begun in Level 7 is continued in Level 8. In the initial chapters of the Level 8 text, pupils build spelling and vocabulary skills through an intensive study of the spellings and meanings of prefixes and roots. In all, pupils study the meanings and spellings of more than twenty Latin prefixes including their variant forms and thirty-five key Latin roots.

Pupils begin by noting how prefixes affect the meaning of the words to which they are affixed and how prefixes and roots form eye-syllables which can be considered "little words" for purposes of spelling. This leads logically to a consideration of words formed by combining prefixes with Latin roots which do not appear as English words but which nevertheless have meaning and form eye-syllables for spelling.

The next component of multisyllabic words to be taken up in Level 8 is the suffix. The root-suffix combinations most common in English words are presented according to the part of speech formed by the use of that group of suffixes. First the suffixes used to convert adjectives and verbs to nouns are examined. Then attention is directed to suffixes which change nouns and verbs into adjectives, and finally to suffixes which change verbs into nouns and adjectives. Throughout this study of commonly used English suffixes, pupils note how suffixes, like prefixes, form eye-syllables for spelling. Special attention is consistently given to the spelling problems caused by the variant forms of certain suffixes and by the unstressed vowels which occur in the final syllable of certain root-suffix combinations.

Because the meaning and spelling of hundreds of English words can be deduced from their prefixes, roots, and suffixes, pupils are given considerable practice in analyzing the spelling and meaning of the prefix-root-suffix elements of the words introduced in Chapter 3. Moreover, the pupils' store of familiar word parts is enlarged by the introduction of additional high-frequency roots and suffixes.

Although Latin is the source of most English word parts, Greek and French spellings occur with sufficient frequency to warrant attention. In Chapter 4, the unusual spelling patterns found in words of Greek and French origin are systematically examined. Special attention is given to the more than forty Greek word parts which appear fre-quently in our scientific and technical vocabulary.

The next chapter addresses itself to several categories of spelling problems which are the result of the imperfect sound-symbol relationship in English. Specifically this chapter deals with the problems of double-consonant spellings, the three spelling options for /s/, *ei-ie* spellings, irregular plurals, troublesome root-suffix combinations, and homonyms.

The final chapter reviews all the material included in Level 8 in a proofreading context. Words appearing in the first five chapters are presented in sentences. By reading these sentences carefully for words which are misspelled or used incorrectly, pupils enhance not only their spelling skills but also their proofreading and vocabulary skills.

SKILLS OUTLINE

LEVEL 7 SKILLS

GENERALIZATION		CHAPTER
Many short-vowel mono-syllables have regular vowel and consonant symbol spellings.	Short-vowel spellings: /a/ *a*, /e/ *e*, /i/ *i*, /o/ *o*, /ô/ *o*, /u/ *u*	1A–B, D–F; 7A*
	Regular consonant spellings: /b/ *b*, /d/ *d*, /g/ *g*, /h/ *h*, /l/ *l*, /m/ *m*, /n/ *n*, /p/ *p*, /r/ *r*, /t/ *t*, /v/ *v*, /w/ *w*, /y/ *y*, /z/ *z*, /kw/ *qu*, /hw/ *wh*, /th/ *th*, /ŦH/ *th*	1B–H, 7A
Some monosyllables have consonant spelling options.	/f/ *f, ph, gh* /j/ *j, g(e, i, y), dge* /k/ *c, k, ck, ch* /s/ *s, c(e, i, y), sc(e, i, y)* /z/ *s, z* Doubled consonants	1D–H, 7A
	/sh/ *sh, ch* /ch/ *ch, tch* /ng/ *ng, n(k), n(c)* /ks/ *cks, x*	1F–H, 7A
Some monosyllables have long-vowel spelling options.	/ā/ *ai, ay, a-consonant-e* /ē/ *e, ee, ea, e-consonant-e* /ī/ *y, i(gh), i(nd), ie, i-consonant-e* /ō/ *o, o(ld), oa, oe, ow, o-consonant-e* /ū/ or /ü/ *ue, ui, ew, u-consonant-e*	1C–D, F–G; 7A

*Letters in this column represent sections of the chapters.

GENERALIZATION		CHAPTER
Some monosyllables have digraphic vowel spelling options.	/ü/ oo, ew, ue, ui, u-consonant-e	1C, G; 7A
	/ů/ oo /oi/ oi, oy /ou/ ou, ow /ô/ aw, au, a(l)	1G, 7A
Some monosyllables have vowel-r spellings.	/är/ ar	1H, 7A
	/our/ our /ůr/ oor	2B(4)*
Some monosyllables have vowel-r spelling options.	/ār/ are, air /ôr/ or, ore, oar /ėr/ er, ir, ur /ir/ ear, eer	1H, 7A
Some monosyllables have silent-consonant spellings.	Silent-consonant spellings: *thigh, knee, write, gnaw, lamb, walk, half, pitch, edge, rhyme, hour, debt, sword, whoop, sign*	2A(1–8), 7B
Some monosyllables have irregular vowel spellings.	Short-vowel snurks (70)	2B(1), 7B
	Long-vowel snurks (81)	2B(2), 7B
	Digraphic-vowel snurks (10)	2B(3), 7B
	Vowel-r snurks (36)	2B(4), 7B
Homonyms are words with the same sounds but with different meanings and spellings.	Short-vowel homonyms	3A–B, 7C
	Short-vowel homonym snurks	3B, 7C
	Long-vowel homonyms	3C–D, 7C
	Long-vowel homonym snurks	3D, 7C
	Digraphic and vowel-r homonyms and snurks	3E, 7C

*Numerals in parentheses represent subsections of the chapter sections.

GENERALIZATIONS		CHAPTER
We spell compounds by dividing them into eye-syllables that have the same spelling options as mono-syllabic words.	Short- and long-vowel compounds	4A–B, 7D
	Digraphic-vowel compounds	4C, 7D
	Vowel-*r* compounds	4D, 7D
	Snurk compounds	4E, 7D
Disyllabic words with soft syllable endings have spelling options for the unstressed endings.	/ē/ jell*y*, jock*ey*	5A(1–6), 7E
	/əl/ litt*le*, lev*el*, med*al*, id*ol*, penc*il*, fert*ile*	5B(1–6), 7E
	/ər/ bett*er*, doct*or*, doll*ar*, murm*ur*	5C(1–5), 7E
Inflectional elements affect the spellings of root words.	Plural noun forms: changing *y* to *i* before *es*	5A(3), 7E
	Verb forms: changing *y* to *i* before *es* and *ed*	5A(4), 7E
	Adjective forms: changing *y* to *i* before *er*, *est*	5A(5), 7E
	Participial forms: dropping *e* before *ing;* doubling final consonant before *ing*	5B(6), 7E
The use of eye-syllables provides spelling option cues by restoring the vowel sounds of unstressed syllables.	VC/CV patterns	6A, B, F; 7F
	V/CCV patterns	6C, F; 7F
	VCC/V patterns	6C, 7F
	VC/CCV patterns	6D, F; 7F
	VCC/CV patterns	6D, 7F
	V/CV patterns	6E, F; 7F
	VC/V patterns	6E, F; 7F
	V/V patterns	6G, 7F

GENERALIZATION		CHAPTER
Proofreading eliminates many spelling errors.	In monosyllables with four groups of spelling options	7A
	In silent-letter and snurk spellings	7B
	In homonyms	7C
	In compounds	7D
	In soft syllable endings	7E
	In multisyllabic words with unstressed syllables	7F

LEVEL 8 SKILLS

GENERALIZATION		CHAPTER
Prefixes affect word meaning and form eye-syllables for spelling.	*un* not; *dis* not, down, from, away; *im (in, ir, il, ig)* not; *in* in; *re* back, again; *en* in, make; *de* down, from, away; *ex* out; *com (co, col, con, cor)* with, together; *pre* before; *pro* onward, for; *sub (suc, suf, sug, sup, sus)* under; *super* over, above; *trans* across, over, through; *inter* between, among	1A, 6A
Prefixes are added to word parts, called roots, which have meaning and form eye-syllables for spelling.	*pose* put, place; *tract* pull, draw; *ceed-cede* go; *port* carry; *pel* push; *press* press, squeeze; *scribe-script* write	1B, 6B

GENERALIZATION		CHAPTER
Suffixes form eye-syllables for spelling and change words from one part of speech to another.	Noun suffixes: *ness, ment, ance-ence, ion-sion-tion, ant-ent* Adjective suffixes: *ful, less, ous-ious-eous, able-ible, ant-ent*	2A, B, C; 6C
Some suffixes have spelling options.	/əns/ *ance-ence;* /shən/ *tion-sion;* /ē əs/ *ious-eous;* /shəs/ *cious-tious;* /ə bəl/ *able-ible;* /ənt/ *ant-ent*	2A, B, C; 6C
Many longer English words are formed by combining a prefix, a root, and a suffix.	Examples: *re + trac(t) + tion* *ex + pre(s) + sion* *im + pos(e) + (i)tion* *trans + port + (a)tion* *sub + scrip(t) + tion* *inter + ced + ing* *pro + pel + (l)ing*	3A, 6D
The meaning and spelling of hundreds of English words can be deduced by analyzing the prefixes, roots, and suffixes.	Additional prefixes: *di* away; *ob* in the way; *intro* inside; *ad (ac, af, ag, al, ap, as, at)* to, towards; *per* through; *ab* away, from; *du* two Additional roots: *gress* walk, go; *ject* throw; *duce-duct* lead; *vert-verse* turn; *mit-miss* send; *spect* look; *voke-voc* call; *spire* breathe; *fer* carry; *claim-clam* cry; *sist* stand; *form* shape; *rupt* break; *ceive-cept* take; *clin* lean; *clude-clus* close; *flect-flex* bend; *pend-pense* hang; *struct* build; *sult* jump; *merge-merse* plunge; *dict* speak; *volve* turn; *tain-tin* hold; *sent-sens* feel; *plic-plex* fold; *plore* cry; *sume-sumpt* take Additional suffixes: *ive, al, ate*	3B, 6D
English words borrowed from the Greek language retain their Greek spellings.	/k/ *ch (chord);* /f/ *ph (photographer);* /ī/ and /i/ *y (myth, hyphen);* /r/ *rh (rhythm);* /s/ *ps (psalm);* /n/ *pn (pneumatic);* /m/ *mn (hymn)*	4A, 6E

GENERALIZATION		CHAPTER
The meaning and spelling of English words formed by combining Greek word parts can be deduced by analyzing the Greek word parts.	*logy-logue* speak, study; *astro* star; *bio* life; *eco* house; *geo* earth; *myth* story; *meteor* air things; *physio* nature; *psycho* mind; *theo* god; *zoo* animal; *mono* one; *dia* through; *cata* down; *graphy-gram* write, draw; *auto* self; *tele* far; *topo* place; *photo* light; *para* beside; *biblio* book; *meter-metry* measure; *micro* small; *thermo* heat; *peri* around; *chrono* time; *baro* weight; *opto* eye; *sym-syn* with; *onym* name; *an* no; *anti* against; *homo* same; *acro* tip; *phone-phon-phony* sound; *mega* great; *scope* view; *stetho* chest; *sphere* round; *atmo* vapor; *hemi* half; *cracy-crat* rule; *demo* rule; *aristo* best	4B, 6E
English words which were borrowed from the French language retain their French spellings.	/sh/ *ch (brochure)*; /zh/ *ge* or *s (beige, pleasure)*; /ü/ or /u̇/ *ou (route, tourist)*; /ō/ *eau (bureau)*; /n/ *gn (reign)*; /g/ *gue (fatigue)*; /ā/ *et (ballet)*; /et/ *ette (cigarette)*; /k/ *que (plaque)*; /wär/ *oir(e) (memoir)*; /ər/ *eur (amateur)*; /ən/ *eon (pigeon)*	4C, 6F
Sometimes it takes two consonant letters to spell one consonant sound.	Examples: *accommodate, sheriff, roommate, overrate, accurate, parallel*	5A, 6G
The /s/ sound is sometimes spelled with *s*, sometimes with *c* followed by *e*, *i*, or *y*, and sometimes with *sc* followed by *e*, *i* or *y*.	Examples: *rinse, verse, mercy, source, scene, sessions*	5B, 6G
Most *ei-ie* spellings are governed by one of several generalizations.	/ā/ and /ã/ are spelled *ei (weigh)*. Before *gn*, use *ei (foreign)*. When *c* spells /s/, the *ei* spelling follows *(ceiling)*.	5C, 6G

Most *ei-ie* spellings are governed by one of several generalizations.	*(continued)* When *ci, ti,* or *si* spell /sh/, use the *ie* spelling *(species, patient, transient).* Use the *ie* spelling before *r (cashier).* The /ē/ sound is usually spelled *ie (field, piece).*	5C, 6G
Some *ei-ie* spellings must be remembered.	*sheik, seize, either, neither, leisure, protein, caffein, seizure, friend, view, review, sieve, their, pie, die, lie, tie, forfeit, counterfeit*	5C, 6G
The plural forms of some nouns take special spellings.	Nouns ending with *y* preceded by a vowel form their plurals by adding *s (decoys).* Nouns ending with *y* preceded by a consonant form their plurals by changing *y* to *i* and adding *es.* Nouns ending with *i* or vowel-*o* form their plurals by adding *s (skis, patios).* Nouns ending with consonant-*o* form their plurals by adding *s* or *es (altos, broncos, echoes, cargoes).* A few nouns have irregularly spelled plurals *(mice, feet, women, children).* Some nouns ending with *f(e)* form their plurals by changing *f(e)* to *v(e)* and adding *(e)s (calves, knives).* Some nouns have the same spelling for both the singular and plural forms *(deer).* Some nouns have no separate singular form *(news, clothes).* Some nouns from Latin and Greek have two plural forms *(mediums, media).*	5D, 6G

The addition of a suffix sometimes affects the spelling of the root word.	If the suffix begins with a consonant, and the root ends with a *y*, change *y* to *i* before adding the *ment, ness, ful,* or *less* suffix *(merriment, plentiful).*	5E, 6G
	When a word ends with a consonant, the final consonant is sometimes doubled before adding a suffix beginning with a vowel.	
	When a word ends with *e*, this final *e* is sometimes dropped before adding a suffix.	
Homonyms cause many spelling errors.	Examples: *miner-minor; canvas-canvass; affect-effect; waive-wave; capital-capitol; principal-principle; stationary-stationery*	5F, 6G
Proofreading eliminates many spelling errors.	In prefixes	6A
	In prefixes and roots	6B
	In roots and root words with suffixes	6C
	In prefix-root-suffix words	6D
	In words and word parts from Greek	6E
	In words from French	6F
	In words with doubled consonants, *s, c,* or *sc* spellings, *ei-ie* words, and homonyms	6G

SPELLING ALPHABET

The letters of the alphabet are written symbols which we use to spell words. There are twenty-six letters in our alphabet. Each letter of the alphabet has a capital and a lower-case form. The handwriting models below show the way to write the capital and lower-case forms of each letter.

SOUND-SPELLING ALPHABET

We show the pronunciation of a word by using special symbols inside slant marks. There are forty-four sound-spelling symbols, one for each of the dictionary sounds. A sound-spelling symbol always stands for the same sound, no matter how the sound is spelled in a word.

Consonant Symbols

/b/ big	/n/ noon	/ch/ church
/d/ did	/p/ pop	/hw/ when
/f/ fife	/r/ rare	/ng/ sing
/g/ gag	/s/ sense	/sh/ ship
/h/ hot	/t/ tot	/ᴛʜ/ this
/j/ judge	/v/ valve	/th/ thin
/k/ kick	/w/ wet	/zh/ vision
/l/ lull	/y/ yes	
/m/ mum	/z/ zoo	

Vowel Symbols

/a/ ran	/o/ not	/ə/ about
/ā/ rain	/ō/ no	taken
/ã/ care	/ô/ off	pencil
/ä/ car		lemon
	/u/ us	circus
/e/ hen	/ū/ use	
/ē/ he	/ü/ tool	
/èr/ her	/ů/ took	
/i/ in	/ou/ cow	
/ī/ ice	/oi/ boy	

1

1 Prefixes and Roots

A *prefix* is a word part you place at the beginning of a word to change its meaning. The *pre* in *prefix* is itself a prefix. *Pre* means "before or in front of." The word *prefix* means "that which you fix before." If you know the prefix meanings, you will be able to guess the meanings of prefixed words.

Prefixes are short and easy to spell. If you know the common prefixes, you will be able to *see* them as parts of longer words and *spell* each whole word easily.

You often use prefixes with familiar words. But you often add prefixes to word parts that are not English words. These word parts, which are called *roots,* are most commonly taken from Latin words. If you learn the meanings and spellings of the common Latin roots and know the prefixes, you will be able to guess many word meanings as well as be able to spell the words.

 A

Prefixes Change Word Meanings

1 "not–opposite" Prefixes *un dis im*
Several prefixes mean "not" so they cause a word to have an "opposite" meaning. Words which have opposite meanings are called *antonyms.*

2

CHAPTER 1

Many pupils are poor spellers because they look at printed words as total configurations and do not look at words analytically to see the component parts. In this first chapter attention is centered on the common prefixes and roots and their meanings in order to help pupils to see them as visual units in words.

In Section A pupils examine the prefix meanings in conjunction with root words which are also used as English words. By studying the prefixed and unprefixed forms of these root words, students will become aware of the meaning of the prefix and its influence upon the root. The prefixes, however, are more often added to Latin roots that are not common English words. In Section B of this chapter and throughout Chapter 3, thirty-five Latin roots are introduced. These Latin roots occur in so many English words that they cannot sensibly be ignored.

A familiar "not–opposite" prefix is *un*. Note how the *un* prefix changes the meaning of these words.

| fair | un·fair | hap·py | un·hap·py |
| cer·tain | un·cer·tain | a·ble | un·a·ble |

To spell prefixed words, look carefully at the *eye-syllables*. The eye-syllables are simply the best groupings of letters to help you *see* word parts. *Ear-syllables* are the word parts you *hear*. Sometimes the eye- and ear-syllables are the same. Sometimes they are not the same. Compare the eye-syllables marked in these familiar words with the ear-syllables.

eye-syllables	*ear-syllables*
luck·y	/luk′ē/
rab·bit	/rab′it/
east·ern	/ēs′tərn/

You will see that the spelling options you have learned in spelling short words appear again in the eye-syllables of longer words. If you say each eye-syllable to yourself as if it were a little word, you will find long words easier to spell.

Look at the eye-syllables in these *un* words. Note the spellings of the sounds. (See the Sound-Spelling Alphabet chart on page 1.) Listen for the vowel sounds in stressed syllables— those word parts that you say louder. Listen for the vowel sounds in unstressed syllables—those syllables you say softly.

u spells /u/ in the unstressed syllable	un·fair	*air* spells /ãr/ in the stressed syllable
er spells /èr/ in the stressed syllable	un·cer·tain	*ai* would spell /ā/ if in a one-syllable word
a spells /a/ in the stressed syllable	un·hap·py	final *y* spells /e/ in unstressed syllables
a spells /ā/ if ending a stressed syllable	un·a·ble	*le* spells /əl/ in unstressed syllables

3

Section A

You will probably want to read through the introductory material with the class. Pupils should have little difficulty understanding and recognizing prefixes. Be sure that pupils look carefully at the word parts of the example words as directed.

The BASIC GOALS IN SPELLING series stresses the use of *eye-syllables,* as opposed to *ear-syllables.* As the text indicates, eye-syllables are the best *visual* groupings of letters which enable one to see the parts of multisyllabic words and remember the spellings. The ear-syllables shown in dictionary pronunciation guides are *auditory* word parts — parts which are heard, not seen. Eye-syllables and ear syllables may not always coincide. For example, the eye-syllables in *eastern* are *east* and *ern;* however, the ear-syllables are /ēs′/ and /tərn/.

The term *spelling options* refers to the various ways we spell the long-vowel, digraphic-

In the eye-syllables you will also see some familiar *snurks*—words with unexpected **spellings**.

‿un‿friend‿ly‿	*ie* spells /e/ instead of /ī/
‿un‿health‿y‿	*ea* spells /e/ instead of /ē/
‿un‿stead‿y‿	
‿un‿wel‿come‿	*o*-consonant-*e* spells /u/ instead of /ō/
‿un‿worth‿y‿	*or* spells /ėr/ instead of /ôr/

Skill Drill 1 Print the antonyms of these words by adding the *un* prefix. Mark the eye-syllables. Think of the meanings of the *un* words. Compare your work with the answers at the end of Chapter 1.

1 aware	4 bearable	7 easy
2 interesting	5 equal	8 fasten
3 popular	6 true	9 lucky

dis

Another "not–opposite" prefix is *dis*. Note how the *dis* prefix changes the word meanings.

‿com‿fort‿	‿dis‿com‿fort‿	‿be‿lief‿	‿dis‿be‿lief‿
‿hon‿est‿	‿dis‿hon‿est‿	‿ap‿prove‿	‿dis‿ap‿prove‿
‿loy‿al‿	‿dis‿loy‿al‿	taste	‿dis‿taste‿

Skill Drill 2 Print the antonyms of these words by adding the *dis* prefix. Mark the eye-syllables. Think of the meanings of the *dis* words. Compare your work with the answers at the end of Chapter 1.

1 connect	4 please	7 similar
2 trust	5 obey	
3 appear	6 continue	

4

---

vowel, and vowel-*r* sounds. These monosyllabic spelling options have been stressed throughout the series and were reviewed thoroughly in the Level 7 text. Pupils using the BASIC GOALS IN SPELLING series are accustomed to applying these spelling options to unstressed syllables by "thinking" stress on the vocally unstressed syllables.

Pupils who have used earlier levels of BASIC GOALS IN SPELLING will be familiar with the term *snurk,* which is used throughout the series to designate words with irregular or unexpected spellings. The *friend* syllable, for example, in *unfriendly* is a snurk because normally we expect *ie* to spell /ī/ as in *pie.* The *health* syllable in *unhealthy* is a snurk because we expect *ea* to spell /ē/ instead of /e/, as does.

The Skill Drills are inserted regularly to enable the pupils to apply the skills which have been introduced in the text. The answers to each Skill Drill are given at the end of each chapter and in the side columns of this Teacher's Edition. Pupils are instructed to check their

im Another "not–opposite" prefix is *im*. There are several different forms of *im*. The most common one is *in*. Note how *im* and *in* give these words opposite meanings.

po lite	im po lite	sane	in sane
prop er	im prop er	act ive	in act ive
ma ture	im ma ture	cor rect	in cor rect

Also, before a word beginning with *r*, the *im* prefix becomes *ir*. Before an *l* word, *im* becomes *il*. Before an *n* word, *im* becomes *ig*.

reg u lar	ir reg u lar	le gal	il le gal
re ver ent	ir rev er ent	log i cal	il log i cal
	no ble		ig no ble

Skill Drill 3 Print the antonyms of these words by adding the correct form of the *im* prefix *(im, in, il,* or *ir)*. Mark the eye-syllables. Think of the meanings of the words. Use your Spelling Dictionary or the classroom dictionary to find the meaning of any unfamiliar word. The last six words are in your Spelling Dictionary. Compare your work with the answers at the end of Chapter 1.

1 personal	5 mortal	8 frequent
2 direct	6 responsible	9 resistible
3 sincere	7 patient	10 legible
4 secure		

Skill Drill 4 Write the regular spellings for these prefixed snurk words. Use the Sound-Spelling Alphabet chart on page 1 to help you translate these sound-spellings. Check the meaning of any unfamiliar word in your Spelling Dictionary or in the classroom dictionary. The last three words are in your Spelling Dictionary. Answers appear at the end of Chapter 1.

1 /un frend′lē/	4 /im pā′shənt/	7 /dis tāst′/
2 /un helth′ē/	5 /un sted′ē/	8 /dis′ə prüv′/
3 /dis bə lēf′/	6 /un wel′kəm/	9 /un wėr′ŦHē/

5

Skill Drill 3 Answers
1 im per son al
2 in di rect
3 in sin cere
4 in se cure
5 im mor tal
6 ir re spons i ble
7 im pa tient
8 in fre quent
9 ir re sist i ble
10 il leg i ble

Skill Drill 4 Answers
1 unfriendly
2 unhealthy
3 disbelief
4 impatient
5 unsteady
6 unwelcome
7 distaste
8 disapprove
9 unworthy

work with the answers given at the end of the chapter.

Pupil performance on the Skill Drills should be monitored closely. If a pupil is performing poorly on these Skill Drills, the material should be gone over thoroughly again before proceeding. If pupils cannot do the Skill Drills reasonably well, they will surely not be able to perform well on the Mastery Test at the end of the chapter.

In the first three Skill Drills, pupils are required to mark the eye-syllables. This is also required in other Skill Drills in the first two chapters. Lead the pupils to understand that the marking of eye-syllables is a matter of personal choice, and that there are no universal rules to prescribe these visual units within words. Even the ear-syllables shown in dictionaries are often the arbitrary choice of a particular lexicographer.

It is important that pupils think about the meanings of the words contained in the Skill Drills. For this reason, the final pages of this text are devoted to a dictionary. The Spelling

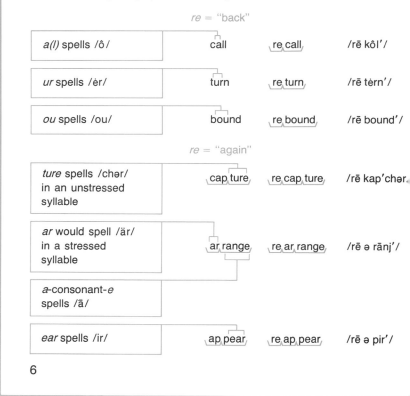

2 "back or again" Prefix *re*

re   The *re* prefix means "back or again." Note how the meanings of the words change when the *re* prefix is added. Note which spelling options are being used in the words.

re = "back"

a(l) spells /ô/	call	re call	/rē kôl′/
ur spells /ėr/	turn	re turn	/rē tėrn′/
ou spells /ou/	bound	re bound	/rē bound′/

re = "again"

ture spells /chər/ in an unstressed syllable	cap ture	re cap ture	/rē kap′chər.
ar would spell /är/ in a stressed syllable	ar range	re ar range	/rē ə rānj′/
a-consonant-*e* spells /ā/			
ear spells /ir/	ap pear	re ap pear	/rē ə pir′/

6

Dictionary does not include the commonly used words from the Skill Drills whose meanings and pronunciations are normally familiar to pupils. When appropriate, the directions to the Skill Drills indicate which words can be found in the Spelling Dictionary.

If there are any pupils who cannot readily read dictionary sound spellings, the symbols should be reviewed for them. A thorough review appears in Chapter 1 of the Level 7 text.

Guide pupils to an understanding of the effect that the prefix has on each root word shown. You may want to ask some pupils to use the prefixed and unprefixed form of each word in a sentence to illustrate its meaning.

Pupils should be familiar with the standard spelling options for the /ô/ sound as in *recall* /rē kôl′/. They are *o* (log), *au* (haul), *aw* (law), and *a* (all).

The standard spelling options for /ėr/, as in *return* /rē tėrn′/, are *er* (her), *ir* (fir), and *ur* (fur).

The /ou/ sound, as in *rebound* /rē bound′/, is always *ou* or *ow*. The *ow* spelling is

Skill Drill 5   Print these words, adding the *re* prefix. Mark the eye-syllables. After each prefixed word, write either *"back"* or *"again"* for the prefix meaning. Compare your work with the answers at the end of Chapter 1.

1 place	5 write	9 join
2 store	6 enter	10 coil
3 build	7 sound	
4 cover	8 count	

3 "make or in" Prefixes   *en   im*

en   The *en* prefix may mean either "make" as it does in *enable*, or "in" as it does in *enclose*. Note how the *en* prefix changes these word meanings.

en = "make"		*en* = "in"	
large	ˌenˌlarge	fold	ˌenˌfold
act	ˌenˌact	trust	ˌenˌtrust
rage	ˌenˌrage	list	ˌenˌlist
gulf	ˌenˌgulf	force	ˌenˌforce
ˌtangˌle	ˌenˌtangˌle	ˌcirˌcle	ˌenˌcirˌcle

im   The *im* prefix may also have the "in" meaning. Note the meanings of these words that show both the *im* and *in* forms of the prefix.

im = "in"			
press	ˌimˌpress	close	ˌinˌclose
print	ˌimˌprint	come	ˌinˌcome
ˌprisˌon	ˌimˌprisˌon	doors	ˌinˌdoors

7

used to spell both /ō/ (show) and /ou/ (cow). The *ou* is an unreliable spelling because it frequently spells other vowel sounds.

Pupils are presumably familiar with the schwa /ə/ symbol, representing the soft, unstressed vowel sound as in *recapture* /rē kap′ chər/ and *rearrange* /rē ə rānj′/. This soft, unstressed vowel sound can be spelled *a* /ə bout′/, *e* /ō′ pən/, *i* /pen′ səl/, *o* /lem′ ən/, and *u* /sėr′ kəs/.

The standard spelling options for /ā/ are *ai*, *ay*, and *a*-consonant-*e*. In *rearrange*, the /nj/ is considered as one consonant sound; therefore, the *a*-consonant-*e* option is used to spell *rearrange*.

The standard spelling options for /ir/ are *ere* (here) and *ear* (hear). The latter option is used to spell *reappear*.

The *im* prefix sometimes means "not" as in the word *improper*. However, this meaning is relatively rare. Because the addition of the *en* and *im* prefix causes very subtle changes in

Skill Drill 6 Answers

1 \en͜cir͜cle͜/ "in"
2 \en͜ti͜tle͜/ "make"
3 \en͜dan͜ger͜/ "in"
4 \en͜li͜ven͜/ "make"
5 \en͜twine͜/ "in"
6 \im͜print͜/ "in"
7 \en͜force͜/ "in"
8 \en͜tang͜le͜/ "make"
9 \en͜rage͜/ "make"
10 \en͜gulf͜/ "make"
11 \en͜dear͜/ "make"
12 \in͜doors͜/ "in"

Skill Drill 6 Print these words, adding the *en* or *im* prefix. Use the *en* prefix ten times. Use the *im* prefix once and use its *in* form once. Mark the eye-syllables. After each prefixed word, write either *"make"* or *"in"* for the prefix meaning. Compare your work with the answers at the end of Chapter 1.

1 circle	5 twine	9 rage
2 title	6 print	10 gulf
3 danger	7 force	11 dear
4 liven	8 tangle	12 doors

4 "down–from–away" Prefixes   *de   dis*

de The *de* prefix usually has the meaning of "down–from–away." A word like *decode* is formed with the prefix *de* and the word *code;* when you *decode,* you write the code "down" into ordinary language. The word *defraud* is formed by the prefix *de* and the word *fraud,* which is a cheating; when you *defraud* you cheat "away" someone's money or property.

dis The *dis* prefix may also have this "down–from–away" meaning.

Note how the *de* and *dis* prefixes change these word meanings.

de = "down–from–away"   *dis* = "down–from–away"

face	\de͜face͜/	arm	\dis͜arm͜/
part	\de͜part͜/	card	\dis͜card͜/
tour	\de͜tour͜/	mount	\dis͜mount͜/

8

meaning, you may want to go over each word emphasizing the way the prefix alters the meaning.

As the *de* and *dis* prefix-root combinations demonstrate, it is not always possible to "read" the meanings of prefix-root combinations literally. In other words, the meaning of the whole word may not be the same as the sum of its parts because such words often undergo shifts in meaning through the years.

Skill Drill 7 Print these words, adding the *de* or *dis* prefix to the regular spelling. Mark the eye-syllables. Use the Sound-Spelling Alphabet chart on page 1 to help you translate these sound-spellings. Compare your work with the answers at the end of Chapter 1.

1 /grād/
2 /thrōn/
3 /kred'ət/
4 /pres/

5 /man'təl/
6 /ə rānj'/
7 /ə pir'/
8 /lō'kāt/

9 /fôrm/
10 /fā'vər/
11 /fās/
12 /chärj/

Skill Drill 7 Answers

1 de grade
2 de throne
3 dis cred it
4 de press
5 dis man tle
6 dis ar range
7 dis ap pear
8 dis lo cate
9 de form
10 dis fa vor
11 de face
12 dis charge

5 "out," "with," "before," and "onward or for" Prefixes
ex com pre pro

ex The *ex* prefix usually means "out" as in *express,* to press "out." When you *express* yourself, you press your thoughts "out." With a hyphen, the *ex* prefix may also be used to show that a person formerly held a position, such as *ex-champion,* a person who was but is no longer champion.

com The *com* prefix means "with–together." You use the *com* prefix before words that begin with *b, p,* or *m.* So *compress* means to press "together"; *combat* means to bat, strike, or fight "with" someone; *commingle* means to mingle or mix "with." Like the *im* prefix, *com* has several different forms. Before words that begin with *l,* you change the *com* prefix to *col* as in *collapse,* to lapse or fall "together." Before *r* words you change the *com* prefix to *cor* as in *correlate,* to relate "with." You sometimes use the *co* prefix form also, as in *cooperate,* to operate "with," and in *copilot,* "with" another pilot. The *con* form also appears often.

9

As noted in the directions for Skill Drill 7, pupils may need to refer to the Sound-Spelling Alphabet chart on page 1. Be sure all pupils are reading the dictionary sound spellings accurately.

Help pupils to note the distinctions between the "out" meaning of *ex* in *express* and the "former" meaning of *ex* in *ex-champion.* Emphasize that the "former" meaning is always signaled by a hyphen.

So *conform* means to get into form or agreement "with"; to *contest* means to test one's ability or strength "with" another; to *condense* means to make dense, to squeeze "together."

pre   The *pre* prefix means "before" as in *prefix,* to fix "before," or in *prepaid,* paid "before."

pro   The *pro* prefix usually means "onward"; to *promote* means to move a pupil "onward." You may also use the *pro* prefix to mean "for." This meaning expresses "in place of" and "in favor of." A *pronoun* is a word used "in place of" a noun; a *proconsul* is a person acting "in place of" a consul. A *pro*-tax voter is a voter who is "in favor of" a tax.

Skill Drill 8 Write the missing prefixed words in these sentences. Compare your work with the answers at the end of Chapter 1.
1 When you have to make a promise "with" another, you __.
2 Making something firm or sure "with" someone, you __.
3 To operate "with" another person, you __.
4 If you and your friend respond to each other in writing, "together" you two __.
5 If you judge "before" the facts are known, you __.
6 When you attend to the duties of the consul "in place of" him or her, you are then __.

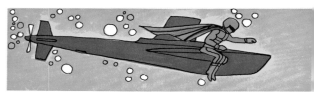

6 "under," "over," "across," and "between" Prefixes
sub   super   trans   inter

sub   The *sub* prefix means "under–below–lower–secondary–next." A *subcontractor* is a person who fills a contract for or "under" the main contractor. A *submarine* is a vessel that goes "below"

10

Note the two meanings of *pro* illustrated by the words *promote* and *pro-tax voter.*

Skill Drill 8 should present no particular problem for pupils. However, allow pupils plenty of time to think about the answers to this exercise.

The *sub, super, trans,* and *inter* prefixes do not appear as frequently in words as some of

the marine or water surface. A *subchief* is a chief ranking "lower" than the head chief. To *sublease* an apartment means to lease it to a "second" person after you have leased the property. A place that is *suburban* is "next" to a city or urban area. You change the *sub* prefix to *suc* in words like *succeed*, to *suf* with *f* word parts such as in *suffer*, to *sug* in words like *suggest*, to *sup* with *p* word parts as in *suppose*, and to *sus* sometimes in words like *suspend* and *sustain*.

super   The *super* prefix means "over–above–superior." A *supersonic* plane flies "over" the speed limit of sound; a *superhighway* is a highway used for speeds "over" those allowed on other roads. Something *supernatural* is "above" the natural, beyond understanding. A *superman* is a "superior" man; the steel framework which gives a structure "superior" strength is called its *superstructure*.

trans   The *trans* prefix means "across–over–through." A *transatlantic* ship goes "across" the Atlantic Ocean. To *transport* means to carry from one place "over" to another place. To *transform* means to make a form different all the way "through."

inter   The *inter* prefix means "between–among–from one to another." *Interstate* agreements are agreements "between" states. An *international* custom is a custom practiced "among" many nations. To *interact* means to act "from one to another."

 Skill Drill 9 Write the missing prefixed words in these sentences. Compare your work with the answers at the end of Chapter 1.

1 In some cities, when you are riding a way on a train "under" the streets, you are on the __.
2 If you feel "below" normal, you feel __.
3 If you are a "superior" human, you are __.
4 When you sail on a ship going "across" the Atlantic Ocean, you are on a __ ship.
5 If your classmates change seats "from one to another," they __ places.

11

Skill Drill 9 Answers
1 subway
2 subnormal
3 superhuman
4 transatlantic
5 interchange

the other prefixes do. Nevertheless, these prefixes do occur frequently enough to merit attention. Pupils should be familiar with the meanings of the example words for each prefix. If necessary, additional examples for each prefix can be found in a dictionary, or pupils can be challenged to supply additional words.

Prefix Review		
Prefix	Meaning	Example
com	with–together	com bat
co		co pi lot
col		col lapse
con		con form
		con test
cor		cor re late
de	down–from–away	de part
dis	not–opposite	dis com fort
	down–from–away	dis mount
en	make	en large
	in	en fold
ex	out	ex press
im	not–opposite	im prop er
ig		ig nore
il		il le gal
in		in cor rect
		in sane
ir		ir reg u lar
im	in	im press
in		in come

Prefix	Meaning	Example
inter	between–among– from one to another	inter act
pre	before	pre paid
pro	onward	pro mote
	for (in place of) (in favor of)	pro noun pro- tax
re	back	re call
	again	re ap pear
sub	under–below–lower– secondary–next	sub ma rine
suc *suf* *sug* *sup* *sus*		suc ceed suf fer sug gest sup pose sus pend sus tain
super	over–above–superior	super nat u ral
trans	across–over–through	trans form
un	not–opposite	un fair

13

B Latin Roots

1 "put–place" Root *pose*

A good example of a Latin root is *pose,* which means to "put," to "place." When models *pose* for an artist, they "put" or "place" themselves into position. When you *pose* as someone else, you "put" or "place" yourself as that person. When you *pose* a question, you "put" the question before others.

Note in the *pose* chart how prefixes can be added to the root to form words. Remember to drop the final *e* in these words before adding the *ing* ending. For example, *repose* becomes *reposing,* and *expose* becomes *exposing.*

		pose = "put–place"		
Prefix	Meaning	Prefix + Root	Meaning	Example
re	back	re‚pose	put back (rest)	to *repose* on a bed
ex	out	ex‚pose	place in full view	to *expose* evil
com	together	com‚pose	put together	to *compose* a poem
im	in	im‚pose	put in or on	to *impose* a fine
pro	for	pro‚pose	put for approval	to *propose* action
de	down	de‚pose	put down	to *depose* a king
dis	away	dis‚pose	put away	to *dispose* of trash
trans	across	trans‚pose	place across (change, reverse)	to *transpose* numbers
sup [sub]	under	sup‚pose	place under (assume)	to *suppose* one is right

14

Section B

This section of Chapter 1 focuses attention on Latin roots. The *pose* root is the first of the 35 Latin roots introduced in this Level 8 text. These Latin roots, when combined with prefixes such as those studied in Section A, account for literally hundreds of English words with their various forms. Familiarity with them will help pupils, not only in spelling, but also in reading, and in enlarging their stock of word meanings. After going over the explanation of the "put–place" root, *pose,* with pupils, take time to explain how the prefixes and the *pose* root are

Skill Drill 10 Write the prefix-*pose* words which have these meanings. Refer to the *pose* chart if you need help. Compare your work with the answers at the end of Chapter 1.

1 remove	4 discard	7 reveal
2 rest	5 assume	8 suggest
3 create	6 change	9 inflict

Skill Drill 10 Answers
1 depose
2 repose
3 compose
4 dispose
5 suppose
6 transpose
7 expose
8 propose
9 impose

2 "pull–draw" Root *tract*

Another example of a common root is *tract,* which in Latin means to "pull," to "draw." A *tractor* is a vehicle for "pulling" farm implements. Note how these prefixes can be added to the *tract* root to form words.

			***tract* = "pull–draw"**	
Prefix	Meaning	Prefix + Root	Meaning	Example
re	back	re‚tract	draw back	to *retract* an offer
ex	out	ex‚tract	pull out	to *extract* a tooth
con [com]	together	con‚tract	draw together	to *contract* an agreement
pro	onward	pro‚tract	draw onward (prolong)	to *protract* a vacation
de	down	de‚tract	pull down (remove some)	to *detract* from a reputation
dis	away	dis‚tract	draw away	to *distract* attention
sub	lower	sub‚tract	draw lower (take from)	to *subtract* numbers

15

combined to form the words. The chart is especially useful for this purpose.

Assign the Skill Drill as usual, and allow pupils to check their answers.

Go over the explanation of the *tract* root with pupils and direct attention to the chart.

The *tract* root comes from Latin *trahere* meaning to pull or draw.

1 subtract
2 protract
3 extract
4 distract
5 retract
6 detract
7 contract

Write the prefix-*tract* words which have these meanings. Refer to the *tract* chart if you need help. Compare your work with the answers at the end of Chapter 1.

1 take from	**4** draw away attention	**7** agree to
2 prolong	**5** draw back	
3 pull out	**6** remove some	

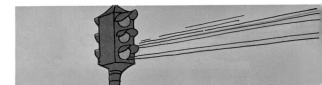

3 "go" Root   *cede–ceed*

A tricky Latin root is *cede–ceed,* meaning to "go." Note the two spelling options for /sēd/. You can solve the spelling problem by remembering that there are only three words with the *ceed* spelling in English—*proceed, succeed,* and *exceed.* All the other /sēd/ spellings are *cede* except for one word.

The one exception is *supersede,* in which *sede* spells /sēd/. The root in *supersede* comes from a different word, the Latin verb *sedere,* "to sit." To *supersede* means to "sit above," that is, to take someone else's position.

Study the next chart, which reviews the *cede–ceed* root that comes from Latin. Note again how prefixes which you learned in Section A of this chapter combine with the root forms to make different words. Think of the meaning of *cede–ceed* and of the prefix, to figure out the meaning of each word example. Then check your meaning with the one given in the chart. Study the phrase examples for uses of the prefix-root words.

In spelling the *ing* form of *cede* words, drop the final *e.* As examples, *recede* becomes *receding,* and *concede* becomes *conceding.*

16

Assign and check the items in the Skill Drill for the *tract* root.

The *cede-ceed* or "go" root in English words originated in the Latin *cedere,* to go. The /sēd/ syllable is a source of many spelling errors. In going over the explanation of this root, stress the three *ceed* spellings, *proceed, succeed,* and *exceed* and the one *sede* spelling of

		Prefix +		
Prefix	Meaning	Root	Meaning	Example
re	back	re cede	go back	to *recede* into the distance
con [com]	with	con cede	go with (give in)	to *concede* a right
pre	before	pre cede	go before (be first)	to *precede* a parade
inter	between	inter cede	go between (help settle differences)	to *intercede* for someone
ex	out	ex ceed	go out (pass beyond)	to *exceed* the speed limit
suc [sub]	next	suc ceed	go next (follow; *now* also means turn out well)	to *succeed* to a throne; to *succeed* in an attempt
pro	onward	pro ceed	go onward	to *proceed* to act

cede–ceed = "go"

Skill Drill 12   Write the prefix-/sēd/ words which have these meanings. Refer to the *cede–ceed* chart if you need help. Compare your work with the answers at the end of Chapter 1.

1 go onward   4 go next   7 go before
2 give in   5 sit above   8 go back
3 go beyond   6 go between

Skill Drill 13   Write the *ing* form of these verbs. Use the Sound-Spelling Alphabet chart on page 1 to help you translate these sound-spellings. Compare your work with the answers at the end of Chapter 1.

1 /rē sēd'/   4 /kəm pōz'/   7 /sə pōz'/
2 /prē sēd'/   5 /suk sēd'/   8 /ek sēd'/
3 /dis pōz'/   6 /eks pōz'/

17

/sēd/ found in *supersede*. All other /sēd/ words are spelled *cede*.

Be sure to give some special attention to the paragraph on spelling the *ing* forms of *cede* words. One of the subsequent Skill Drills is devoted to spelling these *ing* forms.

Have pupils study the chart and work through the Skill Drills.

4 "carry" Root   *port*

Our *port* root comes from the Latin verb *portare,* "to carry." The word *port* means a harbor, a place where vessels unload cargo. This *port* comes from a Latin noun, *portus,* a harbor. Our word *portal* comes from still another Latin noun *porta,* which means gate or door. A *porter* may be a gatekeeper, from Latin *porta,* but he may also be a luggage carrier, from the Latin verb *portare.* Another example is *port* wine, a red wine of rich taste; this *port* word comes from *Pôrto,* the Portuguese city which gave the wine its name.

Study the *port* chart. Note the prefix-root combinations formed with the root derived from *portare.*

		port = "carry"		
Prefix	Meaning	Prefix + Root	Meaning	Example
re	back	re͜port	carry back	to *report* news
ex	out	ex͜port	carry out	to *export* goods
im	in	im͜port	carry in	to *import* goods
de	away	de͜port	carry away (order to leave)	to *deport* a criminal
sup [sub]	under	sup͜port	carry under (hold up)	to *support* a bridge
trans	across	trans͜port	carry across	to *transport* goods

18

After going over the explanation of the *port* root, you may wish to challenge pupils to name other English words containing the *port* root.

Have pupils study the chart carefully before assigning the Skill Drill on page 19. Encourage pupils to try to complete the Skill Drill without turning back to the *port* chart.

Skill Drill 14 Write the missing prefix-*port* words to complete the sentences. Refer to the *port* chart if you need help. Compare your work with the answers at the end of Chapter 1.

1 Large trucking firms __ freight.

2 When criminals are sent out of a country, they are __.

3 Merchants who sell goods in foreign lands __ goods. Merchants who bring goods into a country __ them.

4 Good causes need __.

5 Newspapers __ the news.

5 "push" Root *pel*

The *pel* root means to "push." Note how these prefixes combine with the *pel* root. Remember that you double a final *l* before adding *ed* or *ing*. Words like *repel* become *repelled, repelling,* and *expel* becomes *expelled, expelling.*

		Prefix +		
Prefix	Meaning	Root	Meaning	Example
re	back	re͜pel	push back	to *repel* one's senses or emotions
ex	out	ex͜pel	push out	to *expel* a substance
com	with	com͜pel	push with (force)	to *compel* action
im	in	im͜pel	push in (cause one to act)	to *impel* one to do good
pro	onward	pro͜pel	push onward	to *propel* a boat
dis	away	dis͜pel	push away	to *dispel* gloom

19

The *pel* root in English words comes from Latin *pellere* meaning "to drive" or "to push." Go through the explanation of the *pel* root with pupils noting how the "push" or "drive" meaning is found in each word in the chart. Call particular attention to the fact that the final *l* in these words is doubled before adding *ed* or *ing*. Then assign the Skill Drill on page 20.

Skill Drill 15 Answers

1 compelled
2 dispel
3 propelled; expel
4 impelled
5 repel

Skill Drill 15 Write the missing prefix-*pel* words to complete the sentences. Refer to the *pel* chart if you need help. Compare your work with the answers at the end of Chapter 1.

1 When you are forced to work, you are ___ to work.
2 Having fun will usually ___ sadness and gloom.
3 Sailing ships were ___ by the wind and did not ___ engine fumes.
4 Angry people may be ___ to speak up.
5 Snakes ___ some people.

6 "press–squeeze" Root *press*

The *press* root means just that, to "press," to "squeeze." Study the prefix-root combinations in the *press* chart.

			press = "press–squeeze"	
Prefix	Meaning	Prefix + Root	Meaning	Example
re	back	re press	press back (hold in)	to *repress* anger
ex	out	ex press	press out (speak, send quickly)	to *express* grief; to *express* goods
com	together	com press	press together	to *compress* cotton
im	in	im press	press in (make an imprint of or on)	to *impress* one's listeners
de	down	de press	press down (sadden, lower)	to *depress* spirits
sup [sub]	under	sup press	press under (stop)	to *suppress* power

20

The *press* root in English words comes from the Latin *premere,* meaning "to press." Have pupils study the words in the chart noting how the "press" meaning is included in each word. Another "press" word is *pressure.* If desired, have pupils explain how the "press-squeeze" meaning applies to *pressure, pressure group,* and *pressure suit.*

Skill Drill 16 Write the missing prefix-*press* words to complete the sentences. Refer to the *press* chart if you need help. Compare your work with the answers at the end of Chapter 1.
1 Rainy weather makes some people feel __.
2 Lawyers who can __ themselves will __ juries.
3 A lot of air can be __ into small tanks.
4 Dictators often __ uprisings with force.
5 Shy people often __ their feelings.

7 "write" Root   *scribe*

The *scribe* root means to "write." A *scribe* was a person whose business was "writing." The word *scribble* means to "write" quickly or carelessly. A *script* is a piece of "writing." Actors often use *scripts*. Remember to drop the final *e* in these words before adding the *ing* ending.

scribe = "write"				
Prefix	Meaning	Prefix + Verb	Meaning	Example
in [im]	in	in,scribe	write in	to *inscribe* words
pre	before	pre,scribe	write before	to *prescribe* rest
de	down	de,scribe	write down (inform about)	to *describe* a scene
sub	under	sub,scribe	write under (agree to or with)	to *subscribe* to an opinion
tran [trans]	across	tran,scribe	write across (copy differently)	to *transcribe* shorthand

21

The *scribe* root which occurs in many English words is derived from the Latin *scribere*, meaning "to write." The "write" element in some words in the chart may not be immediately apparent to some pupils. If necessary, take additional time to explain the meanings of *prescribe* and *subscribe*. The *scribe* root can also be illustrated with the word *scripture*.

Skill Drill 17 Answers
1 prescribe
2 inscribed
3 transcribe
4 subscribe
5 describe

Skill Drill 18 Answers
1 propelling
2 inscribing
3 exporting
4 suppressing
5 repelling
6 prescribing
7 deporting
8 compressing
9 transporting
10 subscribing
11 impelling
12 describing
13 reporting
14 dispelling
15 expelling
16 transcribing
17 expressing
18 compelling
19 importing
20 depressing
21 supporting

Skill Drill 17 Write the missing prefix-*scribe* words to com plete the sentences. Refer to the *scribe* chart if you need help Compare your work with the answers at the end of Chapter 1
1 Doctors __ medicine for their patients.
2 Monuments are often __ with words of wisdom.
3 Typists __ letters from shorthand.
4 When we agree with statements, we __ to them.
5 Writers like to __ scenes from their youth.

Skill Drill 18 Write the *ing* form of these verbs. Use the Sound-Spelling Alphabet chart on page 1 to help you translate these sound-spellings. Compare your work with the answer at the end of Chapter 1.

1 /prō pel'/	8 /kəm pres'/	15 /eks pel'/
2 /in skrīb'/	9 /trans pôrt'/	16 /tran skrīb'/
3 /eks pôrt'/	10 /sub skrīb'/	17 /eks pres'/
4 /sə pres'/	11 /im pel'/	18 /kəm pel'/
5 /rē pel'/	12 /dē skrīb'/	19 /im pôrt'/
6 /prē scrīb'/	13 /rē pôrt'/	20 /de pres'/
7 /dē pôrt'/	14 /dis pel'/	21 /sə pôrt'/

Skill Drill 19 Write the *ed* form of these verbs. Use the Sound-Spelling Alphabet chart on page 1 to help you translate these sound-spellings. Compare your work with the answer at the end of Chapter 1.

1 /prē skrīb'/	8 /rē pel'/	15 /sub trakt'/
2 /sə pres'/	9 /prē sēd'/	16 /im pel'/
3 /kəm pel'/	10 /dis pel'/	17 /eks pres'/
4 /trans pôrt'/	11 /kəm pōz'/	18 /dē pôrt'/
5 /prō trakt'/	12 /prō pel'/	19 /eks pel'/
6 /im pōz'/	13 /in skrīb'/	20 /in' tər sēd'/
7 /kən sēd'/	14 /sə pōz'/	21 /dē skrīb'/

22

Skill Drills 18 and 19 provide substantial practice in writing the *ing* and *ed* forms of the words made by combining the prefixes and roots studied in this chapter. Be sure that pupils understand the directions for these Skill Drills before they begin working. Also, it is essential that pupils are reading the dictionary sound-spellings accurately.

The summary allows for a brief review of the chapter before assigning pupils the Mastery

Summary

Prefixes are word parts we affix to the front of English words and Latin roots to change the word or root meanings. The common prefixes are *un, dis, im* ("not–opposite"); *re* ("back or again"); *en* ("make or in") and *im* ("in"); *de, dis* ("down–from–away"); *ex* ("out"); *com* ("with–together"); pre ("before"); *pro* ("onward or for"); *sub* ("under–below–lower–secondary–next"); *super* ("over–above–superior"); *trans* ("across–over–through"); *inter* ("between–among–from one to another").

Latin roots to which we often add these prefixes are *pose* ("put–place"); *tract* ("pull–draw"); *cede–ceed* ("go"); *port* ("carry"); *pel* ("push"); *press* ("press–squeeze"); *scribe* ("write").

When you look at words, you will often see these prefixes and roots as eye-syllables. If you note the spelling options which are being used and you know the meanings of prefixes, you will be able to spell prefix-root words more easily and remember their meanings better.

Skill Drill 19 Answers
1 prescribed
2 suppressed
3 compelled
4 transported
5 protracted
6 imposed
7 conceded
8 repelled
9 preceded
10 dispelled
11 composed
12 propelled
13 inscribed
14 supposed
15 subtracted
16 impelled
17 expressed
18 deported
19 expelled
20 interceded
21 described

23

Test on pages 24 and 25. The Mastery Test is divided into two parts to allow it to be given in two sessions if desired. One longer session may prove to be too tiresome for some pupils. Any pupil unable to perform reasonably well on the Mastery Test should receive some review before going on to Chapter 2. If possible, find a pattern in the pupils' errors and use the chart in the front of this Teacher's Edition to prescribe appropriate review in Level 7 or 8.

Part A Answers

1 illegible
2 uninteresting
3 irresistible
4 insincere
5 illogical
6 unbearable
7 impersonal
8 insecure
9 immature
10 infrequent
11 irresponsible
12 dishonest
13 improper
14 unhealthy
15 ignoble
16 irreverent
17 disconnect
18 discontinue
19 unfasten
20 indirect
21 sublease
22 interchange
23 superstructure
   or substructure
24 transatlantic
25 submarine
26 superhuman *or*
   subhuman
27 subchief
28 subway
29 superhighway
30 transformation
31 subnormal
32 subcontractor
33 interstate

Mastery Test 1

A Write each of the following words with a "not–opposite" prefix

1 legible	8 secure	15 noble
2 interesting	9 mature	16 reverent
3 resistible	10 frequent	17 connect
4 sincere	11 responsible	18 continue
5 logical	12 honest	19 fasten
6 bearable	13 proper	20 direct
7 personal	14 healthy	

Write each of the following words with an "under," "over," "be
tween," or "across" prefix.

21 lease	26 human	31 normal
22 change	27 chief	32 contractor
23 structure	28 way	33 state
24 Atlantic	29 highway	34 natural
25 marine	30 formation	35 national

Write each of the following words with a "make," "in," "down,"
or "back or again" prefix.

36 locate	41 danger	46 throne
37 list	42 close	47 rage
38 print	43 arm	48 prison
39 press	44 come	49 tour
40 grade	45 sure	50 mantle

B Write a word for each definition, using a prefix and the roo
for which the sound-spelling is shown.

/trakt/

1 pull out
2 draw together
3 draw back
4 draw away attention
5 draw lower; take from

24

/pel/

6 push back
7 push onward
8 push out
9 push away
10 push with; force

/pōz/

11 put together
12 put down
13 put for approval; suggest
14 place across; reverse
15 place out in view

/pôrt/

16 carry out goods
17 carry in goods
18 carry across
19 carry back news
20 carry away; order to leave

/pres/

21 press together
22 press in
23 press back
24 press under; stop
25 press out; speak

/sēd/

26 go back
27 go before
28 go between
29 go above; take the place of
30 go onward

/skrīb/

31 write in
32 write down
33 write under; agree
34 write before
35 write across; copy

Part A Answers (cont'd)
34 supernatural
35 international
36 dislocate or relocate
37 enlist
38 imprint or reprint
39 impress, or repress, or depress
40 degrade
41 endanger
42 disclose or enclose
43 disarm or rearm
44 income
45 ensure or insure
46 dethrone or enthrone
47 enrage
48 imprison
49 detour
50 dismantle

Part B Answers
1 extract
2 contract
3 retract
4 distract
5 subtract
6 repel
7 propel
8 expel
9 dispel
10 compel
11 compose
12 depose
13 propose
14 transpose

Part B Answers (cont'd)

15 expose
16 export
17 import
18 transport
19 report
20 deport
21 compress
22 impress
23 repress
24 suppress
25 express
26 recede
27 precede
28 intercede
29 supersede
30 proceed
31 inscribe
32 describe
33 subscribe
34 prescribe
35 transcribe

Skill Drill 1 1 un·a·ware 2 un·in·ter·est·ing
3 un·pop·u·lar 4 un·bear·a·ble 5 un·e·qual 6 un·true
7 un·eas·y 8 un·fast·en 9 un·luck·y

Skill Drill 2 1 dis·con·nect 2 dis·trust 3 dis·ap·pear
4 dis·please 5 dis·o·bey 6 dis·con·tin·ue 7 dis·sim·i·la

Skill Drill 3 1 im·per·son·al 2 in·di·rect 3 in·sin·cere
4 in·se·cure 5 im·mor·tal 6 ir·re·spons·i·ble
7 im·pa·tient 8 in·fre·quent 9 ir·re·sist·i·ble
10 il·leg·i·ble

Skill Drill 4 1 unfriendly 2 unhealthy 3 disbelief
4 impatient 5 unsteady 6 unwelcome 7 distaste
8 disapprove 9 unworthy

Skill Drill 5 1 re·place "again" *or* "back" 2 re·store
"back" *or* "again" 3 re·build "again" 4 re·cover "back"
or "again" 5 re·write "again" 6 re·en·ter "again"
7 re·sound "back" 8 re·count "again" 9 re·join "again"
10 re·coil "back"

Skill Drill 6 1 en·cir·cle "in" 2 en·ti·tle "make"
3 en·dan·ger "in" 4 en·li·ven "make" 5 en·twine "in"
6 im·print "in" 7 en·force "in" 8 en·tang·le "make"
9 en·rage "make" 10 en·gulf "in" 11 en·dear "make"
12 in·doors "in"

Skill Drill 7 1 de·grade 2 de·throne 3 dis·cred·it
4 de·press 5 dis·man·tle 6 dis·ar·range 7 dis·ap·pear
8 dis·lo·cate 9 de·form 10 dis·fa·vor 11 de·face
12 dis·charge

Skill Drill 8 1 compromise 2 confirm 3 cooperate
4 correspond 5 prejudge 6 proconsul

Skill Drill 9 1 subway 2 subnormal 3 superhuman
4 transatlantic 5 interchange

26

Skill Drill 10   1 depose   2 repose   3 compose   4 dispose
5 suppose   6 transpose   7 expose   8 propose   9 impose

Skill Drill 11   1 subtract   2 protract   3 extract   4 distract
5 retract   6 detract   7 contract

Skill Drill 12   1 proceed   2 concede   3 exceed
4 succeed   5 supersede   6 intercede   7 precede
8 recede

Skill Drill 13   1 receding   2 preceding   3 disposing
4 composing   5 succeeding   6 exposing   7 supposing
8 exceeding

Skill Drill 14   1 transport   2 deported   3 export; import
4 support   5 report

Skill Drill 15   1 compelled   2 dispel   3 propelled; expel
4 impelled   5 repel

Skill Drill 16   1 depressed   2 express; impress
3 compressed   4 suppress   5 repress

Skill Drill 17   1 prescribe   2 inscribed   3 transcribe
4 subscribe   5 describe

Skill Drill 18   1 propelling   2 inscribing   3 exporting
4 suppressing   5 repelling   6 prescribing   7 deporting
8 compressing   9 transporting   10 subscribing
11 impelling   12 describing   13 reporting   14 dispelling
15 expelling   16 transcribing   17 expressing
18 compelling   19 importing   20 depressing
21 supporting

Skill Drill 19   1 prescribed   2 suppressed   3 compelled
4 transported   5 protracted   6 imposed   7 conceded
8 repelled   9 preceded   10 dispelled   11 composed
12 propelled   13 inscribed   14 supposed   15 subtracted
16 impelled   17 expressed   18 deported   19 expelled
20 interceded   21 described

27

2 Roots and Suffixes

Just as you add prefixes to the front of root words, you add *suffixes* to the ends of root words to make other words. But the suffixes do not so directly change the meanings of the words or roots to which you add them.

Words are often grouped into the classes which are called "parts of speech." Nouns, verbs, adjectives, and adverbs are examples of these classes of words. Some words are names of places, persons, and things, such as *street, sister,* and *basket.* We call these "naming" words *nouns.* The "doing" words like *speak* are verbs. The classes of "describing" words are *adjectives* and *adverbs.* Adjectives, such as *proud* and *strong,* tell something about nouns. Adverbs, such as *quickly* and *carefully,* tell about verbs. *Nearly* and *very* are adverbs that tell about adjectives. When you add suffixes to words, you change words from one part of speech into another. Sometimes you form a noun by adding a suffix to an adjective or a verb. You may form an adjective by attaching a suffix to a noun or a verb.

Suffixes Change Adjectives and Verbs into Nouns

Some suffixes are noun suffixes. A noun suffix may change adjectives or verbs into nouns. A common noun suffix is *ness,* which usually changes adjectives into nouns. Another common suffix is *ment,* which usually changes verbs into nouns. The *ance* and *ence* suffix forms change verbs and adjectives into nouns. You see *ion* or *sion* or *tion* at the end of many words. Often these words are nouns formed by adding an *ion* or *sion* or *tion* suffix form to verbs.

28

CHAPTER 2

The suffixes cause more spelling problems than do the prefixes because several of them have spelling options, like *ance-ence, ant-ent, tion-sion, ious-eous,* and *able-ible.* Since these suffixes commonly appear in or as unstressed syllables, the vowel sounds are pronounced /ə/, and there are no spelling cues for /ə/.

In addition to mastering the spellings and learning to look for the correct spelling option, the pupils should become aware of the difference in function of the prefixes and suffixes. Whereas the prefixes directly affect the root word meanings, the suffixes, with the exception of *less* and *ful,* do not. Instead of changing the

1 Noun Suffix *ness*

When you attach or affix the *ness* suffix to adjectives, you make nouns out of them. Such words are not hard to spell if you can spell the adjective forms. Study the examples and note the eye-syllables in the first list of nouns.

Many adjectives end in the /ē/ sound, which you usually spell with *y* at the end of a word. When you add the *ness* suffix to such adjectives, you change the final *y* to *i* before adding the *ness* suffix. Note this change in the second list of nouns.

adjective	noun	adjective	noun
bright	bright ness	laz y	laz i ness
kind	kind ness	hap py	hap pi ness
rude	rude ness	read y	read i ness

Skill Drill 1   Change these adjectives into *ness* nouns. Print your answers. Mark the eye-syllables. Compare your work with the answers at the end of Chapter 2.

1 ill	10 steady	19 lively
2 like	11 awkward	20 harsh
3 mad	12 sure	21 greedy
4 heavy	13 holy	22 sober
5 lonely	14 pleasant	23 blessed
6 dizzy	15 rude	24 firm
7 empty	16 still	25 cold
8 friendly	17 stingy	26 fine
9 sick	18 dull	27 lowly

29

Skill Drill 1 Answers

1 ill ness
2 like ness
3 mad ness
4 heav i ness
5 lone li ness
6 diz zi ness
7 emp ti ness
8 friend li ness
9 sick ness
10 stead i ness
11 awk ward ness
12 sure ness
13 hol i ness
14 pleas ant ness
15 rude ness
16 still ness
17 stin gi ness
18 dull ness
19 live li ness
20 harsh ness
21 greed i ness
22 so ber ness
23 bless ed ness
24 firm ness
25 cold ness
26 fine ness
27 low li ness

meaning of words, the suffixes serve to change words from one part of speech to another. The pupils should, therefore, understand the functions of nouns, verbs, adjectives, and adverbs whether the traditional grammar terminology is used or not. A brief review of these parts of speech may be helpful.

Section A

In this first section detailed attention is given to four suffixes which are used to change adjectives and verbs into nouns. In going over the explanation of the *ness* suffix with the pupils, emphasize that the *ness* suffix transforms adjectives into nouns.

30

Skill Drill 2 Answers

1 ap point ment
2 ar range ment
3 gov ern ment
4 man age ment
5 pay ment
6 com mand ment
7 e quip ment
8 ex cite ment
9 ad vance ment
10 a gree ment
11 state ment
12 en gage ment
13 de vel op ment
14 set tle ment
15 em ploy ment
16 en roll ment
17 a chieve ment
18 en force ment
19 ful fill ment
20 com mence ment

2 Noun Suffix *ment*

Usually the *ment* suffix changes verbs into nouns. Study these examples and note the eye-syllables.

verb	noun
treat	treat ment
an nounce	an nounce ment
as sign	as sign ment

Skill Drill 2 Change these verbs into *ment* nouns. Print your answers. Mark the eye-syllables. Compare your work with the answers at the end of Chapter 2.

1 appoint
2 arrange
3 govern
4 manage
5 pay
6 command
7 equip
8 excite
9 advance
10 agree
11 state
12 engage
13 develop
14 settle
15 employ
16 enroll
17 achieve
18 enforce
19 fulfill
20 commence

3 Noun Suffix *ance–ence*

When either the *ance* or *ence* form of this suffix is in a stressed syllable of a word, you can hear the vowel sound clearly. Then you have no spelling problem. But when the *ance–ence* suffix is in a soft or unstressed syllable, you hear /əns/. Then you have to *look* carefully to see which of the two spelling options, *ance* or *ence,* is correct. Study the common *ance–ence* words on the next page. Note the spelling options.

30

After introducing the *ment* suffix and directing pupils' attention to the examples, assign the Skill Drill. Both *enrol* and *enroll* are usually listed in dictionaries. Similarly, *fulfill* and *fulfil* are listed as acceptable spellings.

In studying the *ance-ence* suffix, it particularly important that pupils see how stress clarifies the vowel sound in a syllable and provides a spelling cue. Conversely, they should note how the vowel sound becomes obscure

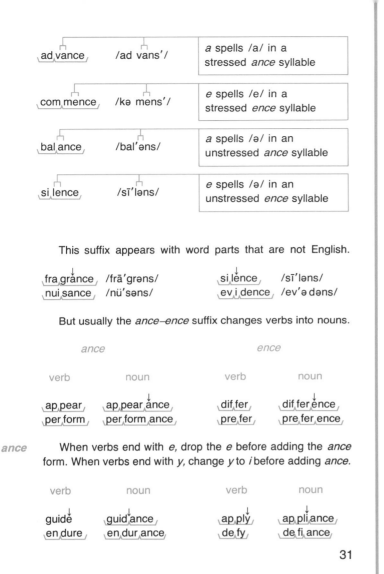

ad vance	/ad vans'/	*a* spells /a/ in a stressed *ance* syllable
com mence	/kə mens'/	*e* spells /e/ in a stressed *ence* syllable
bal ance	/bal'əns/	*a* spells /ə/ in an unstressed *ance* syllable
si lence	/sī'ləns/	*e* spells /ə/ in an unstressed *ence* syllable

This suffix appears with word parts that are not English.

| fra grance | /frā'grəns/ | si lence | /sī'ləns/ |
| nui sance | /nü'səns/ | ev i dence | /ev'ə dəns/ |

But usually the *ance–ence* suffix changes verbs into nouns.

	ance		*ence*
verb	noun	verb	noun
ap pear	ap pear ance	dif fer	dif fer ence
per form	per form ance	pre fer	pre fer ence

ance When verbs end with *e,* drop the *e* before adding the *ance* form. When verbs end with *y,* change *y* to *i* before adding *ance.*

verb	noun	verb	noun
guide	guid ance	ap ply	ap pli ance
en dure	en dur ance	de fy	de fi ance

31

in unstressed syllables and yields no spelling cue. Help pupils to understand the importance of *looking* carefully to see which vowel spelling option *(ance* or *ence)* is correct when the syllable has no stress. Demonstrate how "thinking" stress on unstressed syllables can restore the vowel spelling cue. For example, pronouncing *fragrance* quietly as /frā' grans'/ will make the spelling more apparent.

Skill Drill 3 Answers

1. ac‸quaint‸ance
2. as‸sist‸ance
3. at‸tend‸ance
4. guid‸ance
5. var‸i‸ance
6. ig‸nor‸ance
7. al‸li‸ance
8. as‸sur‸ance
9. re‸li‸ance
10. ap‸pli‸ance
11. ob‸serv‸ance
12. com‸pli‸ance
13. a‸void‸ance
14. ut‸ter‸ance
15. con‸tin‸u‸ance
16. re‸pent‸ance
17. is‸su‸ance
18. dis‸turb‸ance
19. en‸dur‸ance
20. in‸her‸it‸ance

Skill Drill 3 Change these verbs to *ance* nouns. Print your answers. Mark the eye-syllables. Check the meaning of any unfamiliar word in your Spelling Dictionary or in the classroom dictionary. The first four words do not appear in your Spelling Dictionary. Compare your work with the answers at the end of Chapter 2.

1 acquaint	8 assure	15 continue
2 assist	9 rely	16 repent
3 attend	10 apply	17 issue
4 guide	11 observe	18 disturb
5 vary	12 comply	19 endure
6 ignore	13 avoid	20 inherit
7 ally	14 utter	

ence Generally, the *ence* form of this suffix changes *ent*-ending adjectives into *ence*-ending nouns. Study these examples and note the eye-syllables.

adjective	noun	adjective	noun
ab‸sent	ab‸sence	el‸o‸quent	el‸o‸quence
ev‸i‸dent	ev‸i‸dence	pa‸tient	pa‸tience
pres‸ent	pres‸ence	dil‸i‸gent	dil‸i‸gence

Skill Drill 4 Change these *ent* adjectives to *ence* nouns. Print your answers. Mark the eye-syllables. Check the meaning of any unfamiliar word in your Spelling Dictionary or in the classroom dictionary. Compare your work with the answers at the end of Chapter 2.

1 patient	8 violent	15 permanent
2 negligent	9 consequent	16 persistent
3 diligent	10 belligerent	17 emergent
4 penitent	11 concurrent	18 fluorescent
5 eloquent	12 confident	19 resident
6 prominent	13 effervescent	20 correspondent
7 magnificent	14 reverent	

32

After allowing pupils ample time to study the *ance-ence* word charts, assign Skill Drills 3 and 4.

Give the pupils some latitude in marking the eye-syllables in the Skill Drills. Eye-syllables are simply the *best visual groupings of let-*

ters within a word to help one remember the spelling.

In Skill Drill 3 check especially to see that pupils drop the final e and change the final y to i before adding the *ance* suffix. Some of the words in Skill Drill 4 are difficult.

4 Noun Suffix *ion–sion–tion*

The noun suffix *ion–sion–tion* appears in unstressed syllables. The *ion* form spells three different sounds, *sion* spells two, and *tion* spells two. Study the suffix sounds in this first chart and the spelling cues in the second chart.

ion–sion–tion Suffix Sounds

Suffix	Sounds	Example	Sound-Spelling
ion	/ən/	fash ion	/fash'ən/
	/yən/	un ion	/ūn'yən/
	/ē ən/	cham pi on	/cham'pē ən/
sion	/shən/	mis sion	/mish'ən/
	/zhən/	vis ion	/vizh'ən/
tion	/shən/	mo tion	/mō'shən/
	/chən/	sug ges tion	/sug jes'chən/

ion–sion–tion Spelling Cues

Sounds	Example	Sound-Spelling	Spelling Cues
/ən/	fash ion	/fash'ən/	*ion* spells /ən/ after *sh*
	re gion	/rē'jən/	*ion* spells /ən/ after *g*
/yən/	un ion	/ūn'yən/	*ion* spells /yən/ after *n*
	mil lion	/mil'yən/	*ion* spells /yən/ after *l*
/ē ən/	cham pi on	/cham'pē ən/	*ion* spells /ē ən/ after *p*
/shən/	mo tion	/mō'shən/	*tion* generally spells /shən/
	mis sion	/mish'ən/	*sion* generally spells /shən/
	pen sion	/pen'shən/	*sion* spells /shən/ after *n*
/zhən/	vis ion	/vizh'ən/	*sion* spells /zhən/ after a vowel
/chən/	sug ges tion	/sug jes'chən/	*tion* sometimes spells /chən/

33

Skill Drill 4 Answers

1 pa tience
2 neg li gence
3 dil i gence
4 pen it ence
5 el o quence
6 prom i nence
7 mag nif i cence
8 vi o lence
9 con se quence
10 bel lig er ence
11 con cur rence
12 con fi dence
13 ef fer ves cence
14 re ver ence
15 per man ence
16 per sist ence
17 e merg ence
18 flu o res cence
19 res i dence
20 cor re spond ence

The *ion-sion-tion* noun suffix is the source of considerable problems. Be sure the pupils hear the different pronunciations for *ion*, *sion*, and *tion* as shown in the chart.

The spelling cues in the second chart are interesting, but pupils should not be required to memorize them. Memorizing detailed spelling "rules" is not very productive. The subsequent exercises will cause the pupils to examine the spellings more carefully.

Skill Drill 5 Answers
1 cushion
2 opinion
3 division
4 action
5 station
6 religion
7 possession
8 admission
9 billion
10 caution
11 scorpion
12 digestion

If you study the preceding chart carefully, you can find and make use of these spelling cues.

If you hear the ending sounds /ən/, /yən/, or /ē ən/, the suffix spelling will be *ion (fashion, union, champion)*.

If you hear the /shən/ sound, the suffix spelling will be either *sion (mission, pension)* or *tion (motion)*.

If you hear the /zhən/ sound, the spelling will be a vowel letter and the suffix form *sion (vision)*.

If you hear the /chən/ sound, the suffix spelling will be *tion (suggestion)*.

Skill Drill 5 Write the regular spellings of these nouns, using the correct form of the *ion–sion–tion* suffix. Use the Sound-Spelling Alphabet chart on page 1 to help you translate these sound-spellings. Check the meaning of any unfamiliar word in your Spelling Dictionary or in the classroom dictionary. The last five words are in your Spelling Dictionary. Compare your work with the answers at the end of Chapter 2.

1 /kush'ən/   5 /stā'shən/   9 /bil'yən/
2 /ə pin'yən/   6 /rə lij'ən/   10 /kô'shən/
3 /də vizh'ən/   7 /pə zesh'ən/   11 /skôr'pē ən/
4 /ak'shən/   8 /ad mish'ən/   12 /də jes'chən/

tion

The *tion* form of this noun suffix appears more frequently in English words than the *ion* and *sion* forms do. Also, most /shən/ suffix sounds are spelled *tion*. Some *tion* words have meaning only when you see the entire word.

auc tion	/ôk'shən/
fic tion	/fik'shən/
men tion	/men'shən/
na tion	/nā'shən/
sec tion	/sek'shən/
at ten tion	/ə ten'shən/
no tion	/nō'shən/

34

It is particularly important that pupils read the dictionary sound-spellings in Skill Drill 5 accurately in order to make use of the spelling cues for choosing the correct form of the *ion-sion-tion* suffix.

Check to see that pupils know the meanings of the words they write. Pupils will be more motivated to learn the spelling of words they know and can use. Use the example words to demonstrate how changing the final e to a in

You change many *t*-ending verbs to nouns that end with the /shən/ sound by adding *ion.* The final *t* of the verb becomes part of the suffix syllable of the noun.

verb	noun	verb	noun
a.dopt	a.dop.tion	e.lect	e.lec.tion
di.rect	di.rec.tion	at.tract	at.trac.tion

You change many *ate*-ending verbs to *tion* nouns. You drop the final *e* before you add *ion,* to create the /shən/ sound.

But with other vowel-consonant-*e* verbs, you often change the final *e* to *a* before adding the *tion* suffix form to make nouns. The /ā/ makes the word easier to pronounce. Note this change in the second list of nouns.

verb	noun	verb	noun
ro.tate	ro.ta.tion	ad.mire	ad.mir.ā.tion
im.it.ate	im.it.a.tion	im.a.gine	im.a.gin.a.tion
pop.u.late	pop.u.la.tion	civ.il.ize	civ.il.iz.a.tion

Skill Drill 6 Change these verbs to nouns ending with the /shən/ sound. Check the meaning of any unfamiliar word in your Spelling Dictionary or in the classroom dictionary. The first nine words do not appear in your Spelling Dictionary. Compare your work with the answers at the end of Chapter 2.

1 collect
2 correct
3 select
4 edit
5 elect
6 locate
7 communicate
8 create
9 participate
10 decorate
11 situate
12 perspire
13 incline
14 nominate
15 combine
16 dedicate
17 celebrate
18 recite
19 reserve
20 contradict
21 exhibit
22 generate
23 affect
24 regulate
25 inflate
26 vibrate

35

Skill Drill 6 Answers
1 collection
2 correction
3 selection
4 edition
5 election
6 location
7 communication
8 creation
9 participation
10 decoration
11 situation
12 perspiration
13 inclination
14 nomination
15 combination
16 dedication
17 celebration
18 recitation
19 reservation
20 contradiction
21 exhibition
22 generation
23 affection
24 regulation
25 inflation
26 vibration

some vowel-consonant-*e* verbs makes the *tion* form easier to pronounce.

After checking the spellings in Skill Drill 6, you may want to have the pupils use both the verb and noun form of each word in a sentence to illustrate that the meanings and the appropriate usage are familiar. The meaning of *affect* is often confused with *effect.* Use a dictionary to clarify these words if pupils have trouble.

Skill Drill 7 Answers

1 hope, hopeful, hopeless
2 help, helpful, helpless
3 fear, fearful, fearless
4 law, lawful, lawless
5 need, needful, needless
6 shame, shameful, shameless
7 thank, thankful, thankless
8 cheer, cheerful, cheerless
9 faith, faithful, faithless
10 fruit, fruitful, fruitless
11 doubt, doubtful, doubtless
12 thought, thoughtful, thoughtless
13 color, colorful, colorless
14 mercy, merciful, merciless
15 pity, pitiful, pitiless

B

Suffixes Change Nouns and Verbs into Adjectives

1 Adjective Suffixes   *ful   less*

Two common suffixes which we add to nouns and verbs to make adjectives are *ful* and *less*. We do make a few nouns with the *ful* suffix, like *cupful*, but *ful* usually forms adjectives.

The *ful* and *less* suffixes are the only ones which change word meanings directly, as the prefixes do. The *less* suffix adds "without" to the word meaning—*spotless* means "without" a spot. The *ful* suffix adds "having" to the word—*respectful* means "having" respect; *wrongful* means "having" wronged.

Note that in *y*-ending words you change *y* to *i* before adding the *ful* and *less* suffixes: *bounty* becomes *bountiful; pity* becomes *pitiful* or *pitiless; penny* becomes *penniless.*

noun *or* verb	*ful* adjective	*less* adjective
care	care ful	care less
pain	pain ful	pain less
use	use ful	use less

Skill Drill 7   Write the regular spellings of these nouns and verbs. Make two adjectives of each one by adding the *ful* suffix and then the *less* suffix. Use the Sound-Spelling Alphabet chart on page 1 to help you translate these sound-spellings. Answers appear at the end of Chapter 2.

1 /hōp/	5 /nēd/	9 /fāth/	13 /kul′ər/
2 /help/	6 /shām/	10 /früt/	14 /mėr′sē/
3 /fir/	7 /thangk/	11 /dout/	15 /pit′ē/
4 /lô/	8 /chir/	12 /thôt/	

36

Section B

The three subsections contained in this section of Chapter 2 examine the suffixes which are used to change nouns and verbs into adjectives. Although the material can be dealt with independently by the pupils, it is usually preferable to go over each explanation with them. Have pupils make particular note of the fact that the *ful* and *less* suffixes directly affect the

2 Adjective Suffix *ous*

ous The *ous* suffix appears in unstressed syllables and is pronounced /əs/, instead of /ous/ as it would be in a stressed syllable. We may add the *ous* adjective suffix to words we use as English nouns.

noun	adjective	sound-spelling
joy	joy ous	/joi′əs/
dan ger	dan ger ous	/dān′jər əs/
hu mor	hu mor ous	/hū′mər əs/

ious–eous An *i* comes before *ous* in many adjectives. When it does, you pronounce the syllables /ē əs/. There are some words in which *e* comes before *ous*. In these words, you also pronounce the syllables /ē əs/. You have *two* spelling options, then, for /ē əs/ words. Look to see which spelling is correct, *ious* or *eous*.

ious		*eous*	
ser i ous	/sir′ē əs/	hid e ous	/hid′ē əs/
cur i ous	/kūr′ē əs/	court e ous	/kėr′tē əs/
la bor i ous	/lə bôr′ē əs/	pit e ous	/pit′ē əs/

Skill Drill 8 Print the regular spellings of these nouns. Make adjectives out of them by adding the *ous* suffix. Mark the eye-syllables in the adjectives. Use the Sound-Spelling Alphabet chart on page 1 to help you translate these sound-

neaning of the word to which they are affixed. Assign the Skill Drill as usual.

The *ious* and *eous* spelling options do cause confusion. Go through the charts thoroughly and be sure that the pupils are alerted to pay close attention to the correct option in each case.

Skill Drill 8 Answers

1 danger, ⌄dan⌄ger⌄ous⌄
2 joy, ⌄joy⌄ous⌄
3 humor, ⌄hu⌄mor⌄ous⌄
4 marvel, ⌄mar⌄vel⌄ous⌄
5 murder, ⌄mur⌄der⌄ous⌄
6 peril, ⌄per⌄il⌄ous⌄
7 hazard, ⌄haz⌄ard⌄ous⌄
8 scandal, ⌄scan⌄dal⌄ous⌄
9 vigor, ⌄vig⌄or⌄ous⌄
10 venom, ⌄ven⌄om⌄ous⌄

Skill Drill 9 Answers

1 ⌄cur⌄i⌄ous⌄
2 ⌄ser⌄i⌄ous⌄
3 ⌄no⌄tor⌄i⌄ous⌄
4 ⌄court⌄e⌄ous⌄
5 ⌄ob⌄vi⌄ous⌄
6 ⌄bount⌄e⌄ous⌄
7 ⌄pit⌄e⌄ous⌄
8 ⌄hid⌄e⌄ous⌄
9 ⌄la⌄bor⌄i⌄ous⌄

spellings. Check the meaning of any unfamiliar word in your Spelling Dictionary or in the classroom dictionary. The last five words are in your Spelling Dictionary. Compare your work with the answers at the end of Chapter 2.

1 /dān′jər/	5 /mėr′dər/	9 /vig′ər/
2 /joi/	6 /per′əl/	10 /ven′əm/
3 /hū′mər/	7 /haz′ərd/	
4 /mär′vəl/	8 /skan′dəl/	

Skill Drill 9 Print the regular spellings of these /ē əs/ words. Use the *ious* spelling option for five of the words and the *eous* spelling option for four words. Mark the eye-syllables. Use the Sound-Spelling Alphabet chart on page 1 to help you translate these sound-spellings. Check the meaning of any unfamiliar word in your Spelling Dictionary or in the classroom dictionary. All the words except the first one appear in your Spelling Dictionary. Answers appear at the end of Chapter 2.

1 /kūr′ē əs/	4 /ker′tē əs/	7 /pit′ē əs/
2 /sir′ē əs/	5 /ob′vē əs/	8 /hid′ē əs/
3 /nō tôr′ē əs/	6 /boun′tē əs/	9 /lə bôr′ē əs/

cious–tious

When you hear /sh/ before the /əs/ sound, the *ous* suffix sound becomes /shəs/. In /shəs/ words, /sh/ will usually be spelled *ci* or *ti*. When you hear a word ending with /shəs/, *look* at that written word to see which spelling option is used.

cious		*tious*	
gra⌄cious⌄	/grā′shəs/	cau⌄tious⌄	/kô′shəs/
spa⌄cious⌄	/spā′shəs/	am⌄bi⌄tious⌄	/am bish′əs/

ous

Some nouns and verbs end with silent *e*. When you change them to *ous* adjectives, you drop the *e* before adding *ous*. The ending sound becomes simply /əs/.

famė	fam⌄ous⌄	/fā′məs/
pore	⌄por⌄ous⌄	/pôr′əs/

Skill Drill 8 should cause no particular trouble unless some pupils are still experiencing difficulty with the sound-spellings. If so, review the sound-spellings on page 1.

The *cious* and *tious* suffixes cause spelling problems because there are no cues to indicate which option is used. Therefore, allow ample time for pupils to study the examples.

ious

Other nouns and verbs end with final *y*. When you change them to *ous* adjectives, you change the *y* to *i* before adding *ous*. They then become /ē əs/ words.

glor.y   glor.i.ous   /glôr′ē̄ əs/
mys.ter.y   mys.ter.i.ous   /mis tir′ē əs/

Skill Drill 10   Print the regular spellings of these /shəs/ words. Use the *tious* spelling option for four words and the *cious* spelling option for nine words. Mark the eye-syllables. Use the Sound-Spelling Alphabet chart on page 1 to help you translate these sound-spellings. Check the meaning of any unfamiliar word in your Spelling Dictionary or in the classroom dictionary. All the words except the first one appear in your Spelling Dictionary. Compare your work with the answers at the end of Chapter 2.

1 /vish′əs/   6 /də lish′əs/   11 /ô spish′əs/
2 /mə lish′əs/   7 /kô′shəs/   12 /nù trish′əs/
3 /grā′shəs/   8 /presh′əs/   13 /jù dish′əs/
4 /səs pish′əs/   9 /am bish′əs/
5 /fik tish′əs/   10 /spā′shəs/

Skill Drill 11   Make *ous* adjectives from these nouns and verbs. Print the regular spellings. Mark the eye-syllables. Use the Sound-Spelling Alphabet chart on page 1 to help you translate these sound-spellings. Check the meaning of any unfamiliar word in your Spelling Dictionary or in the classroom dictionary. The last five words appear in your Spelling Dictionary. Compare your work with the answers at the end of Chapter 2.

1 /glôr′ē/   5 /mis′tər ē/   9 /fūr′ē/
2 /fām/   6 /ad ven′chər/   10 /pôr/
3 /stud′ē/   7 /nėrv/   11 /här′mə nē/
4 /in′jər ē/   8 /en′vē/   12 /grēv/

39

Skill Drill 10 Answers

1 vi.cious
2 ma.li.cious
3 gra.cious
4 sus.pi.cious
5 fic.ti.tious
6 de.li.cious
7 cau.tious
8 pre.cious
9 am.bi.tious
10 spa.cious
11 aus.pi.cious
12 nu.tri.tious
13 ju.di.cious

Skill Drill 11 Answers

1 glor.i.ous
2 fa.mous
3 stu.di.ous
4 in.jur.i.ous
5 mys.ter.i.ous
6 ad.vent.ur.ous
7 ner.vous
8 en.vi.ous
9 fur.i.ous
10 por.ous
11 har.mo.ni.ous
12 griev.ous

The spellings called for in Skill Drills 10 and 11 are tricky and some of the meanings are difficult. Check pupil response to these exercises carefully. It may be advisable to have pupils write the correct spellings of the words they missed, study these spellings, and redo the Skill Drills.

3 Adjective Suffix *able–ible*

There are a few nouns, like *table, cable, gable, stable, vegetable* and *Bible, dirigible,* which end with the *able* and *ible* spellings. But usually the *able–ible* suffix changes verbs and nouns into adjectives. You use the *able* spelling form more often than the *ible* form, but there are enough *ible* words to cause spelling problems.

The *able–ible* suffix is always pronounced /ə bəl/. You cannot tell from the pronunciation which of the two spelling options is correct. You need to *see*—and remember—which option is being used.

Here are some commonly used *able–ible* words. Study them and note the suffix spellings.

able adjectives		*ible* adjectives	
read able	a dapt able	flex ible	pos sible
break able	en joy able	leg ible	ter rible
ac cept able	at tain able	forc ible	hor rible
rea son able	hon or able	el ig ible	vis ible
laugh able	a gree able	di vis ible	aud ible
suit able	tax able	feas ible	

Skill Drill 12   Write these /ə bəl/ words, noting the spellings. Use the Sound-Spelling Alphabet chart on page 1 to help you translate these sound-spellings. Check the meaning of any unfamiliar word in your Spelling Dictionary or in the classroom dictionary. All words except the first five are in your Spelling Dictionary. Compare your work with the answers at the end of Chapter 2.

1 /laf′ə bəl/   6 /rē′zən ə bəl/   11 /ə dap′tə bəl/
2 /ak sep′tə bəl/   7 /fôr′sə bəl/   12 /el′ə jə bəl/
3 /viz′ə bəl/   8 /on′ər ə bəl/   13 /fē′zə bəl/
4 /süt′ə bəl/   9 /ô′də bəl/
5 /tak′sə bəl/   10 /lej′ə bəl/

40

The *able-ible* spelling option does cause some troublesome problems, and there is no practical formula for choosing the correct spelling. The *able* suffix appears much more frequently, but the *ible* suffix occurs often enough to cause mischief. It is usually helpful to center attention on the *ible* words. Once this shorter list is mastered, pupils can safely assume that nearly all other /ə bəl/ suffixes will be spelled *able*. At any rate, the pupils should be alerted to the options and to the need for noting the correct form, so allow plenty of time

able

Verbs and nouns which end in silent *e* drop the *e* before the *able* suffix form is added. Study these examples and observe the change in spelling from the verb to the adjective form. Note the eye-syllables. Be sure you know the word meanings.

verb	adjective	verb	adjective
like	lik·able	a·dore	a·dor·able
love	lov·able	ad·vise	ad·vis·able
move	mov·able	im·a·gine	im·a·gin·able
note	not·able	val·ue	val·u·able
ad·mire	ad·mir·able	ar·gue	ar·gu·able

But you do *not* drop the *e* when you add *able* to words ending in *ce* or *ge*. The *c* spells /s/ before *e* and the *g* spells /j/ before *e*. We have to keep the *e* in such words. If we did not, the *c* would spell /k/ and the *g* would spell /g/. Study these examples and note the *e* is not dropped when *able* is added to form the adjective.

ge word		ce word	
noun *or* verb	adjective	noun *or* verb	adjective
change	change·able	trace	trace·able
man·age	man·age·able	no·tice	no·tice·able

Skill Drill 13 Make /ə bəl/ adjectives from these verbs. Compare your work with the answers at the end of Chapter 2.

1 love	5 change	9 value
2 move	6 trace	10 imagine
3 manage	7 advise	11 notice
4 admire	8 charge	12 embrace

41

for pupils to study the list of *able* and *ible* adjectives before assigning the Skill Drill.

Unfortunately, most dictionaries list variant spellings for some of these *e*-ending words, such as *likable-likeable, loveable-lovable, movable-moveable*. However, the form given in the text is almost always shown as the preferred form. Others, such as *notable* and *adorable*, are shown with only one spelling.

Be sure the pupils understand why the *e*'s must be retained in verbs ending in *ce* and *ge*. Then assign the Skill Drill.

Suffixes Change Verbs into Nouns and Adjectives

A word part you often use to change many verbs into nouns or adjectives is the *ant–ent* suffix. In a stressed syllable, *ant* spells /ant/ and *ent* spells /ent/. But both the *ant* and *ent* spellings appear frequently as unstressed syllables. When they are not stressed, they are each pronounced /ənt/. You cannot tell from the pronunciation which of the two spelling options is used. You must *look* carefully at /ənt/ words and note the spelling. The *ant–ent* suffix appears both as a noun ending and as an adjective ending.

1 Noun Suffix   *ant–ent*

Here are some common words that show you the *ant* and *ent* spellings in nouns. Study these examples, and note that even easy words that end with *ant* or *ent* have to be observed closely. Study the eye-syllables. Be sure to note carefully which spelling option is used for the /ənt/ sound. Try to remember the correct spelling of its /ənt/ sound. Be sure you know the meaning of these common *ant–ent* words.

ant nouns		*ent* nouns	
mer chant	/mėr′chənt/	pres ent	/prez′ənt/
hy drant	/hī′drənt/	tal ent	/tal′ənt/
page ant	/paj′ənt/	ro dent	/rō′dənt/
pen nant	/pen′ənt/	pat ent	/pat′ənt/
pheas ant	/fez′ənt/	par ent	/pār′ənt/
ten ant	/ten′ənt/	cur rent	/kėr′ənt/
tru ant	/trü′ənt/	cres cent	/kres′ənt/
ty rant	/tī′rənt/	ac cid ent	/ak′sə dənt/
war rant	/wär′ənt/	quo tient	/kwō′shənt/
el e phant	/el′ə fənt/	con tin ent	/kon′tən ənt/
con so nant	/kon′sə nənt/	lig a ment	/lig′a mənt/

42

Section C
This section gives sustained attention to the troublesome *ant-ent* suffix which can convert verbs into both nouns and adjectives. Generally, the *ant-ent* spelling errors occur when *e* is substituted for *a* in *ant* words. Here again, remind students that "thinking" stress on the unstressed suffix syllable will provide a cue to the spelling of the vowel sound.

42

You change verbs into nouns with the *ant* or *ent* form of this suffix. Study each of these examples, and note any change in spelling from the verb to the noun.

ant		*ent*	
verb	noun	verb	noun
serve	ser vant	as cend	as cent
as sist	as sist ant	op pose	op po nent
oc cu py	oc cu pant	pre side	pre sid ent
mi grate	mi grant		

Skill Drill 14   Change these verbs into nouns, using the correct form of the *ant–ent* suffix. Check the meaning of any unfamiliar word in your Spelling Dictionary or in the classroom dictionary. The first two words are not in your Spelling Dictionary. Answers appear at the end of Chapter 2.

1 attend	**4** apply	**7** ascend
2 serve	**5** oppose	**8** occupy
3 migrate	**6** stimulate	**9** preside

2   Adjective Suffix   *ant–ent*

Both spellings of /ənt/ appear as adjective endings. Study the eye-syllables and the spelling options in these examples.

ant adjectives		*ent* adjectives	
va cant	/vā′kənt/	ab sent	/ab′sənt/
pleas ant	/plez′ənt/	de cent	/dē′sənt/
stag nant	/stag′nənt/	si lent	/sī′lənt/

43

Skill Drill 14 Answers

1 attendant
2 servant
3 migrant
4 applicant
5 opponent
6 stimulant
7 ascent
8 occupant
9 president

The pupils will become more familiar with the verb-noun relationship if they change verbs to nouns in illustrative sentence pairs using words from the lesson. For example, pupils can work individually or in pairs reciting sentences like, "I *assist* the manager. I am the *assistant* to the manager." Assign and check the Skill Drill.

Skill Drill 15 Answers

1 consistent
2 defiant
3 ignorant
4 dominant
5 absorbent
6 triumphant
7 confident
8 observant
9 hesitant

Skill Drill 16 Answers

1 pleasant
2 accident
3 frequent
4 decent
5 parent
6 talent
7 absent
8 hydrant
9 pennant
10 tyrant
11 evident
12 current
13 tenant
14 arrogant
15 truant
16 vacant
17 stagnant
18 pageant

You can change verbs into adjectives with the *ant* or *er* form. Note any spelling change in these examples.

ant		*ent*	
verb	adjective	verb	adjective
ob serve	ob serv ant	urge	ur gent
tol er ate	tol er ant	dif fer	dif fer ent
tri umph	tri um phant	ab sorb	ab sorb ent
re ly	re li ant	con sist	con sist ent

Skill Drill 15 Change these verbs into adjectives, using the correct form of the *ant–ent* suffix. Check the meaning of any unfamiliar word in your Spelling Dictionary or in the classroom dictionary. All the words except the first one appear in your Spelling Dictionary. Answers appear at the end of Chapter 2.

1 consist	4 dominate	7 confide
2 defy	5 absorb	8 observe
3 ignore	6 triumph	9 hesitate

Skill Drill 16 Write the regular spellings for these nouns and adjectives. Use the Sound-Spelling Alphabet chart on page to help you translate these sound-spellings. Check the meaning of any unfamiliar word in your Spelling Dictionary or in the classroom dictionary. The first seven words do not appear in your Spelling Dictionary. Compare your work with the answers at the end of Chapter 2.

1 /plez'ənt/	7 /ab'sənt/	13 /ten'ənt/
2 /ak'sə dənt/	8 /hī'drənt/	14 /ār'ə gənt/
3 /frē'kwənt/	9 /pen'ənt/	15 /trü'ənt/
4 /dē'sənt/	10 /tī'rənt/	16 /vā'kənt/
5 /pār'ənt/	11 /ev'ə dənt/	17 /stag'nənt/
6 /tal'ənt/	12 /kėr'ənt/	18 /paj'ənt/

44

Illustrative verb-adjective sentences using the *ant-ent* word pairs will again help to make the relationship clearer to the pupils. For example, pupils can practice saying sentence pairs such as, "The boss will *tolerate* no errors. The boss is not *tolerant.*"

The suffix reference chart is useful to review the suffix spellings and their functions.

44

Suffix Review		
Suffix	Kind	Example
able–ible	adjective	laugh able vis ible change able trace able
ance–ence	noun	ac cept ance con fer ence
ant–ent	noun	as sist ant pre sid ent
	adjective	ob serv ant dif fer ent
ful	adjective	care ful
ion–sion–tion	noun	fash ion un ion cham pi on mis sion vis ion mo tion sug ges tion
less	adjective	pain less
ment	noun	treat ment
ness	noun	bright ness
ous	adjective	joy ous ser i ous court e ous gra cious am bi tious

45

as parts of speech. Pupils should be able to supply additional examples of each suffix.

This chart and the summary which follows should be used to review the suffixes before the Mastery Test is assigned. Because the Mastery Test is so comprehensive, it is given in two parts. This allows the test to be given in two short sessions.

Summary

We use prefixes to change the meanings of root words directly, but generally suffixes change words from one part of speech to another. Common noun suffixes are *ness, ment, ance–ence,* and *ion–sion–tion.* Common adjective suffixes are *ful, less, ous* (with its several forms), and *able–ible.* The *ant–ent* suffix can make both nouns and adjectives.

The *ance–ence* suffix appears in unstressed syllables and is pronounced /əns/. The *sion* and *tion* suffix forms most often are pronounced /shən/. The *able–ible* suffix is pronounced /ə bəl/. The *ant–ent* suffix is pronounced /ənt/. Because these suffixes have more than one spelling option, you must look carefully to see which spelling option is used in a particular word.

Review the preceding chart that shows the common suffixes. Study the eye-syllables in the examples.

46

If the prefix material of Chapter 1 and the suffix material of Chapter 2 are not reasonably mastered by the pupils, Chapter 3, in which the prefix-root-suffix patterns are studied, will be extremely difficult. Therefore, any pupil unable to perform reasonably well on the Mastery Test should receive some review before going on. If possible, find a pattern in the pupils' errors and use the chart which appears in the front of this Teacher's Edition to prescribe appropriate review in Levels 7 or 8.

Mastery Test 2

A Use the *ness*, *ment*, or *ion–tion* suffix to spell a noun form of each word for which the sound-spelling is shown.

1 /red'ē/   6 /rō'tāt/   11 /sel'ə brāt'/
2 /ə ranj'/   7 /ə trakt'/   12 /ə nouns'/
3 /trēt/   8 /ə sīn'/   13 /hev'ē/
4 /kīnd/   9 /man'ij/   14 /sik/
5 /ek sīt'/   10 /frend'lē/   15 /siv'ə līz/

Use *ful*, *less*, or an *ous* suffix form to spell an adjective made from each word for which the sound-spelling is given.

16 /spot/   20 /dan'jər/   24 /boun'tē/
17 /rē spekt'/   21 /glôr'ē/   25 /pit'ē/
18 /rông/   22 /fām/   26 /pit'ē/
19 /lā'bər/   23 /vig'ər/   27 /pit'ē/

Write each word with the correct spelling option of the *ance–ence* noun suffix.

28 sil_nce   32 perform_nce   36 endur_nce
29 evid_nce   33 differ_nce   37 assur_nce
30 appli_nce   34 abs_nce   38 pati_nce
31 guid_nce   35 prefer_nce   39 appear_nce

Write each word with the correct spelling option of the *able–ible* adjective suffix.

40 break_ble   44 mov_ble   48 change_ble
41 forc_ble   45 notice_ble   49 invis_ble
42 divis_ble   46 imagin_ble   50 admir_ble
43 accept_ble   47 flex_ble

Write each word with the correct spelling option of the *ant–ent* noun and adjective suffix.

51 assist_nt   53 occup_nt   55 absorb_nt
52 confid_nt   54 observ_nt   56 conson_nt

47

Part A Answers (cont'd)
34 absence
35 preference
36 endurance
37 assurance
38 patience
39 appearance
40 breakable
41 forcible
42 divisible
43 acceptable
44 movable
45 noticeable
46 imaginable
47 flexible
48 changeable
49 invisible
50 admirable
51 assistant
52 confident
53 occupant
54 observant
55 absorbent
56 consonant

Part B Answers
1 triumphant champion
2 gracious attendant
3 glorious mission
4 serious president
5 current fashion
6 hideous accident
7 pleasant region
8 frequent truant

B

Write the regular spellings for each adjective-noun phrase.

1 /trī um'fənt/ /cham'pē ən/

5 /kėr'ənt/ /fash'ən/

2 /grā'shəs/ /ə ten'dənt/

6 /hid'ē əs/ /ak'sə dənt/

3 /glôr'ē əs/ /mish'ən/

7 /plez'ənt/ /rē'jən/

4 /sir'ē əs/ /prez'ə dənt/

8 /frē'kwənt/ /trü'ənt/

48

9 /ab′sənt/ /tī′rənt/   15 /kėr′tē əs/ /ə ten′shən/
10 /kūr′ē əs/ /nō′shən/   16 /sī′lənt/ /ad′mə rā′shən/
11 /tol′ə rənt/ /pār′ənts/   17 /am bish′əs/ /sėr′vənt/
12 /spā′shəs/ /sek′shən/   18 /dif′ə rənt/ /sich′ü ā′shən/
13 /dē′sənt/ /pen′shən/   19 /də viz′ə bəl/ /kwō′shənt/
14 /kô′shəs/ /mėr′chənt/   20 /mis tir′ē əs/ /ə trak′shən/

 9 absent tyrant
10 curious notion
11 tolerant parents
12 spacious section
13 decent pension
14 cautious merchant
15 courteous attention
16 silent admiration
17 ambitious servant
18 different situation
19 divisible quotient
20 mysterious attraction

Answers for Chapter 2 Skill Drills

Skill Drill 1   1 ill ness   2 like ness   3 mad ness
4 heav i ness   5 lone li ness   6 diz zi ness
7 emp ti ness   8 friend li ness   9 sick ness
10 stead i ness   11 awk ward ness   12 sure ness
13 hol i ness   14 pleas ant ness   15 rude ness
16 still ness   17 sting i ness   18 dull ness   19 live li ness
20 harsh ness   21 greed i ness   22 so ber ness
23 bless ed ness   24 firm ness   25 cold ness
26 fine ness   27 low li ness

Skill Drill 2   1 ap point ment   2 ar range ment
3 gov ern ment   4 man age ment   5 pay ment
6 com mand ment   7 e quip ment   8 ex cite ment
9 ad vance ment   10 a gree ment   11 state ment
12 en gage ment   13 de vel op ment   14 set tle ment
15 em ploy ment   16 en roll ment   17 a chieve ment
18 en force ment   19 ful fill ment   20 com mence ment

Skill Drill 3   1 ac quaint ance   2 as sist ance
3 at tend ance   4 guid ance   5 var i ance   6 ig nor ance
7 al li ance   8 as sur ance   9 re li ance   10 ap pli ance
11 ob serv ance   12 com pli ance   13 a void ance
14 ut ter ance   15 con tin u ance   16 re pent ance
17 is su ance   18 dis turb ance   19 en dur ance
20 in her it ance

49

Skill Drill 4 1 pa·tience 2 neg·li·gence 3 dil·i·gence
4 pen·it·ence 5 el·o·quence 6 prom·i·nence
7 mag·nif·i·cence 8 vi·o·lence 9 con·se·quence
10 bel·lig·er·ence 11 con·cur·rence 12 con·fi·dence
13 ef·fer·ves·cence 14 re·ver·ence 15 per·man·ence
16 per·sist·ence 17 e·merg·ence 18 flu·o·res·cence
19 res·i·dence 20 cor·re·spond·ence

Skill Drill 5 1 cushion 2 opinion 3 division 4 action
5 station 6 religion 7 possession 8 admission 9 billion
10 caution 11 scorpion 12 digestion

Skill Drill 6 1 collection 2 correction 3 selection
4 edition 5 election 6 location 7 communication
8 creation 9 participation 10 decoration 11 situation
12 perspiration 13 inclination 14 nomination
15 combination 16 dedication 17 celebration
18 recitation 19 reservation 20 contradiction
21 exhibition 22 generation 23 affection 24 regulation
25 inflation 26 vibration

Skill Drill 7 1 hope, hopeful, hopeless 2 help, helpful,
helpless 3 fear, fearful, fearless 4 law, lawful, lawless
5 need, needful, needless 6 shame, shameful, shameless
7 thank, thankful, thankless 8 cheer, cheerful, cheerless
9 faith, faithful, faithless 10 fruit, fruitful, fruitless
11 doubt, doubtful, doubtless 12 thought, thoughtful,
thoughtless 13 color, colorful, colorless 14 mercy,
merciful, merciless 15 pity, pitiful, pitiless

Skill Drill 8 1 danger, dan·ger·ous 2 joy, joy·ous
3 humor, hu·mor·ous 4 marvel, mar·vel·ous 5 murder,
mur·der·ous 6 peril, per·il·ous 7 hazard, haz·ard·ous
8 scandal, scan·dal·ous 9 vigor, vig·or·ous 10 venom,
ven·om·ous

50

Skill Drill 9 1 cur i ous 2 ser i ous 3 no tor i ous
4 court e ous 5 ob vi ous 6 bount e ous 7 pit e ous
8 hid e ous 9 la bor i ous

Skill Drill 10 1 vi cious 2 ma li cious 3 gra cious
4 sus pi cious 5 fic ti tious 6 de li cious 7 cau tious
8 pre cious 9 am bi tious 10 spa cious 11 aus pi cious
12 nu tri tious 13 ju di cious

Skill Drill 11 1 glor i ous 2 fa mous 3 stu di ous
4 in jur i ous 5 mys ter i ous 6 ad vent ur ous
7 ner vous 8 en vi ous 9 fur i ous 10 por ous
11 har mo ni ous 12 griev ous

Skill Drill 12 1 laughable 2 acceptable 3 visible
4 suitable 5 taxable 6 reasonable 7 forcible
8 honorable 9 audible 10 legible 11 adaptable
12 eligible 13 feasible

Skill Drill 13 1 lovable 2 movable 3 manageable
4 admirable 5 changeable 6 traceable 7 advisable
8 chargeable 9 valuable 10 imaginable 11 noticeable
12 embraceable

Skill Drill 14 1 attendant 2 servant 3 migrant
4 applicant 5 opponent 6 stimulant 7 ascent
8 occupant 9 president

Skill Drill 15 1 consistent 2 defiant 3 ignorant
4 dominant 5 absorbent 6 triumphant 7 confident
8 observant 9 hesitant

Skill Drill 16 1 pleasant 2 accident 3 frequent
4 decent 5 parent 6 talent 7 absent 8 hydrant
9 pennant 10 tyrant 11 evident 12 current 13 tenant
14 arrogant 15 truant 16 vacant 17 stagnant
18 pageant

51

52

1 interaction
2 transformation
3 cooperation
4 impoliteness
5 distrustful
6 reappearance
7 superintendent
8 prepayment
9 collapsible
10 comfortless
11 ungracious
12 correlation

3 Prefix-Root-Suffix Compounds

In Chapter 1 you wrote words which were compounded by prefixes and root words. Those prefixes directly influenced the meanings of the root words. In Chapter 2 you wrote words which were compounded by root words and suffixes. Those suffixes, except for *ful* and *less,* did not directly influence the meanings of the root words. They did change the words from one part of speech into another part of speech. They changed adjectives and verbs into nouns; nouns and verbs into adjectives; and verbs into nouns and adjectives.

In this chapter you will write some of the many English words which are composed of a prefix *and* a root word *and* a suffix. If you learn to look at words to see the prefix-root-suffix parts, you will find the words easier to spell. You will also be able to guess many of the word meanings if you know the meaning of each word part.

Study the chart of prefixes, roots, and suffixes on the next page. Note the prefixes you wrote in Chapter 1 and the suffixes you wrote in Chapter 2.

In the chart, find the prefix-root-suffix words for these phrases. Compare your work with the Answers for Introductory Exercise, on page 84.

1 action between forces
2 a great change
3 a working together
4 not being courteous
5 not having trust
6 an appearing again
7 an overseer
8 a paying before
9 able to be folded
10 having no comfort
11 not being kind
12 a bringing together

52

CHAPTER 3

The spelling vocabulary of this chapter stresses the common prefix-root-suffix pattern of many English words. The common prefixes studied in Chapter 1 and the suffixes presented in Chapter 2 are summarized in the prefix-suffix chart on page 53.

Some pupils may tend to look at these multisyllabic words as total configurations and try to memorize the letter sequences of the words. The objective in this chapter is to teach the pupils to see the component parts of multisyllabic words.

It is obviously impossible to present all of the words pupils will need to spell. Only if pupils learn to look analytically at all words as they see them in print will they continue to improve in spelling ability.

The teaching of the prefix and root meanings and of the suffix functions through spelling activities has an obvious relationship to the reading skills. There is clear evidence that the primary factors of what we vaguely call "comprehension" in reading are syntax and word meanings. It follows then that reading compre-

Prefixes, Roots, Suffixes

Prefix	Meaning	Root	Suffix	Speech Part	Prefix + Root + Suffix
re	again	appear	ance	n.	re appear ance
de	down	fend	ant	n.	de fend ant
dis	away	trust	ful	adj.	dis trust ful
un	not	grac*(e)*	*(i)*ous	adj.	un gra cious
im	not	polite	ness	n.	im polite ness
in	not	differ	ence	n.	in differ ence
en	make	force	ment	n.	en force ment
ex	out	pres*(s)*	sion	n.	ex pres sion
com	with	fort	less	adj.	com fort less
con	with	dens*(e)*	*(a)*tion	n.	con dens a tion
cor	with	rel*(ate)*	*(a)*tion	n.	cor rel a tion
col	with	laps*(e)*	ible	adj.	col laps ible
co	with	oper*(ate)*	*(a)*tion	n.	co oper a tion
pre	before	pay	ment	n.	pre pay ment
pro	onward	pel	*(l)*ant	n.	pro pel lant
sub	under	divi*(de)*	sion	n.	sub divi sion
sup	under	port	able	adj.	sup port able
super	over	intend	ent	n.	super intend ent
trans	across	form	*(a)*tion	n.	trans form a tion
inter	between	act	ion	n.	inter ac tion

53

...ension can be materially improved by a systematic study of word meanings, especially for pupils who do not read extensively. Hence, these spelling activities are closely related to the word perception skills in reading and are designed to strengthen both the spelling and the reading skills.

The content of this chapter is quite substantial. Each Skill Drill should be checked before the pupils proceed to the next section. The Mastery Test should be used to determine whether the material needs to be reviewed.

The chart gives illustrations of the use of all of the prefixes and suffixes introduced earlier. It will be helpful to go over the chart with the pupils. Stress particularly the eye-syllables.

Answers for Multiple
Choice Sentences

1 retraction
2 extraction
3 contraction

Changing Verbs into Nouns

1 "pull" Root Words

In Chapter 1 you wrote seven verbs which were compounded by seven prefixes and the *tract* root, which means to "pull." You can make prefix-root-suffix nouns out of those verbs by simply adding the *ion* suffix to them. These verbs end with *t*, so the *t* becomes part of the *ion* syllable, which is then pronounced /shən/.

meaning	verb	noun	meaning
pull back	re tract	re trac tion	a pulling back
pull out	ex tract	ex trac tion	a pulling out
pull together	con tract	con trac tion	a pulling together
pull onward	pro tract	pro trac tion	a pulling onward
pull down	de tract	de trac tion	a pulling down
pull away	dis tract	dis trac tion	a pulling away
pull lower	sub tract	sub trac tion	a pulling lower

Now you should be able to choose the correct *tract* noun for each of these sentences. Compare your work with the Answers for Multiple Choice Sentences, Section A 1, on page 84.

1 "You have insulted me!" cried the senator. "I demand that you make a *(retraction, detraction, distraction)!*"
2 "The tooth is bad," said the dentist, "and *(subtraction, protraction, extraction)* is necessary."
3 "Anybody knows that cold, not heat, causes *(detraction, contraction, extraction),*" said the scientist.

54

Section A

In this section attention is given to prefix-root-suffix nouns formed from verbs. Go over the explanation of the "pull" root words with pupils. It may be helpful to have pupils use the seven *tract* verb and noun pairs in sentences which illustrate their relationship.

The three multiple choice sentences may also be done orally, of course, and then dis

Answers for Multiple Choice Sentences
1 suppression
2 expression
3 repression
4 depression

2 "press" Root Words

Each of these six verbs is formed with a familiar prefix and the *press* root. Study the meaning of the root and the prefix added. Note that these prefixed *press* verbs become nouns when we add *ion*. The verbs end with doubled *s*, so the final *s* becomes part of the *ion* syllable, and the suffix is pronounced /shən/.

meaning	verb	noun	meaning
press back	re press	re pres sion	a pressing back
press out	ex press	ex pres sion	a pressing out
press with	com press	com pres sion	a pressing with
press in	im press	im pres sion	a pressing in
press down	de press	de pres sion	a pressing down
press under	sup press	sup pres sion	a pressing under

Choose the correct *press* noun for each of these sentences. Compare your work with the Answers for Multiple Choice Sentences, Section A 2, on page 84.

1 "This is a *(suppression, depression, impression)* of our free speech, Tyrant!" cried the rebels.

2 "No," replied the tyrant. "I favor free *(expression, compression, impression)* of ideas."

3 "Some *(compression, depression, repression)* of loud laughter is necessary," said the principal.

4 "Is our country in a *(suppression, depression, compression)?*" asked the employees when they lost their jobs.

55

ussed and amplified. If desired, additional multiple choice sentences can be composed.

The procedure for the "press" root words is similar to that for the "pull" root. Again it will probably be useful to discuss the material with the pupils and to allow them to use each word in a sentence.

3 "put" Root Words

The *pose* or "put" root word ends with *e*. You change the
to *i* before adding the *tion* noun suffix, to make the noun easie
to pronounce. You drop the final *e* before adding *ing* to thes
verbs.

verb	noun	*ing* form
ex pose	ex pos i tion	ex pos ing
com pose	com pos i tion	com pos ing
im pose	im pos i tion	im pos ing
pro pose	pro pos i tion	pro pos ing
de pose	de pos i tion	de pos ing
dis pose	dis pos i tion	dis pos ing
trans pose	trans pos i tion	trans pos ing
sup pose	sup pos i tion	sup pos ing

Choose the correct *pose* noun. Compare your work with th
answers for Section A 3, on page 84.

1 "The correct answer is 31, not 13," said the teacher. "You
mistake was in *(disposition, transposition, exposition)* of th
numbers."

2 "The king is a tyrant!" screamed the rebels. "We deman
his *(imposition, deposition, composition)!*"

3 "I've studied your offer, but I can't accept the *(depositior
composition, proposition)*," said the young man.

4 "I don't like the taste of this mixture," said the woman. "Wh
is its *(composition, exposition, supposition)?*"

56

Go through the explanation of the "put"
root words with pupils. Allow pupils to recite
and listen to the words in an illustrative sentence. One method for doing this would be to
go over the multiple choice sentences at th
bottom of the page orally with pupils. The pu
pils can then be challenged to create sentence
using the unused words.

Skill Drill 1 Write the correct *tract, press,* and *pose* verbs and also the /shən/-suffix noun of each to complete the sentences. Compare your work with the answers at the end of Chapter 3.

1 If something becomes smaller, it __, and you see a __.

2 If you hide your feelings, you __ them, and there is a __ of your emotions.

3 If you take something for granted, you __ it to be true, or make a __.

4 If you influence people, you __ them, and you may make a very good __.

5 If you can't pay attention, you are __, and you may regret the __ later.

6 If you get rid of trash, you __ of it, or make __ of it.

7 If you switch two letters, you __ them, or make a __ of them.

8 If you take back a statement, you __ it, or make a __.

9 If you write music, you __ it, and it becomes your __.

10 If you speak up, you __ yourself, or give __ to your thoughts.

11 If the dentist must remove your tooth, she will __ it, and the __ may hurt.

12 If you put down a rebellion, you __ it, and the rebels may suffer from __ of their rights.

13 If people take advantage of you, they __ on you, and you suffer an __.

14 If you get more time to use, time is __, or a __ occurs.

15 If you squeeze clothes into a bag, you __ them, and they may be wrinkled by the __.

16 If you make a suggestion, you __ it, or you offer a __.

17 Ugly sights may __ you, and you will suffer __.

18 If you speak ill of people, you __ from their good name, and their reputation may be hurt by the __.

19 If a king is removed, he is __, and suffers __.

20 If you take away when working with numbers, you __, or perform __ in arithmetic.

57

Assign Skill Drill 1 and have pupils correct their work. It may be helpful to go over the first sentence orally with pupils and amplify the prefix-root-suffix components in the answer.

This first Skill Drill may be a difficult exercise for some pupils. Be sure to allow ample time for all pupils to complete the work. Give individual help as needed.

4 "carry" Root Words

Many *port* or "carry" verbs become nouns by addition of **t**
tion suffix. But you insert an *a* between the root and the suf

verb	noun
ex‚port↓	ex‚port‚a‚tion↓
im‚port	im‚port‚a‚tion
de‚port	de‚port‚a‚tion
trans‚port	trans‚port‚a‚tion

Choose the *port* noun. Answers for Section A 4 appear
page 84.

1 "Flee, Robin Hood!" yelled Little John. "You can be su
of *(deportation, importation, exportation)* from England if you
caught."

2 "You'll like this necklace," said the jeweler. "It's a recent *(i.
portation, transportation, deportation)* from Mexico."

5 "write" Root Words

When some verbs change to nouns, the spelling of the ro
changes. The *scribe* or "write" root becomes *scrip* in /shə
nouns. In the *ing* form, you drop the final *e* of the root.

58

Encourage pupils to approach the spelling
of these "carry" root words eye-syllable by
eye-syllable. Spelling problems sometimes occur in the unstressed syllables of these multisyllabic words. Emphasize the fact that vowel

sounds become clear when we "think" stre
on the unaccented syllables. Demonstrate th
fact to pupils by putting stress on every syllab
as you pronounce each word. Go over th
multiple choice questions orally. Challenge p

verb	noun	*ing* form
in scribe	in scrip tion	in scrib ing
pre scribe	pre scrip tion	pre scrib ing
de scribe	de scrip tion	de scrib ing
sub scribe	sub scrip tion	sub scrib ing
tran scribe	tran scrip tion	tran scrib ing

Answers for Multiple Choice Sentences
1 description
2 inscriptions

Choose the correct *scrip* noun. Compare your work with the answers for Section A 5, on page 84.

1 "Take your choice," said the baker. "We have pies of every *(prescription, subscription, description)*."

2 "The *(transcriptions, inscriptions, prescriptions)* on some of these old tombstones are very hard to read," observed the granddaughter.

6 "go" Root Words

Most *cede–ceed* or "go" verb roots change to the spelling *ces* before you add the *sion* suffix to form nouns. You drop the final *e* before adding *ing* to the root *cede*.

verb	noun	*ing* form
re cede	re ces sion	re ced ing
con cede	con ces sion	con ced ing
inter cede	inter ces sion	inter ced ing
suc ceed	suc ces sion	suc ceed ing
pro ceed	pro ces sion	pro ceed ing

59

Is to use both the verb and noun form of each ord in an original sentence.

In going over the list of "write" root words, oint out that the spelling of the root changes hen the verb is changed to a noun. This may be a good time to review the meaning of the prefixes which appear in these words.

In studying the "go" root words, review the fact that *succeed, proceed,* and *exceed* are the only *ceed* spellings.

Choose the correct *ces* noun. Compare your work with the answers for Section A 6, on page 84.

1 "There must be no dispute about the rightful *(recession, succession, intercession)* to the throne," said the dying king.

2 "As a special *(concession, procession, recession)*, I'll let you ride your bike to the circus today," said Mother.

3 "If you hurry," the director called to the driver, "you probably can join the *(intercession, procession, succession)* of cars at the next intersection."

7 "push" Root Words

With few exceptions, the *pel* or "push" root becomes *pul* when you change the verbs into nouns by adding the *sion* suffix. You double the final *l* before adding *ing* to *pel* verbs.

verb	noun	*ing* form
re pel	re pul sion	re pel ling
ex pel	ex pul sion	ex pel ling
com pel	com pul sion	com pel ling
pro pel	pro pul sion	pro pel ling

Choose the correct *pul* noun. Compare your work with the answers for Section A 7, on page 84.

1 "You won't enjoy fishing if you feel a *(repulsion, compulsion, propulsion)* for baiting fishhooks," the old man pointed out.

2 "Everyone must obey the law," declared the judge, "either willingly or under *(expulsion, compulsion, repulsion)*."

60

Have pupils study the list of "push" root words. Explain that when adding a suffix beginning with a vowel such as *ing*, we double the final consonant symbol in roots which end with one vowel and one consonant and which have stress on the final syllable. Pupils having difficulty with spelling the *ing* form of words may review Chapter 5 of Level 7.

Skill Drill 2 Transcribe the simplified verb meanings, choosing from these prefix-root verbs: *describe, expel, deport, compel, subscribe, repel, succeed, transport, transcribe, proceed, import, concede, inscribe, prescribe, export, intercede, propel, recede.* Then change the verbs into /shən/ nouns. Compare your work with the answers at the end of Chapter 3.

1 push back
2 write before
3 write down
4 push with; force
5 write across; copy
6 carry in goods
7 push out
8 carry out goods
9 write in, or on
10 go onward
11 carry away
12 go between
13 go back
14 carry across
15 go with; admit
16 push onward
17 write under; agree
18 go next

Skill Drill 3 Write the *ing* form of these verbs. Compare your work with the answers at the end of Chapter 3.

1 repel
2 proceed
3 compel
4 transcribe
5 recede
6 expel
7 prescribe
8 describe
9 concede

B Additional Latin Roots and Affixes

1 "walk–go" Root   *gress*

The Latin *gress* root means to "walk or go." When you add prefixes to the *gress* root, you make both verbs and nouns. A word like *progress* may serve as both a noun and a verb. You place the stress on the first syllable in the noun

61

Skill Drill 2 Answers
1 repel, repulsion
2 prescribe, prescription
3 describe, description
4 compel, compulsion
5 transcribe, transcription
6 import, importation
7 expel, expulsion
8 export, exportation
9 inscribe, inscription
10 proceed, procession
11 deport, deportation
12 intercede, intercession
13 recede, recession
14 transport, transportation
15 concede, concession
16 propel, propulsion
17 subscribe, subscription
18 succeed, succession

Skill Drill 3 Answers
1 repelling
2 proceeding
3 compelling
4 transcribing
5 receding
6 expelling
7 prescribing
8 describing
9 conceding

Assign the Skill Drills as usual and have pupils check their answers. Be sure each pupil has mastered the spelling of the words in this section before going on to Section B.

Section B
In this section pupils are introduced to a substantial number of additional Latin roots and affixes. The "walk-go" root is new to pupils. Go through the explanation carefully.

/prog′rəs/, but on the second syllable in the verb /prə gres′.
The verbs may also become nouns by addition of the *ion* suffix
The word *progression* is also a noun.

ive

You usually can make adjectives out of the verbs by addin
the *ive* suffix. Note, though, that the *ive* suffix is both a nou
and an adjective suffix *(captive)*.

When you add the *ex* prefix to the *gress* root, you omit th
x, forming the noun *egress*. It means an "out walk" or wa
out. It is a antonym of *ingress*, an "in walk" or entrance.

Many Latin root words may no longer have just their simpl
original meanings. *Congress,* for example, should mean
"walk together." A *congress* actually is a "formal meeting
delegates for discussion." The delegates do "walk" to get "to
gether"; so you can see how *congress* got the particular mean
ing given it now. When you *transgress,* you disobey a com
mand, rule, or law; when you do, you "walk across" or do wha
you should not do. When you *digress,* you "walk away"; yo
do not actually walk, but you do "go" aside, or turn your atten
tion "away" from the subject.

The *di* prefix form in *digress* comes from *de* ("away").

verb	noun	adjective
re gress	re gres sion	re gress ive
di gress	di gres sion	di gress ive
pro gress	pro gres sion	pro gress ive
trans gress	trans gres sion	

Choose the correct *gress* word. Compare your work with th
answers for Section B 1, on page 84.
1 "Two traffic tickets in one month!" cried the judge. "Anoth
(progression, transgression, digression) will mean serious trou
ble!"
2 "You didn't stick to the subject," said the teacher. "You
report was too *(digressive, regressive, progressive)*."

62

Demonstrate or ask pupils to demonstrate
the pronunciation of *progress* as both a noun
and a verb, using the word in a sentence. Lead
pupils to analyze each of the words by parts,
then go through the multiple choice question
orally. Help pupils to speculate about the way
which the "walk" meaning comes to be r
stricted in these words.

2 "throw" Root *ject*

The Latin *ject* root means to "throw." When you say you *reject* an offer, you do not mean that you actually "throw" the offer "back" but that you refuse it, as if you were throwing it back. When doctors *inject* medicine into a vein, they do not really "throw" it "in." When you feel *dejected,* you have not really "thrown" yourself "down" but your spirits are low as if you had. When you *interject,* you do not "throw" something "between" but you do break into another person's speech with your own words.

The word *subject* is used both as a noun /sub′jəkt/ and as a verb /səb jekt′/. The *subject* of a book is what is "thrown under" your attention, or presented to you, to be studied and learned. When we *subject* someone to cruelty, we "throw" him "under" cruel treatment. *Project,* too, may be used as a noun /proj′əkt/ or as a verb /prə jekt′/. A *projector* does "throw" an image "onward" or forward to a screen. A *project* is a task to which people "throw" themselves "onward" to complete, so to speak.

ob   The prefix *ob* means "in the way." An *object* /ob′jəkt/ is something "thrown in the way." To *object* /ob jekt′/ means to "throw in the way."

verb sound-spelling	verb *or* noun	noun sound-spelling
/səb jekt′/	subject	/sub′jəkt/
/prə jekt′/	project	/proj′əkt/
/ob jekt′/	object	/ob′jəkt/

63

This explanatory matter for the "throw" root will also become more meaningful with teacher help. Lead pupils to perceive that while the literal reading of the prefix and root meanings will give clues to the meaning, the words are now usually used in restricted contexts. This fact is amply illustrated by the examples included in the explanatory material.

The final *t* in each *ject* verb joins the *ion* suffix to form /shən/ noun.

verb	noun	verb	noun
re ject	re jec tion	pro ject	pro jec tion
in ject	in jec tion	sub ject	sub jec tion
de ject	de jec tion	ob ject	ob jec tion
inter ject	inter jec tion		

Choose the correct *ject* noun. Compare your work with the answers for Section B 2, on page 84.

1 "A joke would be a welcome *(interjection, projection, objection)* in this boring speech," complained a weary listener.

2 "It's hard not to show *(injection, dejection, subjection)* when your team has lost the game 18 to 1," sighed the cheerleader.

3 "No man should be under *(subjection, rejection, injection)* to a cruel master," declared the statesman.

3 "lead" Roots   duce   duct

A Latin root with two forms is the "lead" root *duce* or *duct*. We use the *duct* root as an English word as well; a *duct* a pipe, tube, or channel which "leads" or lets something flow through. You use the *in [im]* and *de* prefixes with both *duce* and *duct*. To *induce* means to "lead" someone "in" to do what we wish, that is, to persuade someone. To *induct* also means "lead in" or to involve someone in an organization. Person

64

Be sure the pupils understand the change in stress and meaning that occurs in words such as *subject*, *object*, and *project* when they are used as nouns and as verbs. Assign the

multiple choice questions for oral response and extend the list if necessary.

The explanatory material for the "lead roots is quite comprehensive and it may be in

may be *induced,* or persuaded, to go into the armed forces. After they have been *induced,* they are *inducted.*

To *deduce* now means to trace or to figure out, that is, to "lead from" known information to an answer. To *deduct* means to "lead from" in another sense, to take away, to subtract. Parents may *deduct* an amount from their child's allowance.

intro The prefix *intro* in *introduce* means "inside." To *introduce* means to "lead inside" or to make known.

You know that the *re* prefix means "back." To *reduce,* then, means to "lead back" or to make smaller, to decrease.

To *produce* /prə düs′/ means to make or manufacture something, that is, to "lead onward" to another stage. *Produce* may be used also as a noun /prō′dūs/, something which is *produced,* like crops. *Product* is also a noun and means what is *produced,* too. Factories turn out *products.* A *production* is also something which is *produced.* Movies or shows are often called *productions.*

Conduct /kon′dukt/, used as a noun, means behavior, a way of "leading with." To *conduct* /kən dukt′/ means to "lead with," that is, to guide someone or move something along; some metals *conduct* heat easily.

The *duce* root becomes *duc* in nouns, dropping the *e* when the suffix *tion* is added. To the *duct* root you add the *ion* noun suffix, but the *t* joins *ion* to make a /shən/ syllable.

verb	noun
re duce	re duc tion
in duce	in duc tion
de duce	de duc tion
intro duce	intro duc tion
pro duce	pro duc tion
in duct	in duc tion
de duct	de duc tion
con duct	con duc tion

65

appropriate to assign this as independent study for some pupils. If so, guide pupils through the explanation slowly and patiently. Call particular attention to the fact that the *duce* root becomes *duc* in nouns. The arrow in the chart points this out. Be sure pupils understand the meaning of all words. Allow ample time for pupils to study the eye-syllables in the words.

Answers for Multiple Choice Sentences
1 induction
2 reduction
3 conduction

Skill Drill 4 Answers
1 conduct
2 reduction
3 induce
4 transgression
5 rejection
6 ingress
7 dejection
8 progress
9 interjection
10 deduction
11 interject
12 reject
13 objection
14 produce
15 deduce
16 egress
17 deduct
18 transgress
19 object
20 congress

Choose the correct *duct* noun. Compare your work with th[e] answers for Section B 3, on page 84.

1 "The *(induction, conduction, deduction)* of new members w[ill] take place at the next meeting," said our club president.

2 "Are your tax bills too high? Vote for me and I'll work fo[r] *(conduction, reduction, introduction)* of taxes," declared th[e] campaigning senator.

3 "Copper wire is excellent for *(production, reduction, conduc[c]tion)* of electricity," the scientist explained.

Skill Drill 4 Write the *gress, ject,* or *duce–duct* synonym[s] choosing from these words: *egress, deduce, object, interje[ct]* *deduction, ingress, reduction, transgress, produce, reject, reje[c]* *tion, dejection, congress, conduct, objection, interjection, [in]* *duce, progress, deduct, transgression.* Compare your work wi[th] the answers at the end of Chapter 3.

1 behavior	**8** gain	**15** conclude
2 loss	**9** interruption	**16** exit
3 persuade	**10** subtraction	**17** subtract
4 violation	**11** interrupt	**18** violate
5 refusal	**12** refuse	**19** complain
6 entrance	**13** complaint	**20** legislature
7 sadness	**14** manufacture	

4 "turn," "send," "look," "call," and "breathe" Roots
vert verse mit miss spect voke voc spire
If you know the common Latin root and prefix meanings, yo[u] will usually be able to understand how compounded words fir[st] got their meanings. Sometimes the meanings change som[e]

Go through the multiple choice questions orally. Have pupils supply additional sentences using the words from the list on page 65. Assign the Skill Drill and check pupil progress.

As in the previous subsection, the expla[n]atory material for the "turn," "send," "look[,]" "call," and "breathe" roots is quite detaile[d] and may not be appropriate as independe[nt]

what. Sometimes we use the words differently than our ancestors did.

Some roots have more than one spelling. The Latin root which means "turn" is spelled both *vert* and *verse* in English words. The first example in the next chart is *advert*.

ad   The prefix *ad* means "to–toward" and has several forms. Before a *c, k,* or *q* root, it becomes *ac* as in *accede,* to go "toward" or agree, consent. The prefix *ad* becomes *af* before roots that begin with *f* as in *affirm; ag* before *g* roots *(aggressive); al* before *l* roots *(allocate); ap* before *p* roots *(appeal); as* before *s* roots *(assign);* and *at* before *t* roots *(attract).*

vert   To *advert* literally means to "turn to," refer to. You might say
verse that persons often *advert* to books to prove they are right. When we *advertise,* we "turn to" to notify, in an *advertisement.* The adjective *adverse,* however, means "against"; you might say that the umpire made an *adverse* decision.

al   *Reverse* is an example of the *verse* spelling. A noun form, in which you see the suffix *al,* is *reversal,* "a turning back," a loss. An adjective form is *reversible,* able to be "turned back."

mit   The Latin root which means "send" is spelled *mit* or *miss.*
miss   You see it in words like *missile,* something which is "sent." A *missive* is a letter, something "sent." To *dismiss* is to "send away." *Emit* is really *exmit,* with the *x* omitted. You can see that *emit* must mean to "send out." We might say that a car *emits* gases. *Admit* means to "send to."

per   *Permit* uses the prefix *per* with the *mit* root. Per means "through." To *permit* literally means to "send through." You might *permit* someone to put books in your locker.

The *mit* spelling changes to *miss* when *ion, ive,* or *ible* is added, as for example in *admission, permission, permissive, permissible.* You double the *t* in the *mit* root when you spell nouns like *remittance* and *admittance* and adjectives with the suffix *al* like *transmittal.*

spect   The *spect* root means to "look." You see it in words like *spectacles, spectator,* and *spectacle* (something to "see"). To *expect* should mean to "look out"; if you "look

udy. These roots appear frequently in English ocabulary and deserve careful attention.

In guiding pupils through the explanatory aterial, call attention to the prefix-root-suffix components. Even though the prefix and root meanings are often less than apparent in the way we use these words today, there is usually a hint of the original meaning in the modern

1a commit, remit, admit, submit, transmit

1b commitment, commission; remission, remittance; admission, admittance; submission, submittal; transmission, transmittal

2a subvert, divert, invert, revert, convert

2b subversion, diversion, inversion, reversion, conversion

3 inspect, respect, prospect, suspect

4a invoke, evoke, convoke, provoke

4b invocation, evocation, convocation, provocation

5a expire, conspire, inspire, transpire, aspire

5b expiration, conspiration, inspiration, transpiration, aspiration

out," you do *expect*. To *suspect (sub + spect)* means t "look under," as when you *suspect* something happened The *spect* root spelling changes to *spic* in the adjective *susp cious.* People may act in a *suspicious* manner if they take some thing from others without asking.

voke   The Latin root which means to "call" is spelled *voke* or *vo* *voc*   *Vocal* is voice music, a "calling" sound. To *revoke* must mea to "call back." When a driver's license is *revoked,* it is "calle back."

The *voke* spelling changes to *voc* in noun and adjectiv forms like *revocation* and *revocable.*

spire   The *spire* root means to "breathe." To *perspire* means t sweat. You can guess how *perspire* got its meaning. The mois ture "breathes through" your pores.

Study the meanings of these roots and note the eye-sylla bles of the examples in the next chart.

vert verse mit miss spect voke voc spire Root Words				
Root	Meaning	Verb	Noun	Adjective
vert verse	turn	ad vert re verse	ad vert ise ment re vers al	ad verse re vers ible
mit miss	send	e mit per mit dis miss	e mis sion per mis sion dis miss al	per miss ible
spect	look	ex pect	ex pect a tion	ex pect ant
voke voc	call	re voke	re voc a tion	re voc able voc al
spire	breathe	per spire	per spir a tion	

68

meaning. In addition, looking at the meaning of prefixes and roots serves to reinforce the requisite analytical approach to multisyllabic words. The chart on this page serves to sum-

marize the roots introduced in Subsection Each root is shown with a prefix and a nou suffix. Words are also shown in their adje tive form when possible. Have pupils study t

Skill Drill 5 Use the chart on page 68 to help you follow these directions. Compare your work with the answers at the end of Chapter 3.

1a Form five verbs by affixing the *com, re, ad, sub,* and *trans* prefixes to the *mit* ("send") root.

1b Use the *ment, ion, ance,* and *al* suffixes to form ten *mit* or *miss* nouns from the five *mit* verbs you wrote in 1a. The verbs can be used more than once.

2a Form five *vert* ("turn") verbs by affixing the *sub, di [de], in [im],* re, and *con [com]* prefixes to the root.

2b Change the preceding five *vert* verbs into nouns by changing the root to *vers* and adding the *ion* suffix.

3 Form four *spect* ("look") verbs by affixing the *in [im],* re, *pro,* and *sus [sub]* prefixes to the root.

4a Form four *voke* ("call") verbs by affixing the *in [im], e [ex], con [com],* and *pro* prefixes to the root.

4b Change the preceding four *voke* verbs into nouns by changing the root to *voc,* adding *a,* and affixing the *tion* suffix.

5a Form five *spire* ("breathe") verbs by affixing the *ex, con [com], in [im], tran [trans]* and *as [ad]* prefixes to the root.

5b Change the five preceding *spire* verbs into nouns by changing final *e* to *a* and adding the *tion* suffix.

Skill Drill 6 Follow these directions. Compare your work with the answers at the end of Chapter 3.

1 Write *ible* adjectives from the verbs *permit, admit, convert,* and *reverse.*

2 Write *able* adjectives from the verbs *revoke* and *respect.*

3 Write *ive* adjectives from the verbs *prospect, permit,* and *subvert.*

4 Write the *ous* adjective from the verb *suspect.*

5 Write the *ant* adjective from the verb *expect.*

6 Write the *ion* noun from the verb *inspect.*

7 Change the spelling of the root in *emit* from *mit* to *miss* and form the *ion* noun.

69

1 permissible, admissible, convertible, reversible
2 revocable, respectable
3 prospective, permissive, subversive
4 suspicious
5 expectant
6 inspection
7 emission

hart, noting carefully the eye-syllables in each word. Then assign Skill Drills 5 and 6 as usual.

The five items in Skill Drill 5 cover the five roots studied in Subsection 4 as well as the variant spelling of each root. It may be advisable to check pupil performance carefully and review any parts necessary before having pupils go on to Skill Drill 6.

70

1a *prefer* — carry before; rather have *defer* — carry down or away; put off *infer* — carry in; reason out, conclude *confer* — carry with; discuss, talk over *transfer* — carry across; move from one place to another
1b preference, deference, inference, conference, transference
2a *exclaim* — cry out *reclaim* — cry back; get back *proclaim* — cry onward; announce *declaim* — cry down or away; speak out *acclaim* — cry to; hail, praise
2b exclamation, reclamation, proclamation, declamation, acclamation

5 "carry," "cry," "stand," "shape," and "break" Roots
fer   claim   clam   sist   form   rupt

fer The *fer* root means to "carry." When you *prefer,* you "carry before," in your mind. You regard it as better. When your ideas *differ,* they do "not carry," that is, they are unlike. The *fer* nouns are formed by adding the *ence* suffix, as in *difference*

claim The *claim* root spelling changes to *clam* in nouns. You can
clam guess from *exclaim* that the root meaning is to "cry," that is to cry out, to raise the voice—not to weep. You can see the roots in words like *clamor,* loud voices, and *claimant,* a person who makes claims or raises his voice.
You insert an *a* before adding *tion* to form the *clam* nouns

sist The *sist* root means to "stand" so *resist* literally means to "stand back." Some of the *sist* verbs, like *resist* and *assist* take the *ance* and *ant* suffix forms to make nouns and adjectives. Others, like *insist, persist, subsist,* and *exist,* take the *ence* and *ent* suffix forms. Look carefully at *sist* nouns and adjectives to see which suffix spelling option is being used. When you add *ex* to *sist,* you drop the first *s* in the root to form *exist* to "stand out," that is, to be.

form The *form* root means to "shape" or what it says, to "form." If you *inform,* you give shape, or form, or meaning to something. For nouns, we again add an *a* and the *tion* suffix.

rupt The *rupt* root means to "break." To *interrupt* means to "break in between." You *interrupt* someone who is speaking. The adjective *abrupt* consists of the prefix *ab* and *rupt.*

ab The *ab* prefix means "away–from." An *abrupt* move is sudden move, a "breaking away" move.
Study the next chart. Note the eye-syllables in examples

70

The material included in Subsection 5 is again quite comprehensive in that it includes five roots which occur with some frequency in English words. Consequently, it is preferable in most cases to work through the explanatory materials with pupils.

The goal of these lessons is to make these common Latin roots familiar to pupils and t

| fer | claim | clam | sist | form | rupt | Root Words |

Root	Meaning	Verb	Noun	Adjective
fer	carry	pre͵fer͵	pre͵fer͵ence͵	pre͵fer͵able͵
claim clam	cry	ex͵claim͵	ex͵clam͵a͵tion͵ clam͵or͵	clam͵or͵ous͵
sist	stand	re͵sist͵	re͵sist͵ance͵	re͵sist͵ant͵
form	shape	in͵form͵ per͵form͵	in͵form͵a͵tion͵ per͵form͵ance͵	in͵form͵a͵tive͵
rupt	break	inter͵rupt͵	inter͵rup͵tion͵	in͵ter͵rupt͵ible͵

Skill Drill 7 Use the chart above to help you follow these directions. Answers appear at the end of Chapter 3.

1a Combine the *pre, de, in [im], con [com]*, and *trans* prefixes with the *fer* ("carry") root to write five verbs. Give the meanings.

1b Form *fer* nouns by appending *ence* to the verbs in 1a.

2a Combine the *ex, re, pro, de*, and *ac [ad]* prefixes with the *claim* ("cry") root to write five verbs. Explain the meanings.

2b Form nouns with the *claim* verbs in 2a by changing the root spelling to *clam*, adding *a*, and appending the *tion* suffix.

3a Combine the *re, ex, de, sub, con [com], in [im], as [ad]*, and *per* prefixes with the *sist* ("stand") root to write eight verbs. Explain the meanings.

3b Change the *re, ex, sub, in [im], as [ad]*, and *per* verbs to *sist* nouns by appending the correct *ance–ence* suffix form.

4a Combine the *in [im], re, con [com], de*, and *trans* prefixes with *form* ("shape") to write five verbs. Explain the meanings.

4b Make nouns by adding *a* and *tion* to the verbs in 4a.

5a Combine the *inter, e [ex], cor [com]*, and *dis* prefixes with the *rupt* ("break") root to write four verbs. Give the meanings.

5b Add the suffix *ion* to the *rupt* verbs in 5a to form nouns.

71

help pupils develop skill in observing the roots as they occur in English words.

Use the chart to review the five roots. Be sure pupils note the eye-syllables. Assign the

Skill Drill as usual. Again the five items in the Skill Drill correspond to the five roots studied in this subsection. The "Give the meanings" part should be used as an oral activity.

6 "take," "lean," "close," "bend," and "hang" Roots

ceive cept cline clude clus flect flex pend pense

ceive
cept

The "take" root has two spellings. The *ceive* spelling appears in the verb *perceive*. Since the *per* prefix means "through," to *perceive* means to "take through," that is, to understand.

The *ceive* root becomes *cept* in nouns like *perception, deception,* and *reception,* and in the verb *accept (ad + cept).*

cline

The *cline* root means to "lean" as in *recline.* When you *recline,* you "lean back" or lie down.

clude
clus

The *clude* or *clus* root means to "close." When you *include* you "close in." When you *exclude,* you "close out." When you *conclude,* you "close with," that is, you finish.

The *clude* spelling changes to *clus* in noun and adjective forms like *conclusion* and *conclusive.*

flect
flex

The *flect* or *flex* root means to "bend." When light is *reflected,* it is "bent back" or sent back.

The *flect* spelling changes to *flex* in some adjective forms like *reflexive* and *inflexible.*

pend
pense

The *pend* or *pense* root means to "hang" or to weigh. Long ago, scales, or weighing instruments, were made so that weights could be hung on one side or the other to balance the scale. When you *suspend (sub + pend)* an object in the air, you "hang it under," so to speak, as if weighing it. A person may be *suspended* from office for not bearing its weight.

The *pend* spelling changes to *pens* in noun forms like *suspension* and adjective forms like *expensive.*

The *pense* spelling is seen in *dispense,* to "hang away," that is, to hand out, to give out, to spend.

Study the roots and the examples in the next chart.

72

The explanatory material in Subsection 6 will probably be too difficult to assign as independent silent reading for many pupils. Instead go over each of the five roots patiently with pu-

pils. Providing an illustrative sentence for each sample word may help pupils remember the meaning of unfamiliar words. Be sure pupils note the variant spellings of four of the roots.

ceive cept cline clude clus flect flex pend pense Root Words				
Root	Meaning	Verb	Noun	Adjective
ceive cept	take	per ceive ac cept	per cep tion ac cept ance	per cep tive ac cept able
cline	lean	re cline		
clude clus	close	con clude	con clu sion	con clus ive
flect flex	bend	re flect	re flec tion	re flec tive re flex ive
pend pense	hang, weigh	sus pend dis pense	sus pen sion dis pens a tion	

Skill Drill 8 Use the chart above to help you follow these directions. Answers appear at the end of Chapter 3.

1a Combine the *per, re, de,* and *con [com]* prefixes with the *ceive* ("take") root to write four verbs. Explain the meanings.
1b Change the preceding four *ceive* verbs into nouns, by changing the *ceive* spelling to *cept* and adding the *ion* suffix.
2 Combine the *ex, ac [ad],* and *inter* prefixes with the *cept* root to spell three verbs. Explain the meanings.
3 Combine the *re, in [im],* and *de* prefixes with the *cline* ("lean") root to write three verbs. Explain the meanings.
4a Combine the *con [com], in [im],* and *ex* prefixes with the *clude* ("close") root to write three verbs. Explain the meanings.
4b Change the verbs in 4a to nouns with the *clus* root and *ion.*
5 Combine the *re, de,* and *in [im]* prefixes with the *flect* ("bend") root to write three verbs. Explain the meanings.
6 Combine the *sus [sub], de, im, ex,* and *ap [ad]* prefixes with the *pend* ("hang") root to write five verbs. Give the meanings.

73

Skill Drill 8 Answers
1a *perceive*—take through; see, understand, grasp *receive*—take back; get, accept *deceive*—take down; fool, cheat *conceive*—take with; think, understand
1b perception, reception, deception, conception
2 *except*—take out; exclude *accept*—take to; receive *intercept*—take between; seize, catch between
3 *recline*—lean back *incline*—lean in; lean toward *decline*—lean away; refuse
4a *conclude*—close with; end *include*—close in; take in *exclude*—close out; leave out
4b conclusion, inclusion, exclusion
5 *reflect*—bend back; shine back, think over *deflect*—bend down or away; turn aside *inflect*—bend in; change voice tone, change word ending
6 *suspend*—hang under; hang down or in place, stop for a while, remove *depend*—hang down; rely upon *impend*—weigh in; be about to happen *expend*—weigh out; spend, measure out *append*—hang to; fasten to

Go through the chart with the class to review the meanings of the roots and help pupils see the eye-syllables in the sample words. Assign and check Skill Drill 8 before going on to Skill Drill 9. It is suggested that the meaning of each word be discussed when the responses are checked. Review the explanatory material on page 72 if necessary.

Skill Drill 9 Answers

1 transferable, acceptable, preferable, expendable, dependable

2 existent, consistent, insistent, persistent, dependent

3 receptive, deceptive, perceptive

4 conclusive, inclusive, exclusive

5 expensive, disruptive, informative

Skill Drill 10 Answers

1 *construct*—build with; make, build *construction*—a building; a structure *constructive*—building with; helpful *obstruct*—build in the way; block, get in the way of *obstruction*—a building in the way; a blocking *obstructive*—building in the way; blocking *instruct*—build in; teach, show how *instruction*—a building in; a teaching *instructive*—building in; helpful in learning

2 *insult*—jump in; offend, hurt feelings *result*—jump back; end in, final happening *consult*—jump with; talk with, confer

Skill Drill 9 Follow these directions. Compare your work with the answers at the end of Chapter 3.

1 Use the *able* suffix form to change the verbs *transfer, accept, prefer, expend,* and *depend* into adjectives.

2 Use the *ent* suffix form to change the verbs *exist, consist, insist, persist,* and *depend* into adjectives.

3 Use the *cept* root and the *ive* suffix to change the verbs *receive, deceive,* and *perceive* into adjectives.

4 Use the *clus* root and the *ive* suffix to change the verbs *conclude, include,* and *exclude* into adjectives.

5 Write the *ive* adjective form of *expend, disrupt,* and *inform.*

7 "build," "jump," "plunge," "speak," and "turn" Roots

struct   sult   merge   merse   dict   volve

struct   The Latin root *struct* means to "build." A *structure* is a building. Although the verb is *destroy,* the noun form is *destruction,* a "building down." Since the *ob* prefix means "in the way," to *obstruct* literally means to "build in the way" or to block.

sult   The *sult* root means to "jump." When you *consult,* you "jump with" or speak with or get advice from someone.

You add an *a* and the *tion* suffix to form nouns, as in *consultation.* When you add *ex* to *sult,* you drop the *s* from *sult* to form *exult,* to "jump out," that is, to be happy.

merge   *Merge* means to "bring together" now. A *merger* of compa-
merse   nies is a joining of companies. But *merge* originally meant "plunge" or to be swallowed up. To *submerge,* of course, means to "plunge under," as a submarine *submerges.*

Note the *merse* root in *immerse,* to "plunge in" or under.

74

Assign the Skill Drill 9 exercises and have pupils check their answers as directed.

Follow the same procedure in Subsection 7 as you have in previous lessons in this chapter. In order to help pupils retain the meaning of the roots, ask pupils to compose a sentence using each of the sample words from the explanatory material.

dict

As you can guess from *diction* or *dictate*, the *dict* root means to "speak." A *verdict* is a "thing spoken," a judgment. To *predict* means to "speak before" or to foretell.

volve

The *volve* root means to "turn." To *revolve* means to "turn again." You omit the *x* from the *ex* prefix to form *evolve*, which literally means to "turn out." A frog *evolves* from a tadpole.

struct	sult	merge	merse	dict	volve	Root Words		
Root	Meaning	Verb		Noun		Adjective		
struct	build	ob‚struct‚		ob‚struc‚tion‚		ob‚struct‚ive‚		
sult	jump	con‚sult‚		con‚sult‚a‚tion‚				
merge	plunge	sub‚merge‚		sub‚mer‚sion‚		sub‚mers‚ible‚		
merse		im‚merse‚		im‚mer‚sion‚		im‚mers‚ible‚		
dict	speak	pre‚dict‚		pre‚dic‚tion‚		pre‚dict‚able‚		
volve	turn	e‚volve‚		e‚volve‚ment‚		e‚volv‚ing‚		

 Skill Drill 10 Use the chart above to help you follow these directions. Answers appear at the end of Chapter 3.

1 Add the *con [com]*, *ob*, and *in [im]* prefixes to the *struct* ("build") root to form verbs. Then add *ion* and *ive* to change the verbs into nouns and into adjectives. Give the meanings.

2 Add the *in [im]*, *re*, *con [com]*, and *ex* prefixes to the *sult* ("jump") root to form verbs. Then add *a* and *tion* to the *con [com]*, and *ex* verbs to form nouns. Explain the meanings.

3 Add the *pre*, *ad*, *e [ex]*, and *contra* ("against") prefixes to the *dict* ("speak") root. Then add the *ion* suffix to the *pre*, *ad*, and *contra* verbs to form nouns. Explain the meanings.

4 Add the *re*, *in [im]*, and *e [ex]* prefixes to the *volve* ("turn") root. Also write each *ing* verb form. Give the meanings.

5 Add the *e [ex]* and *sub* prefixes to *merge* ("plunge"). Add *im* to *merse*. Write each *ing* verb form. Give the meanings.

75

Use the chart as usual to review the meanings and to help pupils see the eye-syllables.

Assign the Skill Drill as usual. Allow ample time for pupils to complete this exercise. Again the "Give the meanings" portion of the directions should be handled as an oral activity when you go over the answers. Review the explanatory material if necessary.

Skill Drill 11 Answers

Skill Drill 11 Answers

1 *complicate*—fold with; make difficult *complication*—a folding with; difficulty *supplicate*—fold under; plead, beg, appeal to *supplication*—a folding under; a begging, a pleading *implicate*—fold in; involve, mix in *implication*—a folding in; involvement, suggestion, hint *duplicate*—fold twice; copy *duplication*—a folding twice; a copy

2 *resume*—take again; begin again *resumption*—a taking again; another beginning *assume*—take to; suppose, take for granted *assumption*—a taking to; a supposition *consume*—take with; use up *consumption*—a taking with; a using up *presume*—take before; suppose, assume *presumption*—a taking before; a supposition, an assumption

8 "hold," "feel," "fold," "cry," and "take" Roots
tain tin sent sens plic plex plore sume sumpt

tain
tin
The *tain* root means to "hold." To *detain* means to "hold back. To *pertain* literally means to "hold through" or to belong to

You see the *tin* spelling in the adjective form *pertinent* "holding through," relating. You may say that someone's remarks are not *pertinent* to the subject being talked about.

sent
sens
The *sent* or *sens* root means to "feel." *Sentiment* is "feeling." *Presentiment* is a "feeling before," for example, a feeling of approaching danger. When you *resent,* you literally "feel back" or "feel against" or are angry about. The *sens* form of *sent* appears in words like *supersensitive* and *insensible.*

plic
plex
The *plic* root, which sometimes changes to the *plex* form literally means to "fold."

du
ate
When you use the prefix *du,* which means "two," with *plic* and the *ate* verb suffix, you get *duplicate.* Duplicate literally means to "fold two" or make another thing like the first. When you *implicate,* you "fold someone in" as when a person is *implicated,* or mixed up in a crime.

You see the *plex* root in the noun *duplex* and verb *perplex.*

plore
The *plore* root means to "cry." *Explore* got its meaning from the fact that an *ex* ("out")–*plorer* ("crier") "cries out" in surprise when making new discoveries. To *implore* is to "cry in" or to beg. To *deplore* is to "cry down," to regret.

sume
sumpt
The *sume* verbs become *sumpt* when they are changed into nouns. Both roots come from a Latin verb which means to "take." To *resume* means to "take up again," to continue. A *resumption* is a "taking up again," a continuation.

Study the next chart, which summarizes these roots.

76

The explanatory material for Subsection 8 should be amplified with sentences to illustrate the meaning of the example words. Call particular attention to the variant spellings of the roots presented in this subsection. Help pupils to see how the literal meanings of words such as *duplicate, implicate,* and *explore* have changed with use over the years.

tain tin	sent sens	plic plex	plore	sume sumpt	Root Words

Root	Meaning	Verb	Noun	Adjective
tain tin	hold	per.tain, con.tin.ue	per.tin.ence, con.tin.u.ance,	per.tin.ent, con.tin.u.ous,
sent sens	feel	re.sent,	re.sent.ment,	re.sent.ful, in.sens.ible,
plic	fold	du.plic.ate, com.plic.ate,	du.plic.a.tion, com.plic.a.tion,	com.plex,
plex		per.plex,	per.plex.i.ty,	
plore	cry	ex.plore,	ex.plor.a.tion,	
sume sumpt	take	re.sume, pre.sume,	re.sump.tion, pre.sump.tion,	pre.sumpt.ive,

Skill Drill 11   Use the chart above to help you follow these directions. Compare your work with the answers at the end of Chapter 3.

1 Combine the *com, sup [sub], im,* and *du* prefixes with the *plic* ("fold") root and the *ate* suffix to form verbs. Then change each verb into a noun with the *ion* suffix. Explain the meanings.
2 Add the *re, as [ad], con [com],* and *pre* prefixes to the *sume* ("take") root to form verbs. Then change the verbs into nouns by changing the root spelling to *sumpt* and adding the *ion* suffix. Explain the meanings.
3 Add the *ex, de,* and *im* prefixes to the *plore* ("cry") root to form verbs. Then write each *ing* form. Explain the meanings.
4 Add the *ob, con [com], enter [inter], de, re, per,* and *sus [sub]* prefixes to the *tain* ("hold") root to form verbs. Explain the meanings.
5 Add the *con [com], re, dis,* and *as [ad]* prefixes to the *sent* ("feel") root to form verbs. Explain the meanings.

77

Skill Drill 11 Answers (cont'd)

3 *explore*—cry out; examine, look into *exploring*—crying out; examining, looking into *deplore*—cry down; regret *deploring*—crying down; regretting *implore*—cry in; beg, plead *imploring*—crying in; begging, pleading
4 *obtain*—hold in the way of; get, secure *contain*—hold with; include *entertain*—hold between; amuse, think of *detain*—hold down; delay *retain*—hold back; keep *pertain*—hold through; have to do with *sustain*—hold under; support
5 *consent*—feel with; agree *resent*—feel back; be angry about *dissent*—feel away; disagree *assent*—feel to; consent, agree

Use the chart to review the roots and help pupils see the parts of these multisyllabic words. Then assign the Skill Drill as usual. The "Explain the meaning" part of the directions should be done orally. Rather than having pupils write the meaning of each word in this exercise, go over the meaning of each word orally when the answers are discussed.

Latin Roots		
Roots	Meaning	Prefix + Root + Suffix
cede–ceed ces	go	pre ced ing, suc ceed ing, inter ces sion
ceive cept	take	re ceiv able, ac cept ance
claim clam	cry	ex claim ing, pro clam a tion
cline	lean	in clin a tion
clude clus	close	ex clud ing, con clus ive
dict	speak	pre dict able
duce duct	lead	in duce ment, intro duc tion
fer	carry	de fer ence
flect flex	bend	re flec tion, re flex ive
form	shape	re form a tion
gress	walk–go	di gress ive
ject	throw	ab ject ness
merge merse	plunge	e merg ence, im mer sion
mit miss	send	ad mit tance, per miss ible
pel pul	push	re pel lent, com pul sion
pend pense	hang	ex pend able, sus pense ful
plic plex	fold	du plic ate, per plex ing
plore	cry	ex plor a tion

78

This Latin roots reference chart includes the thirty-five roots which appear again and again in English words. Take time to review these roots and their meaning to be sure that all of the pupils have mastered them before assigning Mastery Test 3 which concludes this chapter. Pupils should be able to supply the one-word meanings for these roots instantly.

Roots	Meaning	Prefix + Root + Suffix
port	carry	un im port ant
pose	put	sup pos i tion
press	squeeze	com pres sion
rupt	break	cor rup tion
scribe scrip	write	sub scrib ing tran scrip tion
sent sens	feel	re sent ment super sens it ive
sist	stand	as sist ance
spect	look	re spect ful
spire	breathe	in spir a tion
struct	build	ob struc tion
sult	jump	con sult ant
sume sumpt	take	con sum able as sump tion
tain tin	hold	con tain ing con tin u ous
tract	pull	dis trac tion
vert verse	turn	con vert ible re vers ible
voke voc	call	pro vok ing in voc a tion
volve	turn	in volve ment

79

They should also be able to supply several examples of each root in English words.

It is advisable to review all of the prefixes, suffixes, and roots studied in the first three chapters in conjunction with the summary on page 80. The usefulness of these elements can be made clear to pupils by having them scan several pages of any of their other textbooks

Summary

In this chapter you reviewed the prefixes and suffixes that you
worked with in Chapters 1 and 2. We add these prefixes and
suffixes to some English words. More often we add them to
Latin roots. You, therefore, have learned the meanings and
spellings of thirty-five frequently used Latin roots.

If you know prefix and root meanings, you can often guess
the meaning of many words. If you know noun and adjective
suffixes, you will be able to understand how the words are
used. If you learn to see long words as eye-syllables—consisting of a prefix, a root, and a suffix—you will find them much
easier to read and spell.

The reference chart of Latin roots on the preceding two
pages lists the thirty-five roots and their meanings, and shows
them with the prefixes and suffixes you used in Chapters 1
and 2, as well as with the affixes presented in this chapter.

80

to find examples of their use. Lead pupils to
understand that the learning material in these
first three chapters is useful both in reading
and spelling.

The Mastery Test is divided into two parts.
This allows the test to be administered in two
shorter sessions if a longer session is inappro-
priate for you or the pupils.

Carefully check the results of the Mastery
Test. Use the chart which appears in the front
of this Teacher's Edition to prescribe appropriate review in Levels 7 or 8.

Mastery Test 3

A

Write a word for each meaning, using a prefix, the root which is shown in sound-spelling, and a /shən/ suffix form.

/trakt/

1 withdrawal of a statement
2 process in arithmetic
3 a drawing out

/skrip/

4 a copy
5 words engraved on stone or metal
6 a picture in words

/pres/

7 a feeling or notion
8 low place
9 a speaking out

/klam/

10 official announcement
11 sudden cry
12 a putting back into good condition

/pōz/

13 a show or display
14 opinion
15 make-up of anything

/ses/

16 persons riding or marching forward or onward
17 plea for another person
18 a moving backward

Write a word for each meaning, using a prefix, the root which is shown in sound-spelling, and an /əns/ suffix form.

/sist/

19 a sticking to your point
20 a help

/mėrj/ or /pôrt/

21 a coming out
22 significance, worth

/fėr/

23 disagreement
24 first choice
25 great respect

26 discussion meeting
27 conclusion

81

Part A Answers (cont'd)

28 exclusive
29 conclusive
30 dependable
31 expendable
32 compulsive
33 repulsive
34 reversible
35 convertible
36 destructive
37 constructive
38 predictable
39 deplorable

Part B Answers

1 reflection
2 presentiment
3 instruction
4 exploration
5 immersion
6 admission
7 admittance
8 inducement
9 invocation
10 dependent
11 dejection
12 corruption

Write a word for each meaning, using a prefix, the root which is shown in sound-spelling, and either the /iv/ suffix or an /ə bəl/ suffix form.

/klüs/

28 shutting out others
29 final, decisive

/pend/

30 reliable
31 worth giving up for a cause

/puls/

32 having a forceful drive or urge
33 causing strong dislike

/vėrt/ *or* /vèrs/

34 able to be turned inside out or back
35 possible to be folded or changed

/strukt/

36 able to destroy
37 having a helpful influence

/dikt/ *or* /plôr/

38 able to foretell
39 regretful

B Write a word for each definition, using a prefix, the root which is shown in sound-spelling, and a noun suffix.

1 /flekt/   image in a mirror
2 /sent/   a feeling of approaching danger
3 /strukt/   the teaching of, guidance
4 /plôr/   a careful going over
5 /mèrs/   a plunging into
6 /mis/   price paid to enter
7 /mit/   right to enter
8 /düs/   something that persuades
9 /vōk/   prayer for help
10 /pend/   one reliant upon another for support
11 /jekt/   sadness; discouragement
12 /rupt/   decay, dishonesty

82

Write a word for each definition, using a prefix, the root which is shown in sound-spelling, and an adjective suffix.

13	/tin/	connected, going on
14	/fleks/	not easily bent, rigid, firm
15	/sept/	worth accepting, agreeable
16	/mis/	allowable
17	/pôrt/	meaning much, necessary
18	/gres/	tending to get off the main subject
19	/spekt/	polite
20	/fėr/	not alike
21	/pens/	having suspense
22	/vōk/	able to be withdrawn
23	/sept/	observant, very aware
24	/gres/	advancing or moving to something better
25	/pens/	costly

83

Chart   1 interaction   2 transformation   3 cooperatio
4 impoliteness   5 distrustful   6 reappearance
7 superintendent   8 prepayment   9 collapsib
10 comfortless   11 ungracious   12 correlatic

Answers for Multiple Choice Sentences

Section A 1   1 retraction   2 extraction   3 contraction
A 2   1 suppression   2 expression   3 repression
4 depression
A 3   1 transposition   2 deposition   3 proposition
4 composition
A 4   1 deportation   2 importation
A 5   1 description   2 inscriptions
A 6   1 succession   2 concession   3 procession
A 7   1 repulsion   2 compulsion

Section B 1   1 transgression   2 digressive
B 2   1 interjection   2 dejection   3 subjection
B 3   1 induction   2 reduction   3 conduction

84

Skill Drill 1 1 contracts, contraction 2 repress, repression
3 suppose, supposition 4 impress, impression
5 distracted, distraction 6 dispose, disposition
7 transpose, transposition 8 retract, retraction
9 compose, composition 10 express, expression
11 extract, extraction 12 suppress, suppression
13 impose, imposition 14 protracted, protraction
15 compress, compression 16 propose, proposition
17 depress, depression 18 detract, detraction
19 deposed, deposition 20 subtract, subtraction

Skill Drill 2 1 repel, repulsion 2 prescribe, prescription
3 describe, description 4 compel, compulsion 5 transcribe,
transcription 6 import, importation 7 expel, expulsion
8 export, exportation 9 inscribe, inscription 10 proceed,
procession 11 deport, deportation 12 intercede,
intercession 13 recede, recession 14 transport,
transportation 15 concede, concession 16 propel,
propulsion 17 subscribe, subscription 18 succeed,
succession

Skill Drill 3 1 repelling 2 proceeding 3 compelling
4 transcribing 5 receding 6 expelling 7 prescribing
8 describing 9 conceding

Skill Drill 4 1 conduct 2 reduction 3 induce
4 transgression 5 rejection 6 ingress 7 dejection
8 progress 9 interjection 10 deduction 11 interject
12 reject 13 objection 14 produce 15 deduce
16 egress 17 deduct 18 transgress 19 object
20 congress

Skill Drill 5 1a commit, remit, admit, submit, transmit
1b commitment, commission; remission, remittance;
admission, admittance; submission, submittal; transmission,
transmittal

85

2a subvert, divert, invert, revert, convert   2b subversion, diversion, inversion, reversion, conversion

3 inspect, respect, prospect, suspect   4a invoke, evoke, convoke, provoke 4b invocation, evocation, convocation, provocation   5a expire, conspire, inspire, transpire, aspire 5b expiration, conspiration, inspiration, transpiration, aspiration

Skill Drill 6   1 permissible, admissible, convertible, reversible 2 revocable, respectable 3 prospective, permissive, subversive 4 suspicious 5 expectant 6 inspection 7 emission

Skill Drill 7   1a prefer—carry before; rather have defer—carry down or away; put off infer—carry in; reason out, conclude confer—carry with; discuss, talk over transfer—carry across; move from one place to another 1b preference, deference, inference, conference, transference 2a exclaim—cry out reclaim—cry back; get back proclaim—cry onward; announce declaim—cry down or away; speak out acclaim—cry to; hail, praise 2b exclamation, reclamation, proclamation, declamation, acclamation 3a resist—stand back; stand or be against exist—stand out; be, live desist—stand down; stop subsist—stand under; barely live consist—stand with; include insist—stand in; stand firm assist—stand to; help persist—stand through; refuse to stop   3b resistance, existence, subsistence, insistence, assistance, persistence 4a inform—form in; let know, tell reform—form again; change for the better conform—form with; obey, agree with deform—form down; change or spoil shape transform—form across; change form   4b information, reformation, conformation, deformation, transformation 5a interrupt—break between; break into erupt—break out; burst forth, explode corrupt—break with; spoil, make bad disrupt—break down or away; break up, interfere 5b interruption, eruption, corruption, disruption

86

Skill Drill 8 1a <u>perceive</u>—take through; see, understand, grasp <u>receive</u>—take back; get, accept <u>deceive</u>—take down; fool, cheat <u>conceive</u>—take with; think, understand
1b perception, reception, deception, conception
2 <u>except</u>—take out; exclude <u>accept</u>—take to; receive <u>intercept</u>—take between; seize, catch between
3 <u>recline</u>—lean back <u>incline</u>—lean in; lean toward <u>decline</u>—lean away; refuse
4a <u>conclude</u>—close with; end <u>include</u>—close in; take in <u>exclude</u>—close out; leave out   4b conclusion, inclusion, exclusion
5 <u>reflect</u>—bend back; shine back, think over <u>deflect</u>—bend down or away; turn aside <u>inflect</u>—bend in; change voice tone, change word ending
6 <u>suspend</u>—hang under; hang down or in place, stop for a while, remove <u>depend</u>—hang down; rely upon <u>impend</u>—weigh in; be about to happen <u>expend</u>—weigh out; spend, measure out <u>append</u>—hang to; fasten to

Skill Drill 9 1 transferable, acceptable, preferable, expendable, dependable 2 existent, consistent, insistent, persistent, dependent 3 receptive, deceptive, perceptive
4 conclusive, inclusive, exclusive 5 expensive, disruptive, informative

Skill Drill 10 1 <u>construct</u>—build with; make, build / construction—a building; a structure / constructive—building with; helpful   <u>obstruct</u>—build in the way; block, get in the way of / obstruction—a building in the way; a blocking / obstructive—building in the way; blocking   <u>instruct</u>—build in; teach, show how / instruction—a building in; a teaching / instructive—building in; helpful in learning
2 <u>insult</u>—jump in; offend, hurt feelings   <u>result</u>—jump back; end in, final happening   <u>consult</u>—jump with; talk with, confer / consultation—a jumping with; a meeting,

87

conference   exult—jump out; rejoice, be happy /
exultation—a jumping out; a rejoicing, being happy
3 predict—say before; foretell / prediction—a saying before
a foretelling   addict—say to; form a habit /
addiction—a saying to; habit   edict—say out;
command   contradict—speak against; disagree /
contradiction—a speaking against; disagreement
4 revolve—turn again; turn in a circle / revolving—
turning again; turning in a circle   involve—turn
in; take in, include / involving—turning in; taking in,
including   evolve—turn out; become,
change into / evolving—turning out; becoming,
changing into
5 emerge—plunge out; appear / emerging—plunging
out; appearing   submerge—plunge under; go under /
submerging—plunging under; going under   immerse—
plunge in; shove under / immersing—plunging in;
shoving under

Skill Drill 11 1 complicate—fold with; make difficult /
complication—a folding with; difficulty   supplicate—fold
under; plead, beg, appeal to / supplication—a folding
under; a begging, a pleading   implicate—fold in; involve,
mix in / implication—a folding in; involvement, suggestion,
hint   duplicate—fold twice; copy / duplication—a folding
twice; a copy
2 resume—take again; begin again / resumption—a taking
again; another beginning   assume—take to; suppose,
take for granted / assumption—a taking to; a supposition
consume—take with; use up / consumption—a taking with;
using up   presume—take before; suppose, assume /
presumption—a taking before; a supposition, an assumption

88

3 explore—cry out; examine, look into / exploring—crying out; examining, looking into   deplore—cry down; regret / deploring—crying down; regretting
implore—cry in; beg, plead / imploring—crying in; begging, pleading

4 obtain—hold in the way of; get, secure   contain—hold with; include   entertain—hold between; amuse, think of
detain—hold down; delay   retain—hold back; keep
pertain—hold through; have to do with   sustain—hold under; support

5 consent—feel with; agree   resent—feel back; be angry about   dissent—feel away; disagree
assent—feel to; consent, agree

89

4 Greek and French Spellings

Our English language uses more words than any other language. The big dictionaries you see in libraries have more than 600,000 words. As you saw in Chapter 3, the majority, if not most, of our words come from Latin. But, thousands of words came from other languages.

In this chapter you will meet words that have Greek and French spellings. These spellings are different from our usual English spellings. You will also meet some Greek word parts which we often join together to form words.

Greek Spellings

Many years ago English scholars studied and wrote Greek as well as Latin. The Greeks had written great literature, especially plays, and many Greek drama words came into English.

As science, medicine, and technology discover new concepts and processes, we make new English words to name them from Greek word parts. The Greek spellings of these word parts do not always agree with our English spellings.

1 *ch* Spells /k/

In words taken from Greek, *ch* spells the /k/ sound, as in *chord*, *choral, anchor,* or *echo.* You often see this *ch* spelling in words like these. Check the meaning of any unfamiliar word.

chasm	or,chid,	sched,ule,
char,ac,ter,	or,ches,tra,	schol,ar,
cha,os,	ar,chit,ect,	scheme
chem,i,cal,	me,chan,ic,	

CHAPTER 4

Although there are more words of Latin origin than Greek origin in our English vocabulary, the Greek contribution is substantial, and we continue to coin new medical and scientific words from Greek sources. These words of Greek origin are the most frequent violators of our standard English spelling habits. Knowing the Greek prefixes and combining forms is useful in determining both word meanings and spellings.

Similarly, English words of French origin also cause a considerable number of spelling problems. Although the number of French spellings found in English words is relatively small, they present some of the most difficult dilemmas for pupils.

In this chapter, sustained attention is given to Greek spellings, Greek word parts, and some thirteen French spellings which occur frequently in English.

2 *ph* Spells /f/

In words taken from Greek, *ph* spells the /f/ sound. Note the *ph* spelling of /f/ in these words. Check the meaning of any unfamiliar word.

cam phor	pho to graph	as phalt
dol phin	ep i taph	mor phine
pheas ant	cel lo phane	pro phet
al pha bet	diph ther i a	sul phur
ty phoon	or phan	tro phy

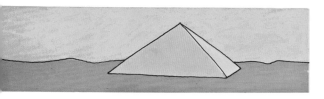

3 *y* Spells /ī/ and /i/

The use of *y* instead of *i* often shows that the word has a Greek origin. Study these examples. Check the meaning of any unfamiliar word.

myth	a sy lum	sys tem
hy phen	dy na mite	ty rant
py thon	cyl in der	hy drant
cy clone	syl la ble	pyr a mid
cym bal	sym phon y	pyg my

91

Skill Drill 1 Answers

 1 myth
 2 rhythm
 3 echo
 4 autumn
 5 cellophane
 6 typhoon
 7 pneumonia
 8 rhubarb
 9 hyphen
10 condemn
11 syllable
12 orchestra
13 pheasant
14 cyclone
15 rhinoceros
16 character
17 photograph
18 scheme
19 cylinder
20 column
21 schedule
22 trophy
23 hydrant
24 mechanic
25 chord
26 symphony
27 alphabet
28 psychology
29 pygmy
30 dolphin
31 anchor
32 psychiatrist
33 system

4   Silent Consonants

Some other unusual spellings in words from Greek are *rh* i◦
which *h* is silent, *ps* in which *p* is silent, *pn* in which *p* is silen◦
and *mn* in which *n* is silent. Note the silent consonant in th◦
consonant pair in each of these examples. Check the meanin◦
of any unfamiliar word in your Spelling Dictionary or in th◦
classroom dictionary.

rhythm   psalm   hymn
rhu barb   psy chi at rist   au tumn
rhet or ic   psy chol o gy   col umn
rhi noc er os   pneu mat ic   con demn
rheu mat ism   pneu mon i a

Skill Drill 1   Write the regular spellings for these words ◦
Greek origin. Compare your work with the answers at the en◦
of Chapter 4.

 1 /mith/
 2 /riŦн′əm/
 3 /ek′ō/
 4 /ô′təm/
 5 /sel′ə fān′/
 6 /tī fün′/
 7 /nü mōn′yə/
 8 /rü′bärb/
 9 /hī′fən/
10 /kən dem′/
11 /sil′ə bəl/
12 /ôr′kəs trə/
13 /fez′ənt/
14 /sī′klōn/
15 /rī nos′ər əs/
16 /kar′ək tər/
17 /fō′tə graf′/
18 /skēm/
19 /sil′ən dər/
20 /kol′əm/
21 /skej′ùl/
22 /trō′fē/
23 /hī′drənt/
24 /mə kan′ik/
25 /kôrd/
26 /sim′fə nē′/
27 /al′fə bet/
28 /sī kol′ə jē/
29 /pig′mē/
30 /dol′fən/
31 /ang′kər/
32 /sī kī′ə trist/
33 /sis′təm/

92

The fourteen words listed in the text are those which the pupils will be most likely to see and have to spell. Be sure pupils know the meaning of each word in the list. Assign Skill Drill 1 in the usual manner and check pupil responses.

Section B

The Greek word parts, which are examined i◦ this section, are more conspicuous than Lati◦ roots in English words and have fewer spellin◦ variations. Greek word parts are not usual◦ responsible for serious spelling problems, bu◦ we include them here because they are usefu◦

B Greek Word Parts

You saw that Latin prefixes, roots, and suffixes pieced together neatly made English words. We also form English words from Greek word parts. We piece these Greek word parts together in almost the same way that we combine short words to form English compounds, like *flashlight* and *toothbrush*.

1 "speaking about–study of" Word Parts *logy logue*

The Greek *logos* means "word." *Logos* now converted to the *logy* or *logue* root is attached to many other word parts. It means a "speaking about" or the "study of" or science of.

astr(o)   Another Greek word part, or root, is *aster* or *astr(o)*. It means "star." The flower we call the *aster* has "star-shaped" petals. The *asterisk* [*] is the little "star" printers use. An *asteroid* is a "starlike body." An *astronaut* is literally a "star sailor." You can see the stars in an *astrodome*. The word *disaster* is a combination of the Latin prefix *dis* and the Greek word part *aster*. Long ago, people believed that the stars governed life on earth, so a *disaster* became a "down" or bad happening caused by the wrong position of the "stars."

The word *astrology, astr* plus *o* plus the *logy* root, is a "study of the stars." *Astrology* has come to mean the "study of the influence of the stars" upon people's lives. *Astronomy* now means the "science of the heavenly bodies."

bio   The Greek word for "life" is *bios*. We use the *bio* root and attach *logy* to make *biology*, the "study of living things."

eco   The Greek root *ec* or *eco*, meaning "house," and the *logy* root form the word *ecology*, the "study of living things in their house" or environment.

93

mastering word meanings and because they help pupils identify significant word parts in longer words. Go through the explanation of the "speaking about-study of" word parts with students. The meaning of each word can be further illustrated by using the words in a sentence.

There are scores of other *logy* words in English. Additional examples include *anthology, anthropology, chronology, doxology, etymology, eulogy, genealogy, ideology, ophthalmology, ornithology, penology, pharmacology,* and *technology.*

geo	Greek *ge* or *geo* means "earth." It is used in *geology*, th
	"study of the earth" and its composition. Greek *myth*, c
myth(o)	"story," has become our *mythology*, the "speaking of myths.
	Meteors were to the Greeks "things in the air"; now the coine
meteor(o)	word *meteorology* formed from *meteor* with an *o* and *log*
	means the "study of weather."

Three common word parts that come from Latin and tha combine with *logy* to form familiar words are *socio, minera* and *criminal. Socio* means "associates" and it appears in th word *sociology*, "the study of society." *Mineral* means "rock and it combines with *logy* in the word *mineralogy*, the "stud of minerals." Our word *criminology* comes from the Latin *crim nal*, meaning "wrong doer" and the Greek word part *log* When we speak of *criminology*, we mean the "study of crim nals." Note the spelling of *mineralogy* formed from *mineral* an *logy*, and *criminology* formed from *criminal* and *logy*.

physio	We use *physio* from *physis*, the Greek word for "nature
	in *physiology*, the "study of how our bodily organs work." Fro
psych(o)	the Greek word for "soul" or "mind," *psyche*, we use *psyc*
theo	in *psychology*, the "study of the mind." The word part *the*
	comes from the Greek word *theos* that means "god," so th
zoo	word *theology* is the "study of religion." Our *zoo* root come
	from the Greek word for "animal," so *zoology* means t
	"study of animal life."
mono	The Greek *mono* means "one or alone," as in *monoplar*
	or *monotone*. A *monologue* is a "speaking alone," a spee
dia	by one person. Greek *dia* means "through," or dividing in
	two parts; so a *dialogue* is a "speaking by two persons."

The Latin prefix *pro* may also mean "before." If you cor bine *pro* with *logue*, you have the word *prologue* which mea a "speaking before," an introduction as for a play. Anoth Latin word part that appears with the Greek *logue* is *trav* These two word parts form the word *travelogue*, a "speakir about travel." Note the spelling of *travelogue* formed from *tra el* and *logue*.

cata	Another word that comes from Greek is *catalogue*. Tl

94

Many of the *logue* words are now spelled *log*. The dictionaries list *monologue* and *monolog, dialogue* and *dialog, catalogue* and *catalog, travelogue* and *travelog*.

To help pupils understand the functio of the *logy* root, have them make up nonsen words to describe something they would li to study. For example, the study of candy mig

Greek word part *cata* means "down," so a *catalogue* is a "list of words or things set down."

The next chart shows these English words which we have coined by using Greek word parts.

logy logue = "speaking about–study of"			
Word Part	**Meaning**	**Word**	**Meaning**
astr *(o)*	star	astr͵o͵logy	study of stars
bio	life	bio͵logy	study of life
eco	house	eco͵logy	study of environment
geo	earth	geo͵logy	study of earth
myth *(o)*	story	myth͵o͵logy	study of myths
meteor *(o)*	air things	meteor͵o͵logy	study of weather
socio [L]	associates	socio͵logy	study of society
mineral [L]	rocks	minera͵logy	study of minerals
criminal [L]	wrong doer	crimin͵o͵logy	study of crime
physio	nature	physio͵logy	study of organs
psych *(o)*	mind	psych͵o͵logy	study of the mind
theo	god	theo͵logy	study of religion
zoo	animal	zoo͵logy	study of animals
mono	one	mono͵logue	speech by one
dia	through	dia͵logue	speech by two
pro [L]	before	pro͵logue	introductory speech
travel [L]	travel	trave͵logue	talk about travel
cata	down	cata͵logue	written-down list

Skill Drill 2 Write the word which means the "study of." Answers appear at the end of Chapter 4.

1 the stars' influence 5 environment 9 crime
2 animals 6 religion 10 society
3 rocks 7 minerals 11 weather
4 myths 8 bodily organs 12 living things

95

Skill Drill 2 Answers
1 astrology
2 zoology
3 geology
4 mythology
5 ecology
6 theology
7 mineralogy
8 physiology
9 criminology
10 sociology
11 meteorology
12 biology

by the name candyology. The study of hamburgers might be called hamburgerology.

Use the chart to review the Greek word parts and their meanings. Challenge pupils to give additional examples of each word part. Then assign the Skill Drills and check the pupils' responses.

Skill Drill 3   Write the *logue* words. Compare your work w
the answers at the end of Chapter 4.

1 a travel description   **4** talk between two people
2 a drama introduction   **5** a listing of items
3 a speech by one person

2   "write–draw" Word Parts *graph(y) gram*
The word *graph* comes from the Greek verb *graphein,* whi
means "write–draw." That soft black mineral in pencils is call
graphite because you "write" with it. The Greek *graph(y)* a
gram roots with other word parts mean a "writing."

    We combine *geo* ("earth") and *graphy* ("writing") in *geog*
phy. We combine *bio* ("life") with *graphy* in *biography.*

auto   The Greek word part *auto* means "self" so an *autobio*
raphy is a "self-life-writing," the story of one's own life. An *a*
tograph is a "self-writing," the signing of one's name. Gre

tele   *tele* means "far" so a *telegraph* is a "far writer" and a *telegra*
is a "far writing."

    Since *dia* means "through," a *diagram* is a "through dra*
ing," showing a thing all the way through.

topo   The word part *topo* comes from the Greek word *top*
which means "place" so *topography* is a "place writing." *T*
pography has now come to mean a description of the surfa
of a place, its hills, valleys, streams, lakes, and cities.

    The *picto* root is from Latin and means a "picture" so
pictograph is "picture writing."

    A *monograph* is a "one-writing," an essay on one subje
A *monogram* is "one letter" or letters grouped or intertwine

96

    The "write-draw" word parts occur with some frequency in English and deserve careful attention. Go over the explanatory material with pupils or assign it as independent work. The more commonly used *graph* words are in-cluded in the explanation. There are, of cours many others. Other examples which could k used are *choreography, cryptography, demo raphy, lexicography, lithography, orthograph physiography, stenography* and *typography.*

photo The Greek *photo* means "light," so a *photograph* is literally a picture made by the "writing of light."

para The Greek prefix *para* means "beside" as in *parallel,* a line running "beside" another. A *parasite* is one eating "beside" or feeding upon another. A *paragraph* is a "beside writing."

biblio The Greek root *biblio* means "book" so a *bibliography* is a listing or "writing" down of "book" titles.

The next chart summarizes these word parts and shows the meanings and spellings.

graph(y) gram = "write–draw"			
Word Part	Meaning	Word	Meaning
auto	self	auto bio graphy	self-life-writing
		auto graph	self (name)-writing
tele	far	tele graph	far writer
		tele gram	far letter
topo	place	topo graphy	place writing
picto [L]	picture	picto graph	picture writing
mono	one	mono graph	one-writing
photo	light	photo graph	light writing
para	beside	para graph	beside writing
biblio	book	biblio graphy	book title writing
geo	earth	geo graphy	earth writing
bio	life	bio graphy	life writing
dia	through	dia gram	through drawing

Skill Drill 4 Write the word which means a "writing about or of." Answers appear at the end of Chapter 4.

1 the earth
2 a book list
3 one's own life
4 someone else's life
5 land surfaces
6 light

97

It will help to review the Greek word parts in the *logy* group with these in the *graph* chart. Be sure pupils note the word parts in each word and understand the meaning. The root meaning will not always give clear clues to the modern meaning. Be prepared to elaborate on the meanings of the words or to use them in a sentence. Assign and check the Skill Drills.

Skill Drill 5 Write the *graph* and *gram* words. Compare you■ work with the answers at the end of Chapter 4.

1 light writing
2 far letter
3 picture writing
4 beside writing
5 far writer
6 one letter
7 a through drawing
8 one's name

3 "measure" Word Parts   *meter   metry*

The Greek word part *meter* or *metry* means "measure." Th■ *metric* system is a system of "measurement." *Meter* itself ■ an English word, as in gas *meter*. Since *dia* means "through a *diameter* is a "measure through" the center of a circle.

micro

Greek *micro* means "small"; *microfilm* is "small film." *micrometer* is an instrument to "measure small distances."

therm(o)

The Greek *therm* means "heat" so a *thermometer* is an i■ strument to "measure heat." Note that you add an *o* to *ther*■ before affixing it to the *meter* root.

peri

The Greek prefix *peri* means "around" so a *perimeter* ■ the "measurement" or distance "around" a figure.

chron(o)

Greek *chron* means "time." A *chronic* illness is an illne■ one has for a long "time." A *chronicle* is an account of even■ over some "time." A *chronometer* is an instrument that "mea■ sures time" very accurately.

bar(o)

Greek *bar* means "weight" so a *barometer* is an instrume■ which "measures weight," the weight of the air. Note that yo■ add an *o* to the word parts *chron* and *bar* before affixing the■ to the *meter* root to spell *chronometer* and *barometer*.

As *geo* means "earth," *geometry* once meant a "measu■

98

The explanatory material can be assigned as independent reading or used as the source of a guided class discussion. In either case, be sure that the activity concludes with a careful study of the word chart. The chart includes some of the more common uses of the "meas■ ure" word part that pupils may encounter.

The word parts studied in this subsectio■ appear in many other words which pupils ■ this level will probably not meet very ofte■

of earth" or land. Now *geometry* means the science of "measuring" surfaces, lines, and angles in space.

opto   Greek *opto* means "eye" so *optometry* is the science of "eye measure." An *optometrist* is a person who "fits" lenses.

sym   Greek *sym–syn* means "with." *Sympathy* means feeling or
syn   suffering "with" someone. A *syndicate* is a group of people who work "with" one another. *Symmetry*, then, is a "with-measure," which now means matching or balancing parts.

Review these spellings and meanings in the next chart.

meter metry = "measure"			
Word Part	Meaning	Word	Meaning
micro	small	micro meter	small measurer
therm(o)	heat	therm o meter	heat measurer
peri	around	peri meter	distance around
chron(o)	time	chron o meter	time measurer
bar(o)	weight	bar o meter	weight (air) measurer
opto	eye	opto metry	science of eye measure
sym–syn	with	sym metry	equal balance
dia	through	dia meter	distance through center
geo	earth	geo metry	science of lines, angles

Skill Drill 6   Write the *meter* and *metry* words. Compare your work with the answers at the end of Chapter 4.

1 distance around   4 science of lens fitting
2 distance through center   5 equal balance
3 science of angles

Skill Drill 7   Write the names of the measuring instruments for these items. Answers appear at the end of Chapter 4.

1 air weight   3 heat
2 time   4 small distances

99

Skill Drill 6 Answers
1 perimeter
2 diameter
3 geometry
4 optometry
5 symmetry

Skill Drill 7 Answers
1 barometer
2 chronometer
3 thermometer
4 micrometer

owever, the following words may be used to inforce the meaning of the root: *microorganism, microwave, thermal, thermonuclear, periphery, chronological, barograph, geophysics, ptician,* and *symposium.*

It will be helpful to review the Greek word parts introduced in the two earlier charts as well as these in the *meter* group. Assign and check the Skill Drill as usual. Review any spellings which appear to be troublesome.

4 "name" Word Part   *onym*

The root *onym* comes from the Greek word for "name,
onyma.

an   You see *an,* meaning "no," and the word part *onym* i
anonymous, which means "no name." *Anonymous* writers d
not give their names.

As *syn* means "with," a *synonym* is literally a "with-name,
or a word which has the same meaning as another word.

anti   The Greek *anti* means "against"; it becomes *ant* in *an*
onym, an "against-name," a word that means the opposite of
another word.

homo   Greek *homo* means "one or same," so a *homonym (ho*
+ *onym)* is a word with the same pronunciation as another
but a different meaning and spelling; for example, *sail* and *sal*

acro   We use *acro* from the Greek *akros,* meaning "highest" or
having to do with the tips or ends. An *acrobat* was once
performer who walked on "tiptoe" to do feats. An *acronym (ac*
+ *onym)* is a word formed from the "first" letters of severa
"words." A VIP is a "Very Important Person."

Because Greek *para* means "beside," a *paronym* is a wor
that comes from the same root as another word. Note th
spelling of *paronym* formed from *para* and *onym.*

Study these word parts in the next chart.

onym = "name"			
Word Part	Meaning	Word	Meaning
an	no	an onym ous	no name
anti	against	ant onym	opposite meaning
homo	same	hom onym	same pronunciation
acro	tip	acr onym	"tip" word
sym–syn	with	syn onym	same meaning
para	beside	par onym	same origin

100

The "name" word part should cause no particular difficulty provided pupils read the explanatory materials carefully. If necessary, go over the explanation with the pupils. Be sure again that pupils study the chart carefully and know the meaning of each word.

Some less frequently occurring *onyr* words could be used to expand the list in th chart; for example, *patronymic* (a name derive from a paternal ancestor), *matronymic* (nam derived from a maternal ancestor), and *pseu donym,* (a fictitious name).

Skill Drill 8 Complete these sentences. Compare your work with the answers at the end of Chapter 4.

1 A word with the same meaning as another word is a __.
2 A word with the opposite meaning of another word is an __.
3 A word with the same pronunciation as another is a __.
4 A word formed from beginning letters is an __.
5 A word with the same origin as another word is a __.

Skill Drill 8 Answers

1 synonym
2 antonym
3 homonym
4 acronym
5 paronym

5 "sound," "view," "round," and "rule" Word Parts

phone phono phony   scope   sphere   cracy crat

phone
phono
phony

The Greek word part *phone* or *phono* or *phony* means "sound."

As *tele* means "far," the *telephone* is a "far sound." A *phonograph* must be "sound writing." *Symphony* means "with" or together "sounds," which you hear of course at a concert. You use a *microphone* to make "small sounds" louder.

mega

Greek *mega* means "great" so a *megaphone* is a device to make voice "sounds" louder or "greater."

scope

Greek *scope* means a "viewing" instrument of some kind. A *telescope* must be a "far viewer." A *microscope* helps you "see small" things. A *periscope* enables submarine sailors to "view" the ocean in "all directions."

steth(o)

Greek *steth* means "chest"; a *stethoscope (stetho + scope)* is a "chest viewer," although the doctor listens through it.

sphere

The Greek word *sphere* means a "round" object.

atmo

Greek *atmos* means "vapor," so *atmosphere (atmo + sphere)* is the air or "vapor" layer around the "sphere" Earth.

hemi

Hemi means "half"; so *hemisphere* means "half a sphere."

101

The *anti* combining form appears in scores other words. Some examples are *antiadministration, antiintellectual, antislavery, antisocial, antiwar, anti-aircraft, antibody, anticlimax, antiseptic, antitoxic.* Assign and check the Skill Drill as usual.

Pupils should recognize most of the word parts introduced and explained on page 101.

The Latin prefix *semi* is more common than the Greek *hemi*, even though both have approximately the same meaning. *Demi* is another Latin "half" prefix.

The familiar word *democracy* is made up of the Greek wor[d]
part *demo,* which means the "people," and the *cracy* word par[t]
which means "rule." A *democracy* then is literally a "people[
rule," a government by the people. *Autocrats* would be "self[-
rule" people who want to rule themselves in an *autocracy.*

The Greek word *aristos* means "best" so an *aristocracy*
(aristo + cracy) should mean a government "ruled" by the
"best" or ablest people.

Study the next chart, which shows these Greek word parts[

cracy
crat

demo

aristo

phone phono phony	scope	sphere	cracy crat	Word Parts

Word Parts	Meaning	Word	Meaning
phone phono phony	sound		
tele	far	tele phone	far sound
graph	write	phono graph	sound writing
sym–syn	with	sym phony	together sounds
micro	small	micro phone	small sound
mega	great	mega phone	great sound
scope	view		
tele	far	tele scope	far viewer
micro	small	micro scope	small viewer
peri	around	peri scope	around viewer
steth *(o)*	chest	steth o scope	chest viewer
sphere	round		
atmo	vapor	atmo sphere	world vapor
hemi	half	hemi sphere	half sphere
cracy crat	rule		
demo	people	demo cracy	people-rule
auto	self	auto crat	self-ruler
aristo	best	aristo cracy	best rule

102

The use of the *cracy* combining form, from Greek *kratos* (strength, power), is a good example of the use of Greek word parts to coin English words. Examples of this process are found in words such as *bureaucracy* (rule [by] administrative officials), *gynecocracy* (rule [by] women), *mobocracy* (rule by mob), *plutocra[cy]* (rule by the wealthy), *theocracy* (rule by divin[e]

Skill Drill 9 Write the words which these pictures represent. Answers appear at the end of Chapter 4.

1

2

3

4

5

6

7

8

9

You studied forty-four Greek word parts in this chapter. The reference chart which appears on the next two pages will help you review these Greek word parts. Study the meaning and example for each word part. Observe the addition of an *o* to some word parts, as with *astr* to make *astronomy* and with *bar* to form *barometer*. Observe, too, that you drop the *o* from some word parts, as with *acro* plus *onym* to form *acronym* and with *homo* plus *onym* to make *homonym*. Also note, for example, that if you know *dia, gram, logue,* and *meter,* you can easily give the meanings for *diagram, dialogue,* and *diameter.*

103

uidance). Pupils might enjoy looking up the meanings of these words or collecting additional examples. After pupils have had ample time to study, assign Skill Drill 9.

Use the reference chart on page 104 and 105 to review all of the Greek word parts studied in this section. Challenge pupils to provide an additional example word for each word part.

Greek Word Parts

Word Part	Meaning	Example
acro	tip	acr·onym
an	no	an·onym·ous
anti	against	ant·onym
aristo	best	aristo·crat
astr(o)	star	astr·onomy
atmo	vapor	atmo·sphere
auto	self	auto·graph
bar(o)	weight	bar·o·meter
biblio	book	biblio·graphy
bio	life	bio·graphy
cata	down	cata·logue
chron(o)	time	chron·o·meter
cracy crat	rule	auto·cracy auto·crat
demo	people	demo·cracy
dia	through	dia·gram
eco	house	eco·logy
geo	earth	geo·graphy
graph(y) gram	write	graph·ite tele·gram
hemi	half	hemi·sphere
homo	same	hom·onym
logy logue	speak–study	geo·logy dia·logue
mega	great	mega·phone

Word Part	Meaning	Example
meteor *(o)*	air things	meteor o logy
meter metry	measure	dia meter geo metry
micro	small	micro phone
mono	one	mono logue
myth *(o)*	story	myth o logy
onym	name	syn onym
opto	eye	opto metry
para	beside	para graph
peri	around	peri meter
phone phono phony	sound	tele phone phono graph sym phony
photo	light	photo graph
physio	nature	physio logy
psych *(o)*	mind	psych o logy
scope	view	tele scope
sphere	round	atmo sphere
steth *(o)*	chest	steth o scope
sym–syn	with	sym pathy syn onym
tele	far	tele graph
theo	god	theo logy
therm *(o)*	heat	therm o meter
topo	place	topo graphy
zoo	animal	zoo logy

105

French Spellings

We have been taking French words into English for hundred of years. More than half of the words in our *big* dictionarie come from Latin, but half of those have come through Frencl During the thirteenth and fourteenth centuries, the Englis occupied large parts of France and many learned French. Th English also imported French goods, ideas, clothing, and man ners—and their names.

Long before, in 1066, the Norman French had conquere England. In that year William of Normandy claimed the Britis throne. His fleet crossed the English Channel. William's arm defeated the Anglo-Saxons at the battle of Hastings. He seize lands for his followers and friends. The Normans became th landlords and nobles. Norman French became the languag of the courts and of high society. Latin continued to be th language of the church and school. The conquered Englis continued to speak their native Anglo-Saxon, but many Frenc words crept into their language. The Norman French scribe did most of the writing, though, and they spelled Anglo-Saxo words as they had spelled their French words. As a resul many of the French words we use in English have spelling which seem strange to us. If you become familiar with som of these French spelling habits, you will spell the words bette

1 *ch* Spells /sh/

You use *ch* or *tch* to spell the /ch/ sound, as in *church* o *catch*. In words from Greek *ch* is used to spell /k/, as i *chorus*. The French, though, use *ch* to spell /sh/. Since *s* also spells /sh/, the *ch* spelling of /sh/ may cause spellin

106

Section C

This very brief summary of the French influence on English spelling can, of course, be amplified in several ways. One interesting way is to compare some words of French origin with words of Anglo-Saxon origin. For example, the French gave us *banquet, beef, pork, venison,* and *par-*

liament. The Anglo-Saxons gave us *food, cow swine, deer* and *law.*

The explanation of the *ch* spelling of /sh which we find in words of French origin, i relatively brief. However, because pupils nee to distinguish this from the use of *ch* to spe

errors. Say these words and note the spellings. Check the meaning of any unfamiliar word in your Spelling Dictionary or in the classroom dictionary.

mus tache	/mus'tash/	chas sis	/shas'ē/
ma chine	/mə shēn'/	bro chure	/brō shùr'/
chif fon	/shi fon'/	par a chute	/par'ə shüt/
chef	/shef/		

2 *ge* or *s* Spells /zh/

The old English writers used *g* to spell only the /g/ sound. The French scribes introduced the rule that *g* should spell /j/ before *e, i,* or *y,* and /g/ before *a, o,* or *u.* The /zh/ consonant sound is typically French, and it is usually spelled with *ge* or *s* in words that come through French. Note the spellings of the /zh/ sound in these words. Check the word meanings in your Spelling Dictionary or in the classroom dictionary.

ge spells /zh/

beige	/bāzh/	cor sage	/kôr säzh'/
rouge	/rüzh/	bar rage	/bə räzh'/
ga rage	/gə räzh'/	pres tige	/pres tēzh'/
mir age	/mə räzh'/	fu se lage	/fū'zə läzh'/
mas sage	/mə säzh'/	cam ou flage	/kam'ə fläzh'/

s spells /zh/

pleas ure	/plezh'ər/	treas ure	/trezh'ər/
meas ure	/mezh'ər/	leis ure	/lē'zhər/

107

/ in Greek words, it may be desirable to go over the explanation with pupils.

Be sure pupils study the word list carefully. There are many more words in which *ch* spells /sh/. Other examples include *chaperon, chagrin,* and *charlatan.*

After going over the explanation of the *ge* or *s* spelling of /zh/, have pupils study the chart. Other words with /zh/ are *montage, cortege, protege, sabotage, espionage, entourage.* In *usury, composure,* and *exposure,* the *s* spells /zh/.

3 *ou* Spells /ü/ or /ů/

You use *ou* or *ow* to spell the /ou/ vowel sound, as in *hou*
or *howl*. But the *ou* usually spells /ü/ or /ů/ in words fr∎
French. Say these words and note the spellings. Check t∎
meaning of any unfamiliar word in your Spelling Dictionary
in the classroom dictionary.

route	/rüt/	tour ist	/tůr′ist/
de tour	/dē′tür/	boul e vard	/bůl′ə värd/
cou pon	/kü′pon/		
sou ve nir	/sü′və nir′/		

4 *eau* Spells /ō/

The spelling options for spelling /ō/ are final *o (no)*, *oa (bo∎*
ow (show), and *o*-consonant-*e (lone)*. The *eau* French spell∎
is unusual in English words like these below. Be sure you kn∎
the word meanings.

bur eau	/bū′rō/
plat eau	/pla tō′/
trous seau	/trü sō′/

108

We have so many words with *ou* spellings
which have come into English through French
that our generalization that *ou* spells /ou/ is
not very reliable. Have pupils read the explanatory material on the *ou* spellings and study the

six sample words in the chart. Less comm∎
examples of this category of words are *troup∎*
bivouac, nougat, and *contour.*

The remaining explanations on these tw∎
pages can be assigned as independent readi∎

5 *gn* Spells /n/

The *g* is silent in French *gn* words like these below. Check the meaning of any unfamiliar word.

re sign	/rē zīn′/	ma lign	/mə līn′/
de sign	/dē zīn′/	cam paign	/kam pān′/
as sign	/ə sīn′/	sov e reign	/sov′rən/
reign	/rān/	fo reign	/fôr′ən/
feign	/fān/		

6 *gue* Spells /g/

The French scribes' spelling rule about the *c* spelling of /s/ and the *g* spelling of /j/ before *e, i, or y* complicated English spelling. For example, the English used *g* to spell only the /g/ sound. They spelled *tongue* the way it sounded—*tung*. Because *g* could spell either /g/ or /j/ in French, the scribes thought they needed *a, o,* or *u* after the *g* to give a signal that *g* was spelling /g/ and not /j/. They could not sensibly spell *tongu*, because the *u* would then spell a sound. They added *e* to make the *ue* silent. Notice the pronunciations and spellings of these words. Check the meaning of any unfamiliar word in your Spelling Dictionary or in the classroom dictionary.

109

f desired. However, be prepared to provide additional help when needed. The unusual *eau* spelling of /ō/ as in *chateau, portmanteau, tableau* does not occur very frequently. It occasionally occurs in proper names.

There are other French *gn* words which are not so frequently used. Examples include *benign, consign, deign, poignant,* and *impugn.*

Be sure the pupils understand why *gue* sometimes spells /g/. There are a number of

Skill Drill 10 Answers

1 tongue
2 corsage
3 tourist
4 garage
5 treasure
6 brochure
7 mustache
8 parachute

tongue	/tungↄ/	plague	/plāg̱/
morgue	/môrg/	league	/lēg/
vague	/vāg/	fa͜tigue	/fə tēg'/
vogue	/vōg/	col͜league	/kol'ēg/

Skill Drill 10 Write the words which these pictures represen⟨t⟩ Answers appear at the end of Chapter 4.

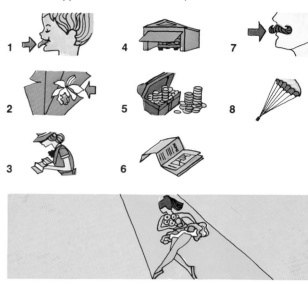

7 *et* Spells /ā/

In English spelling, you expect *et* to spell /et/ as in *let*. Th⟨en⟩ *et* spells /ā/ in words with French pronunciations. Note th⟨e⟩ spellings of these words. Check the meanings.

bal͜let	/bal'ā̱/	cro͜chet	/krō shā̱'/
ber͜et	/bə rā'/	bou͜quet	/bō kā'/
buf͜fet	/bu fā'/	cro͜quet	/krō kā'/

110

these *gue* spellings in English. Other examples that could be used are *brogue, rogue, intrigue, meringue,* and *harangue.* Words like *peda-gogue* and *demagogue* are sometimes spelled *pedagog* and *demagog.* After pupils have stud⟨i⟩ied the *gue* words, assign the Skill Drill.

The remaining explanations of the Frenc⟨h⟩ spelling patterns covered in this section coul⟨d⟩

8 *ette* Spells /et/

The English *et* spelling of /et/ becomes the *ette* spelling in words from French. But sometimes the French *ette* spelling shortens to the *et* spelling in English usage. You may see words like /kwär tet′/ spelled both *quartette* and *quartet*. *Brunette* is sometimes spelled *brunet*. Note the spellings of these words. Check the word meanings.

ci͜gar͜ette͜   /sig′ə ret′/   sil͜hou͜ette͜   /sil′ü et′/
cro͜quette͜   /krō ket′/   stat͜u͜ette͜   /stach′ū et′/
et͜i͜quette͜   /et′ə kət/

9 *que* Spells /k/

In English spelling, *qu* spells the /kw/ sounds, as in *quit*. Usually *k (milk), ck (kick),* or *c (picnic)* spells a final /k/ sound. The *que* spelling of /k/ occurs in these words from French.

plaque   /plak/   ob͜lique͜   /o blēk′/
clique   /klēk/   an͜tique͜   /an tēk′/
pique   /pēk/   u͜nique͜   /ū nēk′/
mosque   /mosk/   phys͜ique͜   /fə zēk′/
brusque   /brusk/   tech͜nique͜ /tek nēk′/

111

e assigned for independent reading and study. However, most pupils will profit from a class discussion. Each word list could be extended, but these words occur most frequently.

Other *ette* spellings include *gazette, layette, marionette, novelette,* and *pirouette.* The *que* spelling also occurs in *critique, masque, opaque, baroque, grotesque,* and *picturesque.*

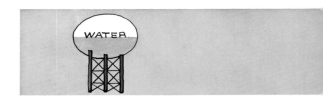

10 *oir(e)* Spells /wär/

In English spelling, *oi* or *oy* spells the /oi/ vowel sound, a in *boil* or *boy*. The *oir* or *oire* French spelling is pronounce /wär/. Look at these spellings and listen to the /wär/ soun Check the meaning of any unfamiliar word in your Spelling Dic tionary or in the classroom dictionary.

mem̦oir̦   /mem'wär/
re̦ser̦voir̦   /rez'ər vwär/
re̦per̦toire̦   /rep'ər twär/

11 *eur* Spells /ər/

In English spelling, you usually spell the unstressed /ər/ end ing with *er (better)*, *or (color)*, or *ar (collar)*. We have kept th *eur* French spelling of /ər/ in some words like these. Chec the word meanings.

am̦a̦teur̦   /am'ə chər/
chauf̦feur̦   /shō'fər/
gran̦deur̦   /gran'jər/

112

The French spelling patterns for the /wär/, /ər/ and /ən/ do not occur very frequently in English words. In fact, only ten words occur with sufficient frequency to be included in these final charts. However, these words includ some of the most difficult spellings that pupi will encounter. Be sure pupils study each li carefully. Assign and check Skill Drills 11 an

12 *eon* Spells /ən/

We use the French *eon* spelling for /ən/ in several words.

dun geon /dun′jən/   sur geon /sėr′jən/
pig eon   /pij′ən/   lunch eon /lunch′ən/

 Skill Drill 11 Write the words which these pictures represent. Answers appear at the end of Chapter 4.

1 4 7

2 5 8

3 6 9

 Skill Drill 12 Write the regular spelling of these words. Compare your work with the answers at the end of Chapter 4.

1 /rüzh/	9 /an tēk′/	17 /krō shā′/
2 /lēg/	10 /shas′ē/	18 /kü′pon/
3 /vāg/	11 /fôr′ən/	19 /mem′wär/
4 /ə sīn′/	12 /mə līn′/	20 /bùl′ə värd/
5 /ū nēk′/	13 /fə tēg′/	21 /am′ə chər/
6 /bu fā′/	14 /kam pān′/	22 /pres tēzh′/
7 /bū′rō/	15 /dun′jən/	23 /sü′və nir′/
8 /pla tō′/	16 /et′ə kət/	24 /kam′ə fläzh′/

113

2. Review any parts of this section which seem
) cause particular problems.

Use the chart on the following page to re-
iew the French spellings. Also use the chart on pages 104 and 105 to review the Greek word parts before giving Mastery Test 4 which begins on page 115. As usual, the Mastery Test is divided into two parts.

This reference chart reviews the typical French spellings which we use in English words. Study the spellings and their corresponding sounds. Compare the French and English spelling.

French Spellings			
Spelling	Sound	Example	Usual English Spelling
ch	/sh/	machine parachute	sh
ge	/zh/	garage beige	
s	/zh/	leisure	
ou	/ü/	coupon route	oo
	/ù/	boulevard tourist	oo, u
eau	/ō/	bureau plateau	o, oa, ow, o-consonant-e
gn	/n/	reign	n
gue	/g/	tongue fatigue	g
et	/ā/	bouquet crochet	ai, ay, a-consonant-e
ette	/et/	silhouette etiquette	et
que	/k/	antique technique	k, ck, c
oir(e)	/wär/	reservoir repertoire	war
eur	/ər/	amateur grandeur	er, or, ar
eon	/ən/	surgeon	en

114

Mastery Test 4

A Write the Greek word parts for these meanings, choosing from this list: *chrono, mega, onym, sphere, zoo, hemi, demo, geo, theo, topo, steth, thermo, peri, homo, astro, opto, micro, mono, psycho, myth.*

1 people	**5** god	**9** earth	**13** around	**17** star
2 animal	**6** name	**10** time	**14** round	**18** great
3 heat	**7** eye	**11** half	**15** small	**19** chest
4 story	**8** one	**12** same	**16** mind	**20** place

Write the meaning for each Greek word part.

21 sym	**23** physio	**25** meter	**27** graph	**29** dia
22 scope	**24** phono	**26** logy	**28** eco	**30** cracy

Write a word for each meaning, using a word part from list A and one from list B.

	A	**B**
31 time measurer	pro	meter
32 opposite meaning	picto	onym
33 introductory speech	chrono	logue
34 picture writing	ant	sphere
35 air around the earth	atmo	graph

B Write the regular spellings for the missing words in each sentence.

1 "It's our ___ /in ten'shən/ to unload the ___ /ship'mənt/ of ___ /mə shēnz'/ on ___ /skej'ùl/," advised the foreman.

2 "We must ___ /shär/ the ___ /chôrz/ or we'll have ___ /kā'os/ in the ___ /kich'ən/," said the ___ /chēf/ ___ /shef/.

3 "___ /tùr'ists/ would be ___ /fül'ish/ not to visit ___ /bùk'stôrz'/ on this ___ /fā'məs/ ___ /bùl'ə värd/," the woman observed.

4 "I'll ___ /rē mān'/ your ___ /sov'rən/ and ___ /rān/ in spite of a ___ /kam pān'/ to ___ /mə līn'/ me," cried the queen.

115

31 chronometer
32 antonym
33 prologue
34 pictograph
35 atmosphere

Part B Answers

1 intention, shipment, machines, schedule
2 share, chores, chaos, kitchen, chief, chef
3 Tourists, foolish, bookstores, famous, boulevard
4 remain, sovereign, reign, campaign, malign
5 assigned, refine, design, souvenir, brochure
6 surely, pleasure, corsage, beige
7 lone, hobo, slowly, plateau
8 insurance, measure, damage, garage
9 banquet, ballet, gay, bouquet
10 antique, plaque, streaks, black
11 points, memoirs, pique, colleagues
12 notion, luncheon, amateur, future

5 "An artist was __ /ə sīnd'/ to __ /rē fīn'/ the __ /dē zīn for the cover of our __ /sü'və nir'/ __ /brō shùr'/," reporte the convention manager.
6 "It's __ /shùr'lē/ a __ /plezh'ər/ to wear this love __ /kōr säzh'/ with my __ /bāzh/ dress," said the girl.
7 "A __ /lōn/ __ /hō'bō/ walked __ /slō'lē/ across th __ /pla tō'/," wrote the author.
8 "The __ /in shùr'əns/ company tried to __ /mezh'ər/ th __ /dam'ij/ to the __ /gə räzh'/ roof," said the repairman.
9 "At the __ /bang'kwət/, the __ /bal'ā/ dancer was give a __ /gā/ __ /bō kā'/ of roses," said the young man.
10 "That __ /an tēk'/ __ /plak/ is spoiled by __ /strēks/ __ /blak/ paint," sighed the shop owner.
11 "Many __ /points/ in my __ /mem'wärz/ will __ /pēk/ m __ /kol'ēgz'/," admitted the author.
12 "I have a __ /nō'shən/ that this __ /lunch'ən/ was pre pared by an __ /am'ə chər/ cook who won't be here in th __ /fū'chər/," complained the guest.

Answers for Chapter 4 Skill Drills

Skill Drill 1 1 myth 2 rhythm 3 echo 4 autumn
5 cellophane 6 typhoon 7 pneumonia 8 rhubarb
9 hyphen 10 condemn 11 syllable 12 orchestra
13 pheasant 14 cyclone 15 rhinoceros 16 character
17 photograph 18 scheme 19 cylinder 20 column
21 schedule 22 trophy 23 hydrant 24 mechanic
25 chord 26 symphony 27 alphabet 28 psychology
29 pygmy 30 dolphin 31 anchor 32 psychiatrist
33 system

116

Skill Drill 2   1 astrology   2 zoology   3 geology
4 mythology   5 ecology   6 theology   7 mineralogy
8 physiology   9 criminology   10 sociology
11 meteorology   12 biology

Skill Drill 3   1 travelogue   2 prologue   3 monologue
4 dialogue   5 catalogue

Skill Drill 4   1 geography   2 bibliography   3 autobiography
4 biography   5 topography   6 photography

Skill Drill 5   1 photograph   2 telegram   3 pictograph
4 paragraph   5 telegraph   6 monogram   7 diagram
8 autograph

Skill Drill 6   1 perimeter   2 diameter   3 geometry
4 optometry   5 symmetry

Skill Drill 7   1 barometer   2 chronometer   3 thermometer
4 micrometer

Skill Drill 8   1 synonym   2 antonym   3 homonym
4 acronym   5 paronym

Skill Drill 9   1 stethoscope   2 telephone   3 phonograph
4 periscope   5 symphony   6 microscope   7 microphone
8 telescope   9 megaphone

Skill Drill 10   1 tongue   2 corsage   3 tourist   4 garage
5 treasure   6 brochure   7 mustache   8 parachute

Skill Drill 11   1 physique   2 chauffeur   3 plaque
4 surgeon   5 mosque   6 bouquet   7 reservoir
8 quartette   9 beret

Skill Drill 12   1 rouge   2 league   3 vague   4 assign
5 unique   6 buffet   7 bureau   8 plateau   9 antique
10 chassis   11 foreign   12 malign   13 fatigue
14 campaign   15 dungeon   16 etiquette   17 crochet
18 coupon   19 memoir   20 boulevard   21 amateur
22 prestige   23 souvenir   24 camouflage

117

118

5 Special Spelling Problems

We have spelling problems in English, because we do not have a perfect alphabet to spell our spoken sounds. Many years ago people like the Chinese and the Egyptians invented writing systems which consisted of pictures. The American Indians, too, developed such a *pictographic* system. But when you want to write words which cannot be pictured, you must invent a symbol for each word. As you increase the number of such symbols, only some people may remember all of them and learn to read and write well.

Many years ago a Semitic tribe invented a new writing system. They realized that human beings can make only a limited number of speech sounds. So they borrowed some Egyptian symbols called hieroglyphics. They used one symbol to represent only one sound. They spelled each sound with only one symbol. We call such a writing system an *alphabetic* writing system.

The Greeks found out about this alphabetic system. They changed some symbols and added others. Then the Romans modified the Greek alphabet to fit the sounds of Latin.

Meanwhile, the people living on the island we now call England had a kind of alphabet, too. They called their symbols the *runes.* The runic alphabet had been developed to fit the sounds of their Germanic language. They were induced to give up their runic alphabet for the Roman alphabet, which did not fit English sounds as an alphabet should.

Our reconstituted Roman alphabet now has twenty-six letters, or symbols, but we have more than twenty-six sounds. So we do not have an efficient spelling alphabet. Because we continue to use it, we will always have spelling problems. In this chapter we will deal with some of these.

118

CHAPTER 5

This chapter focuses attention upon six of the major sources of spelling errors. The first of these is the problem of doubled consonant letters. Words like *accommodate* and *embarrass* are frequently misspelled because there is no auditory clue to the doubled consonant spelling. Similarly the *s*, *c*, and *sc* spelling options for words with the /s/ sound offer no clues to

the spelling. To make matters worse, we have curious inconsistencies when we try to spell words like *census* and *consensus, descent* and *decent.*

The *ie-ei* spellings are notoriously exasperating. In the chapter we suggest several word groupings to help reduce the number of words which would otherwise have to be mem

A Doubled Consonant Letters

One of our difficulties in English spelling is caused by doubling a consonant symbol to spell *one* consonant sound. The dictionary, which always gives the same symbol for the same sound, shows that the two spellings of /b/ below represent only one /b/ sound.

rabbit   /rab′it/

habit   /hab′it/

Since you can spell both *rabbit* and *habit,* this spelling problem may not seem to be difficult. But we make many spelling errors because we do not double some consonant letters when we should, or do double them when we should not. You can hardly ever tell by *hearing* the word whether a consonant letter is doubled or not. You must *look* carefully and remember.

1 Two Pairs of Doubled Consonants

Here are some words you will probably need to write. They have *two* pairs of doubled consonants. Look at the eye-syllables carefully. They will help you remember the doubled consonants. Check the meaning of any unfamiliar word in your Spelling Dictionary or in the classroom dictionary.

ac cess	/ak′ses/	god dess	/god′əs/
suc cess	/suk ses′/	mat tress	/mat′rəs/
pos sess	/pə zes′/	em bar rass	/em bar′əs/
op press	/ə pres′/	com mit tee	/kə mit′ē/
ad dress	/ə dres′/	ag gres sive	/ə gres′iv/
sup press	/sə pres′/	ac com mo date	/ə kom′ə dāt′/

119

rized. Attention is also directed to the spelling of plurals, especially the plural forms of consonant-o–ending words.

Attention in the chapter is also given to the problems of doubling final consonants and dropping final e's before the addition of a suffix. Homonyms are another problem in English spelling taken up in this chapter.

Section A

In this first section, the problem of doubled and undoubled consonants is divided into four smaller parts. As usual, each part includes a brief explanation of the spelling problems and a list of words with their parts clearly marked.

Pupils who have done a great deal of reading may be able to spell the words in this sec-

Skill Drill 1 Answers

1 accommodate
2 corridor
3 address
4 tariff
5 missile
6 announce
7 collide
8 villain
9 embarrass
10 suppress
11 access
12 terrace
13 immigrant
14 dissatisfy
15 committee

2 One Pair of Doubled Consonants

These words have one pair of doubled consonants. Some spell
ing mistakes occur when writers use only one consonant lett
instead of two. Be sure you know all the word meanings.

sher iff	/sher'if/	ap prove	/ə prüv'/
tar iff	/tar'if/	hic cup	/hik'up/
re cess	/rē ses'/	col lide	/kə līd'/
car cass	/kär'kəs/	pen nant	/pen'ənt/
oc cur	/ə kėr'/	ter race	/ter'əs/
mis sile	/mis'əl/	vil lain	/vil'ən/
bag gage	/bag'ij/	as sure	/ə shür'/
chal lenge	/chal'ənj/	dis solve	/də zolv'/
con nect	/kə nekt'/	cor rid or	/kôr'ə dôr/
stir rup	/stėr'əp/	ac cus tom	/ə kus'təm/
an nounce	/ə nouns'/	an nu al	/an'ū əl/
an noy	/ə noi'/	im mi grant	/im'ə grənt/
ap plause	/ə plôz'/	oc cu py	/ok'ū pī'/
ap point	/ə point'/	dis sat is fy	/dis sat'is fī/

Skill Drill 1 Write the regular spelling of these words. Cor
pare your work with the answers at the end of Chapter 5.

1 /ə kom'ə dāt'/	6 /ə nouns'/	11 /ak'səs/
2 /kôr'ə dôr/	7 /kə līd'/	12 /ter'əs/
3 /ə dres'/	8 /vil'ən/	13 /im'ə grənt/
4 /tar'if/	9 /em bar'əs/	14 /dis sat'is fī/
5 /mis'əl/	10 /sə pres'/	15 /kə mit'ē/

3 Doubled Consonants in Compound Words

In most compound words, when the same consonant ends on
word and begins the other, you keep both consonant letters.

news stand	ear ring	room mate
book keeper	under rate	jack knife
dumb bell	over rate	with hold

120

tion simply because they have seen them so
often. Even when such pupils are not certain of
the spelling, they can often write several possible spellings and choose the correct one.

Because there are no auditory clues
these words, it is especially important here th
pupils study the words carefully. The ey
syllable markers are designed to help pup

But compounds do not always include the full spelling of both word parts.

wher|ever   wel|fare   thresh|old   ful|fill

4 Doubled and Undoubled Consonants

It is easier to make double-consonant spelling mistakes in words in which one consonant letter is doubled and one is not. Be sure you know these word meanings.

ac|cur|ate   par|al|lel   ap|pet|ite

syl|la|ble   at|ti|tude   ir|ri|gate

sat|el|lite   hur|ri|cane   o|pos|sum

vac|cin|ate   par|af|fin   ne|ces|sity

moc|ca|sin   op|po|nent   mo|las|ses

oc|ca|sion   co|los|sal   to|bog|gan

to|bac|co   ter|rif|ic

Skill Drill 2 Write the correct spelling. Compare your work with the answers at the end of Chapter 5.

1 mollases	molases	molasses
2 oppossum	oposum	opossum
3 tobacco	tobbaco	tobaco
4 paralel	parallel	parrallel
5 satellite	sattelite	sattellite
6 moccassin	mocassin	moccasin
7 parafin	parraffin	paraffin
8 collosal	colossal	collossal
9 appettite	appetite	apetite
10 terific	terrific	terriffic
11 threshold	threshhold	thresshold
12 welfare	wellfare	welffare

121

)serve the word parts. It may be profitable to ave pupils write the words and mark the eye- llables at least once before you assign the o Skill Drills in this section.

Check pupil performance on the Skill Drills. If any of the four types of double conso- nants is causing difficulty, review that section before going on to the next section.

Skill Drill 3 Answers

1 pierce
2 niece
3 kerosene
4 scissors
5 scepter
6 mercy
7 adversity
8 eclipse
9 ascent
10 rinse

Spelling Options for /s/

In a perfect alphabet we would use only one letter to spell [each] sound like /s/. Not only do we use *s* to spell /z/ *(days)* a[nd] *c* to spell /k/ *(cook)*, but we use *s* and *c* and also *sc* to sp[ell] /s/. We make spelling mistakes by using the wrong one [of] the three options. The French scribes invented the rule th[at] *c* spells /s/ only before *e (cent)*, *i (city)*, or *y (cycle)*. It is [a] dependable rule, but in our spelling *s* and *c* and *sc* all c[an] spell /s/ before *e, i,* or *y.* Compare the spellings and the /[s]/ sounds in these words. Check the meaning of any unfamil[iar] word in your Spelling Dictionary or in the classroom dictiona[ry.]

s spells /s/		*c* spells /s/	
syl·la·ble	ker·o·sene	mer·cy	niece
rinse	e·clipse	pierce	fleece
de·fense	ad·vers·it·y	ounce	nui·sance
of·fense	crease	source	wince
tense	verse	pen·cil	prance

sc spells /s/	
scene	as·cent
scent	de·scent
scep·ter	ab·scess
science	dis·ci·pline
scis·sors	ad·o·les·cent
scythe	mis·cel·la·ne·ous

Skill Drill 3 Write the correct spelling. Compare your wo[rk] with the answers at the end of Chapter 5.

1	pierse	pierce	6	mercy	mersy
2	niese	niece	7	advercity	adversity
3	kerocene	kerosene	8	eclipce	eclipse
4	scissors	sissors	9	ascent	asent
5	septer	scepter	10	rinse	rince

122

Section B

The *s, c,* and *sc* spelling options for the /s/ sound also cause numerous spelling problems because there are no auditory clues to the spelling. Although etymology offers some assistance here, the best approach to mastery of this spelling problem is frequent exposure to the words in print and an awareness of the ey[e?] syllables.

In this section most words exemplify the [c] spelling of /s/ because pupils are inclined t[o] remember these *c* spellings more readily. G[o] through the explanations carefully or assig[n]

You have less spelling confusion when *c* spells /s/ at the beginning of a word, because you are inclined to notice the *c* more readily. Note the *c* spelling of /s/ in these examples. Be sure you know all of the word meanings.

cis tern	cel lar	cyl in der
civ il	ceil ing	cel er y
cir cuit	ce dar	cease
ci gar	cel e brate	cit rus
cy clone	cer e al	cen sus

But you may confuse the *c* and *s* spelling options when the *c* spelling of the /s/ sound occurs inside a word. Check the word meanings.

a cid	dec i mal	crev ice
par cel	re cip e	can cer
con ceal	sac ri fice	pri va cy
fau cet	i ci cle	por ce lain
sau cer	lic or ice	pre cip ice
pen cil	se cre cy	in cid ent
let tuce	sin cere	cap ac it y
li cense	in cense	

Skill Drill 4   Write the regular spelling of these words. Compare your work with the answers at the end of Chapter 5.

1 /siv'əl/
2 /let'əs/
3 /pär'səl/
4 /sī'klōn/
5 /ab'ses/
6 /nü'səns/
7 /sin sir'/
8 /dis'ə plin/

9 /res'ə pē/
10 /sėr'kət/
11 /sēs/
12 /sit'rəs/
13 /ad'ə les'ənt/
14 /in'səns/
15 /lik'ə ris/
16 /sen'səs/

17 /sel'ər ē/
18 /sil'ən dər/
19 /fô'sət/
20 /ī'si kəl/
21 /pres'ə pis/
22 /mis'ə lā'nē əs/

123

Skill Drill 4 Answers

1 civil
2 lettuce
3 parcel
4 cyclone
5 abscess
6 nuisance
7 sincere
8 discipline
9 recipe
10 circuit
11 cease
12 citrus
13 adolescent
14 incense
15 licorice
16 census
17 celery
18 cylinder
19 faucet
20 icicle
21 precipice
22 miscellaneous

em as independent reading. However, be sure at pupils spend ample time studying the ords in each list and noting the word parts fore beginning the Skill Drills. Be sure all pils are reading the sound spellings correctly Skill Drill 4. Pupils should have no difficulty

with these sound spellings. Allow pupils to refer to the Sound-Spelling Alphabet on page 1 if necessary. Check the pupil responses and review as necessary.

The *ie* and *ei* spelling options in English have always cause
trouble. Long ago pupils learned this jingle to help them spe
better.

> *i* before *e* except after *c*
> or when sounded as /ā/,
> as in *neighbor* or *weigh*.

Unhappily there are about thirty words in which *i* does no
come before *e*. There are also many words in which *ie* doe
come after *c*. The only part of the old "rule" that works is "whe
sounded as /ā/." You cannot solve the *ie–ei* spelling problem
by a simple rule. Rather than memorizing the spellings of th
ie–ei words, though, you will help yourself best by rememberin
some general groupings and by memorizing the exceptions.

1   *ei* Spells /ā/ or /ã/

If you know that a word has either the *ie* or *ei* spelling for th
/ā/ or /ã/ vowel sound, you can be sure the spelling will b
ei, not *ie*. Here are some /ā/ and /ã/ words you may need.

weigh	/wā/	rein	/rãn/
neigh	/nā/	vein	/vān/
sleigh	/slā/	veil	/vāl/
eight	/āt/	beige	/bāzh/
weight	/wāt/	feint	/fānt/
freight	/frāt/		
neigh̦bor	/nā′bər/	their	/ŦHãr/
		heir	/ãr/

124

Section C

The *ie-ei* spellings in English are so erratic that they are a constant source of spelling mistakes. The *ei* spelling of /ā/ or /ã/ presented on this page is consistent, and pupils can eliminate some common spelling errors by remembering

it. Emphasize the validity of this spelling cu
before pupils study the list of words.

The spelling problem is complicated by th
fact that *weigh, neigh, sleigh, eight, weigh
rein, vein, veil, feint, their,* and *heir* have hom

124

2   *ei* Before *gn*

You may be sure that words with the French *gn* spelling for /n/ will be spelled *ei*, not *ie*. Check the word meanings in your Spelling Dictionary or in the classroom dictionary.

reign	/rān/
deign	/dān/
feign	/fān/
for eign	/fôr′ən/
sov er eign	/sov′rən/

3   When *c* Spells /s/, *ei* Follows

Both *ie* and *ei* follow a *c* spelling. (Of course, you must know that the /s/ sound is spelled *c* in such words.) When the preceding *c* spells /s/, the *ei* spelling will follow, not the *ie*. Note these word examples. Be sure you know the meanings of the words.

re ceive	con ceit
de ceive	de ceit
con ceive	re ceipt
per ceive	ceil ing

125

ms. Allow pupils ample time to study the list words.

The cues provided for the *ie* and *ei* spelling before *gn* and after /s/ are somewhat less useful. Since these words are commonly mis-

spelled, it will be profitable to call attention to the word parts.

Skill Drill 5 Answers

1 weigh
2 rein or reign
3 eight
4 foreign
5 neighbor
6 quotient
7 their
8 species
9 sufficient

4 When *ci, ti,* or *si* Spells /sh/, *ie* Follows

When the letters *c* and *i* spell /sh/, the *ie* spelling will follow Check the meaning of any unfamiliar word in your Spelling Dictionary or in the classroom dictionary.

spe͜cies	/spē′shēz/	suf͜fi͜cient	/sə fish′ənt/
an͜cient	/ān′shənt/	de͜fi͜cient	/dē fish′ənt/
con͜science	/kon′shəns/	pro͜fi͜cient	/prō fish′ənt/
ef͜fi͜cient	/ə fish′ənt/		

And when *ti* or *si* spells /sh/, the *ie* spelling must follow Check the word meanings.

pa͜tient	/pā′shənt/	tran͜sient	/tran′shənt/
quo͜tient	/kwō′shənt/		

Skill Drill 5 Write the regular spellings of these *ie–ei* words Compare your work with the answers at the end of Chapter 5.

1 /wā/		**4** /fôr′ən/		**7** /ᴛнâr/	
2 /rān/		**5** /nā′bər/		**8** /spē′shēz/	
3 /āt/		**6** /kwō′shənt/		**9** /sə fish′ənt/	

5 *ie* Before *r*

When *r* follows, the spelling will be *ie,* not *ei* (unless the vowel sound is /ā/ as in *their*). There is one exception you need to remember—*weird.* Be sure you know all of these word meanings.

126

The familiar rule, "*i* before *e* except after *c* or when sounded as /ā/ as in *neighbor* or *weigh,*" has exceptions. Note that all seven of the words in the first list violate the "*i* before *e*, except after *c*" rule.

When assigning Skill Drill 5, caution pupils not to write the homonyms for numbers 2, 3, and 7 instead of the *ie* or *ei* word.

After reading the explanation of the spelling before *r,* pupils should study the li

pier↓	cashier↓
tier	glacier
bier	soldier
pierce	premier
fierce	frontier

6 *ie* or *ei* Spells /ē/

The *ie* option spells /ē/ in these words. Check the word meanings.

field↓	piece↓	chief↓	siege↓	retrieve↓
yield	niece	relief	diesel	reprieve
wield	grief	belief	grieve	medieval
shield	thief	shriek	believe	hygiene
fiend	brief	priest	achieve	

But in these exceptions, *ei*, not *ie*, spells /ē/.

sheik↓	leisure↓
seize	protein
either	caffein(e)
neither	seizure

7 *ie* and *ei* Spell Other Sounds

The *ie* spelling can also have the pronunciations in these example words: /e/ in *friend,* /ū/ in *view* and *review,* and /i/ in *sieve*. In monosyllables like *pie, die, lie,* and *tie,* the *ie* spells /ī/.

The *ei* option spells /i/ in *forfeit* and *counterfeit*.

127

arefully. Be sure pupils note that the *r* is almost lways preceded by the *ie* spelling. Be sure that upils also note that *pier, tier, bier,* and *piece* ave homonyms which do not have the *ie* or *i* spelling.

The words provided in the last two subsections may require longer study time because they lack reliable spelling cues. Study the words in groups, giving primary attention to the *ie* spelling of /ē/.

Skill Drill 6 Answers

1 glacier
2 soldier
3 yield
4 fierce
5 fiend
6 niece
7 grieve
8 hygiene
9 sheik
10 either
11 protein
12 leisure
13 friend
14 forfeit
15 counterfeit

Skill Drill 6 Write the regular spelling of these *ie–ei* words. Answers appear at the end of Chapter 5.

1 /glā'shər/   6 /nēs/   11 /prō'tēn/
2 /sol'jər/   7 /grēv/   12 /lē'zhər/
3 /yēld/   8 /hī'jēn/   13 /frend/
4 /firs/   9 /shēk/   14 /fôr'fit/
5 /fēnd/   10 /ē'ᴛHər/   15 /koun'tər fit/

The chart below, of the common *ie–ei* spellings, will help you remember the spellings correctly without memorizing each one separately. Study each clue in the first column.

Spelling *ie–ei* Words

Sound or Spelling Clue	Use	Example	Exception
vowel sound is /ā/ or /ã/	ei	weigh their	
gn follows	ei	foreign	
c spells /s/	ei	ceiling	
ci, ti, and *si* spell /sh/	ie	species patient transient	
r follows	ie	pierce	weird
vowel sound is /ē/	ie	shield	sheik, seize, leisure, caffein(e), protein
other vowel sounds occur	ie	friend, view, sieve, pie	
	ei	forfeit, counterfeit	

128

Assign the Skill Drill. Be sure pupils are pronouncing the sound spelling accurately.

The chart should be used to review the *ie-ei* spellings. Then assign and check Skill Drill 7.

Section D

Fortunately, the spelling of most plural forms is encompassed by the rule that says to add s or es to the singular. Review this rule briefly using the introductory material. Then explain that this section will deal with the plural forms of words

Skill Drill 7 Write the correct spelling. Compare your work with the answers at the end of Chapter 5.

1	recieve	receive	8	peirce	pierce
2	sieze	seize	9	anceint	ancient
3	conceit	conciet	10	acheive	achieve
4	seige	siege	11	cieling	ceiling
5	view	veiw	12	receipt	reciept
6	shriek	shreik	13	sieve	seive
7	weird	wierd	14	pateint	patient

Spelling Plurals

You form the plurals of most consonant-ending words by simply adding *s;* for example: *tub-tubs, stamp-stamps, seed-seeds, lobster-lobsters.* To words which end in /s/-related sounds you add *es: box-boxes, bush-bushes, gas-gases, glass-glasses, buzz-buzzes, scratch-scratches.* But words which end in vowel letters may cause some spelling problems. Also, some irregular plural forms may cause spelling trouble.

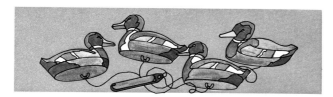

1 *y*-Ending Nouns

Nouns which end in *y* preceded by a vowel letter form the plural by adding *s*. So *journey* becomes *journeys, decoy* becomes *decoys, relay* becomes *relays.*

Nouns which end in *y* preceded by a consonant letter form the plural by changing *y* to *i* and adding *es*. So *company* becomes *companies, baby* becomes *babies, daisy* becomes *daisies.*

129

which end in vowel letters and words with irregular plurals.

The first of these troublesome plurals occurs with *y*-ending nouns. Pupils can probably be allowed to read the explanations and study the examples of these first three problem plurals independently. It may be helpful, however, to demonstrate the *y* to *i* change that occurs in nouns ending in *y* preceded by a consonant.

2   *i*-Ending and Vowel-*o*–Ending Nouns

You form the plural of the few *i*-ending nouns in English by adding *s*.

ski-skis	rabbi-rabbis
taxi-taxis	alibi-alibis

When a vowel letter precedes a final *o,* you form the plural by simply adding *s*.

patio-patios	rodeo-rodeos
radio-radios	cameo-cameos
ratio-ratios	
studio-studios	

Note the few double-*o*–ending nouns. You form the plural of these *oo*-ending nouns by adding *s.*

zoo-zoos	cuckoo-cuckoos	tattoo-tattoos

3   Consonant-*o*–Ending Nouns

Spelling the plurals of consonant-o–ending nouns does cause problems. There are four spelling options. Some of these consonant-*o* nouns take only *s* in the plural form. Some take only *es*. Some take either *s* or *es*, with the *s* form preferred. Some take either *s* or *es*, with the *es* form preferred.

130

The *i*-ending and vowel-*o*–ending nouns are fairly rare. A careful reading of the explanation and an unhurried study of the word list can again be assigned as independent study.

The plural forms of consonant-*o*–ending nouns are a common source of spelling annoyance for even experienced writers because of the lack of tangible and reliable spelling cues.

You can be fairly sure that nouns ending with consonant-*o* and having to do with music will take only *s* in the plural form. Check the meaning of any unfamiliar word in your Spelling Dictionary or in the classroom dictionary.

alto-altos
cello-cellos
piano-pianos

solo-solos
soprano-sopranos
concerto-concertos
banjo-banjos, banjoes

You can be generally certain that consonant-*o* nouns from Spanish will take only *s* in the plural form in English usage. Be sure you know the meanings of these Spanish nouns.

burro-burros
bronco-broncos
pinto-pintos

pimento-pimentos
pueblo-pueblos
sombrero-sombreros
lasso-lassos, lassoes

These nouns always form the plural by adding only *s*. Be sure you know the meanings.

auto-autos
ditto-dittos
ego-egos
hello-hellos
memo-memos

silo-silos
ghetto-ghettos
yoyo-yoyos
kimono-kimonos
dynamo-dynamos

The plural forms of some nouns may be spelled either *s* or *es*. In these nouns the *s* plural is *preferred*. To keep from being uncertain, it is best to learn them as *s*-ending nouns.

halo-halos
hobo-hobos
zero-zeros

memento-mementos
flamingo-flamingos
tuxedo-tuxedos

131

Go through each explanation with pupils and help them to note how the plurals in the various groups of sample words are formed. Most of the musical terms are Italian in origin.

The *s*-plural endings for words of Italian and Spanish origin are reasonably reliable. Be sure pupils know the meaning of each word in the lists.

Skill Drill 8 Answers

1 journeys
2 silos
3 studios
4 potatoes
5 daisies
6 solos
7 dynamos
8 halos
9 alibis
10 burros
11 heroes
12 tattoos
13 radios
14 broncos
15 volcanoes
16 mottoes
17 zeros
18 sopranos

The following nouns have the *es* plural form only. Be su◄ you know the meanings of these words.

echo-echoes	fungo-fungoes
veto-vetoes	potato-potatoes
hero-heroes	tomato-tomatoes

With these nouns, the *es* plural form is *preferred*. It will ◄ easier for you to just write them always with *es*.

cargo-cargoes	tornado-tornadoes
motto-mottoes	volcano-volcanoes
calico-calicoes	mosquito-mosquitoes
buffalo-buffaloes	domino-dominoes

Skill Drill 8 Write the plural form of these words. Compa◄ your work with the answers at the end of Chapter 5.

1 journey	7 dynamo	13 radio
2 silo	8 halo	14 bronco
3 studio	9 alibi	15 volcano
4 potato	10 burro	16 motto
5 daisy	11 hero	17 zero
6 solo	12 tattoo	18 soprano

4 Irregular Plurals

We have a few plural forms remaining in English in which v◄ change the vowel letters within the words instead of addi◄ *s* or *es*.

mouse-mice	foot-feet	man-men
louse-lice	goose-geese	woman-wome◄
	tooth-teeth	

We also change *child* to *children*, *ox* to *oxen*, and *broth◄* to *brethren*, although *brothers* is now generally used.

132

There are other consonant-*o* words, of course. We here include those consonant-*o* words with *es* plurals which are most frequently used. Since these words lack spelling cues, pupils should study the word lists very carefully.

Assign Skill Drill 8. Since this exercis◄ covers some rather difficult spellings, note an◄ categories of the consonant-*o* plurals whic◄ merit review and assign or conduct the revie◄ before going on.

5 f(e)-Ending Nouns

Sometimes the *f* in /f/-ending nouns changes to *v* before adding *es* to form plurals. Study the examples of *f(e)*-ending nouns that require this change in their plural form.

calf-calves	knife-knives
elf-elves	leaf-leaves
half-halves	life-lives
loaf-loaves	self-selves
sheaf-sheaves	thief-thieves
wife-wives	wolf-wolves
beef-beeves	wharf-wharves, wharfs

The plural *ves* forms of *hoof, scarf,* and *dwarf* are now rarely used. Other /f/-ending words generally add *s* to form the plurals.

hoof-hoofs
scarf-scarfs
dwarf-dwarfs

6 Zero Plurals

Some nouns have the same spelling for both the singular and plural forms. You do not add *s* to these nouns. We call these *zero* plural forms. Study these examples of zero plurals. Check the meaning of any unfamiliar word in your Spelling Dictionary or in the classroom dictionary.

bison	sheep
deer	swine
grouse	trout
moose	aircraft

133

The plurals covered in Subsections 4–7 do not cause serious spelling problems for most pupils. Independent study of these groups of plurals will ordinarily be sufficient. Some words usually thought of as having zero plurals, such as *fish, beaver, fox,* and *turtle* will occasionally appear with a plural form when used to indicate a diversity of species. But the zero plural is far more common.

Skill Drill 9 Answers

1 mice
2 knives
3 moose
4 scarfs
5 children
6 thieves
7 women
8 halves
9 sheep

7 s-Ending Nouns

Some nouns have no separate singular form. These noun always have the *s* ending.

news	clothes	politics	scissors
thanks	series	athletics	trousers

Skill Drill 9   Write the plural form of these words. If two form are correct, use the preferred form. Compare your work wi the answers at the end of Chapter 5.

1 mouse	4 scarf	7 woman
2 knife	5 child	8 half
3 moose	6 thief	9 sheep

8 Greek and Latin Plurals

Certain Greek and Latin nouns which we have absorbed in English now usually have two plural forms. In those language the plurals were formed by changing the noun endings, b *not* with *s* or *es*. For example, their *um*-ending nouns becam plurals by changing *um* to *a*. So the plural form of *stadiu* became *stadia*. Because we form English plurals by adding or *es,* we simply add *s* to *stadium*. We use whichever for we prefer, *stadia* or *stadiums*. We often use the Latin plu word *data* ("facts"). We rarely use the singular form, *datu* We never use *datums*. There is no word *datas*.

These *um* nouns have two plural forms. You may correct use either spelling. Be sure you know the word meanings.

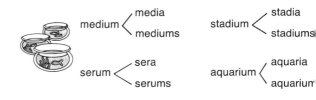

medium ⟨ media / mediums

stadium ⟨ stadia / stadiums

serum ⟨ sera / serums

aquarium ⟨ aquaria / aquarium

134

Assign the Skill Drill and check the answers. Pupils should have no difficulty.

The alternative plural forms of certain words from other languages need not be a source of difficulty. Since there are a substan tial number of words and categories in this sub section, it is generally advisable to go over th explanation and the word list with pupils.

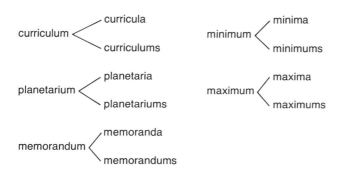

curriculum < curricula / curriculums

minimum < minima / minimums

planetarium < planetaria / planetariums

maximum < maxima / maximums

memorandum < memoranda / memorandums

Another group of nouns which end in *is* form the plural by changing *is* to *es*. These nouns have only one plural form. Check the word meanings in your Spelling Dictionary or in the classroom dictionary.

axis-axes   analysis-analyses
oasis-oases   diagnosis-diagnoses
thesis-theses   emphasis-emphases
crisis-crises   synopsis-synopses
basis-bases   parenthesis-parentheses

These borrowed *a*-ending nouns have two plural forms. The foreign plurals have an *e* added, and the English forms have an *s* affixed. The only exception is *larva* ("early insect form"); the plural form of *larva* is *larvae,* never *larvas.*

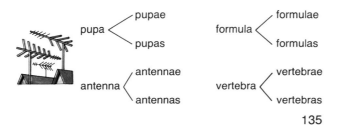

pupa < pupae / pupas

formula < formulae / formulas

antenna < antennae / antennas

vertebra < vertebrae / vertebras

135

Among these Greek and Latin plurals, *media* is more common than *stadia; serums* and *aquariums* are more common than *sera* and *aquaria.*

Pupae, formulae, antennae, and *vertebrae* will often appear in technical publications, but *pupas, formulas, antennas,* and *vertebras* are probably more common.

Skill Drill 10 Answers

1 larvae
2 crises
3 alumni
4 diagnoses
5 stimuli
6 analyses
7 oases
8 parentheses
9 emphases

Skill Drill 11 Answers

1 stadia
2 appendices
3 formulae
4 curricula
5 media
6 nuclei
7 fungi
8 pupae
9 data

With two exceptions, the *us*-ending nouns have two plural forms, the foreign *i* and our English *es*. The plural form of *alumnus* is *alumni*, never *alumnuses;* the plural form of *stimulus* is *stimuli*, never *stimuluses*.

Be sure you know the meanings of these *us* nouns.

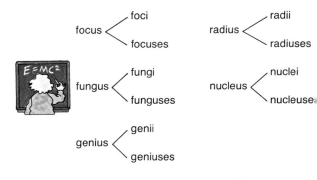

The *x*-ending nouns also have two plural forms.

Skill Drill 10 Write the plural form of these words. Compare your work with the answers at the end of Chapter 5.

1 larva	4 diagnosis	7 oasis
2 crisis	5 stimulus	8 parenthesis
3 alumnus	6 analysis	9 emphasis

Skill Drill 11 Write the foreign plural of these nouns. Compare your work with the answers at the end of Chapter 5.

1 stadium	4 curriculum	7 fungus
2 appendix	5 medium	8 pupa
3 formula	6 nucleus	9 datum

136

Again, the foreign plurals tend to appear in technical publications, the *es* plurals in other writings and speech. *Genii,* however, is rarely seen or heard. *Indices* and *appendices* are fairly common.

After pupils have studied the word charts carefully, assign and check the Skill Drills. Review parts of this section if necessary. Be sure that pupils note that Skill Drill 11 asks for the foreign plurals.

Hitching Suffix Trailers

You must often tinker with a word ending before you can hitch a suffix to it. This tinkering depends partly on whether the suffix begins with a consonant letter or a vowel letter.

1 Consonant Suffixes

If the suffix begins with a consonant letter, you have no serious spelling problem. You simply hitch the suffix to the root word.

```
excite  + ment = excitement
selfish + ness = selfishness
hate    + ful  = hateful
need    + less = needless
```

Of course, the *y*-ending words do change *y* to *i* before these consonant suffixes.

```
merry + ment = merriment
happy + ness = happiness
plenty + ful  = plentiful
penny + less  = penniless
```

Skill Drill 12 Affix the *ment, ness, less,* or *ful* suffix to these words. Compare your work with the answers at the end of Chapter 5.

1 announce	5 merry	9 govern
2 unhappy	6 unkind	10 plenty
3 regard	7 relent	11 gloomy
4 forget	8 regret	12 duty

137

Skill Drill 12 Answers
1 announcement
2 unhappiness
3 regardless
4 forgetful
5 merriment
6 unkindness
7 relentless
8 regretful
9 government
10 plentiful
11 gloominess
12 dutiful

Section E

This section takes up the several spelling problems related to adding suffixes to words. The "rules" which apply to some of these spellings are difficult to remember and therefore are not always properly applied.

Suffixes beginning with a consonant rarely cause much trouble unless they are attached to *y*-ending words. Most pupils can probably do this first subsection independently.

When a word ends with a consonant letter, you must determine whether you do or do not double it before adding a vowel suffix.

The word could end with two different consonant letters. If it does, you do not double the final consonant letter before adding the vowel suffix.

melt   + ed   = melted
start   + ing = starting
perform + ance = performance
remark   + able = remarkable
digest   + ion = digestion
moment   + ous = momentous

When a word ends with *two* vowel letters and a consonant letter, you do *not* double the final consonant before adding a vowel suffix.

need   + ed   = needed
reveal   + ing = revealing
appear   + ance = appearance
avail   + able = available
villain + ous = villainous

You do have a spelling problem when the suffix begins with a vowel letter and when the word ends with a single vowel and a single consonant. Now you must determine if the *last* syllable has any stress. If the syllable has stress, you double the final consonant before adding a vowel suffix. If the syllable does *not* have stress, you do *not* double the final consonant.

You have no spelling problem with one-syllable words which end in a single vowel and a single consonant. All

Attaching suffixes which begin with a vowel to words that end with a consonant is the source of considerable spelling difficulty. Guide pupils through the explanatory material and point out the key elements in the words in each list.

Spelling problems usually occur when a suffix beginning with a vowel is attached to a word ending with a consonant preceded by a single vowel.

Be sure that all pupils can distinguish between stressed and unstressed syllables and one-syllable words have stress, although the dictionary does not show the stress symbol. One-syllable words which end in a single consonant preceded by a single vowel double the final consonant before a vowel suffix.

bat↓   bat↓ted   bat↓ting

When words ending in a single consonant preceded by a single vowel have primary or secondary stress on the last syllable, you double the final consonant before a vowel suffix. When such words have no stress on the last syllable, you do *not* double the final consonant.

Study these examples which show the different stresses and the different spellings with the *ing* form.

	stress↓	double↓
admit	/ad mit′/	admitting
prefer	/prē fėr′/	preferring
occur	/ə kėr′/	occurring
rebel	/rē bel′/	rebelling

	no stress↓	single↓
profit	/prof′it/	profiting
credit	/kred′it/	crediting
differ	/dif′ər/	differing
gossip	/gos′ip/	gossiping

The following "rule" is helpful with words of two or more syllables and with suffixes which begin with vowels: When you add a vowel suffix to a word ending in a single consonant preceded by a single vowel, double the final consonant if there is stress on the last syllable. Note where stress occurs in the following words and if the final consonant is or is not doubled.

139

that they understand that all one-syllable words have stress.

Memorized spelling "rules" are seldom effective unless pupils first study examples of the correct spellings and generalize for themselves. Therefore, even though the common generalization given in the text regarding the doubling of the final consonant is valid, it will be more useful if pupils arrive at it inductively.

Skill Drill 13 Answers

1 omitting
2 leveling
3 auditing
4 suffering
5 compelling
6 committing
7 shivering
8 equaling
9 permitting
10 referring
11 editing
12 propelling
13 covering
14 profiting
15 remitting
16 enrolling
17 conferring
18 labeling
19 rivaling
20 repelling
21 programing
22 focusing
23 kidnaping
24 canceling
25 picnicking
26 mimicking
27 appealing

no	yes	no	yes
↓	↓	↓	↓
libelous	rebellious	difference	occurrence

no	yes	no	yes
↓	↓	↓	↓
profitable	controllable	inheritance	admittance

To keep *c* from spelling /s/ before the *i* in *ing*, we nee to add a *k* to *c*-ending verbs.

	add k		add k
picnic	picnicking	mimic	mimicking
frolic	frolicking	panic	panicking

Skill Drill 13   Write the *ing* form of these verbs. Compare yo work with the answers at the end of Chapter 5.

1 omit	10 refer	19 rival
2 level	11 edit	20 repel
3 audit	12 propel	21 program
4 suffer	13 cover	22 focus
5 compel	14 profit	23 kidnap
6 commit	15 remit	24 cancel
7 shiver	16 enroll	25 picnic
8 equal	17 confer	26 mimic
9 permit	18 label	27 appeal

3   Final *e* Before Suffixes

Dropping or not dropping the *e* at the end of a word whe a suffix is added depends on whether the suffix begins wit a vowel or a consonant. It also depends on the letters tha precede the *e* in the word.

If a final *e* is preceded by a consonant, we usually kee the *e* before a suffix beginning with a consonant.

140

If necessary, help pupils recall that because *c* spells /s/ before *i*, the *k* is added to retain the /k/ sound in words like *picnicking*, *frolicking*, *mimicking*, and *panicking*.

Assign Skill Drill 13 and check it carefully for these words cause many spelling errors Much spelling confusion results becaus the dictionaries show two spellings for word

	keep			*keep*	
love + ly	= lovely		hope + less	= hopeless	
hate + ful	= hateful		excite + ment	= excitement	

If the final *e* is preceded by another vowel letter, we usually drop the *e* before a consonant suffix.

due	duly	awe	awful
true	truly	argue	argument

If final *e* is preceded by a consonant letter, we usually drop the *e* before a vowel suffix.

use	usable	move	movable
come	coming	guide	guidance
sale	salable	nerve	nervous

But remember these exceptions.

	keep		*keep*
mile	mileage	acre	acreage

If final *e* is preceded by *g* or *c*, we usually keep the *e* before a suffix which begins with *a, o,* or *u*. We do so to keep the *g* from spelling /g/ and the *c* from spelling /k/.

keep

change + able = changeable
manage + able = manageable
outrage + ous = outrageous
courage + ous = courageous

keep

notice + able = noticeable
replace + able = replaceable
service + able = serviceable
enforce + able = enforceable

141

like *movable* (also *moveable*), but only one for *mileage* and *acreage*. Again, the generalizations will probably be more useful if pupils first examine the word lists.

Pupils may need help to recall that words ending in *ge* and *ce* need to keep the final *e*. This final *e* retains the /j/ and /s/ in the pronunciations.

Skill Drill 14 Answers

1 diving
2 bathing
3 lying
4 escaping
5 consuming
6 operating
7 guiding
8 hiding
9 hoping
10 imposing
11 racing
12 plunging
13 relating
14 tying
15 obligating
16 participating
17 shaving
18 preparing

Words ending in *ie* usually change *ie* to *y* when *ing* is added.

tie	tying
lie	lying
die	dying

But remember this spelling.

dye	dyeing

Skill Drill 14 Write the *ing* form of these verbs. Compare your work with the answers at the end of Chapter 5.

1 dive	**7** guide	**13** relate
2 bathe	**8** hide	**14** tie
3 lie	**9** hope	**15** obligate
4 escape	**10** impose	**16** participate
5 consume	**11** race	**17** shave
6 operate	**12** plunge	**18** prepare

Skill Drill 15 Affix the *able* suffix to these verbs. Compare your work with the answers at the end of Chapter 5.

1 live	**7** admire	**13** sale
2 love	**8** service	**14** like
3 enforce	**9** manage	**15** exchange
4 pronounce	**10** use	**16** advise
5 notice	**11** blame	**17** embrace
6 move	**12** imagine	**18** excite

Homonyms

Homonyms cause many spelling errors. Homonyms are words which sound the same but have different meanings and spellings. You have learned many of the English homonyms. In this section you will review fifteen of these homonym pairs which you will probably need to write. Study each pair and note the differences in spellings and meanings.

142

Assign these Skill Drills and check them carefully. Review any parts of this section deemed necessary from the results of the Skill Drills before going on to the next section.

Section F

Homonyms are dealt with thoroughly in the Level 7 text. They have also been given constant attention in the earlier levels of this series. The following homonym pairs were also included in

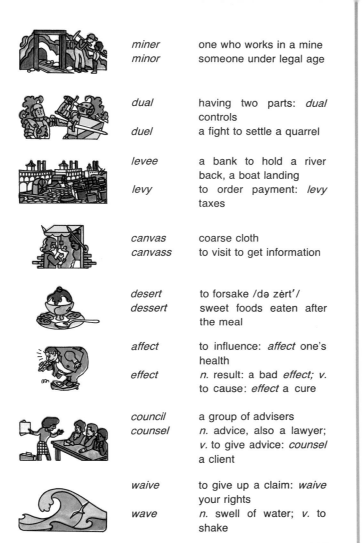

miner	one who works in a mine	
minor	someone under legal age	
dual	having two parts: *dual* controls	
duel	a fight to settle a quarrel	
levee	a bank to hold a river back, a boat landing	
levy	to order payment: *levy* taxes	
canvas	coarse cloth	
canvass	to visit to get information	
desert	to forsake /də zėrt′/	
dessert	sweet foods eaten after the meal	
affect	to influence: *affect* one's health	
effect	*n.* result: a bad *effect; v.* to cause: *effect* a cure	
council	a group of advisers	
counsel	*n.* advice, also a lawyer; *v.* to give advice: *counsel* a client	
waive	to give up a claim: *waive* your rights	
wave	*n.* swell of water; *v.* to shake	

143

the Level 7 text: *colonel, kernel; cymbal, symbol; miner, minor; dual, duel; council, counsel; waive, wave.* They are included here as a means of reviewing these often confused words.

Go over the meanings of these homonyms with the pupils. You might want to illustrate the meaning of each homonym by using it in a sentence.

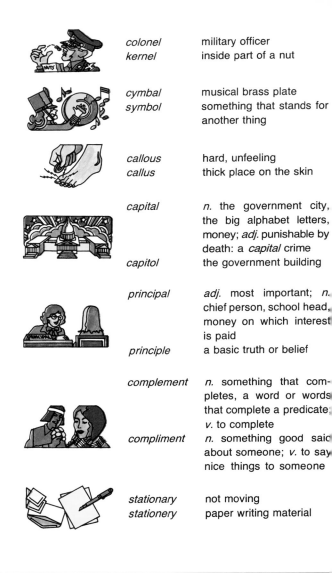

	colonel	military officer
	kernel	inside part of a nut
	cymbal	musical brass plate
	symbol	something that stands for another thing
	callous	hard, unfeeling
	callus	thick place on the skin
	capital	*n.* the government city, the big alphabet letters, money; *adj.* punishable by death: a *capital* crime
	capitol	the government building
	principal	*adj.* most important; *n.* chief person, school head, money on which interest is paid
	principle	a basic truth or belief
	complement	*n.* something that completes, a word or words that complete a predicate; *v.* to complete
	compliment	*n.* something good said about someone; *v.* to say nice things to someone
	stationary	not moving
	stationery	paper writing material

144

The *capital-capitol, principle-principal,* and *complement-compliment* homonym pairs are often confused by pupils and adults. Take additional time with these words. Allow pupils to develop devices for distinguishing these troublesome pairs.

Assign Skill Drill 16. If pupils are having difficulty, go over the answers with them and clarify any confusion about the homonyms.

The two parts of the Mastery Test allow i to be given in two sessions instead of one i desired. Use the results of the Mastery Test and the chart in the front of this Teacher's Edition to prescribe appropriate review in Level 7 o Level 8 if needed.

Skill Drill 16 Complete the sentences by writing the correct homonym. Compare your work with the answers at the end of Chapter 5.

1 A huge __ /wāv/ damaged the __ /lev´ē/.

2 The coal __ /mī´nər/ had a __ /kal´əs/ on his hand.

3 The __ /kan´vəs/ sails flapped and the ship remained __ /stā´shən ər ē/.

4 The __ /prin´sə pəl/ was __ /kal´əs/ to the demands of the parents.

5 Her advisory __ /koun´səl/ is meeting in the __ /kap´ə təl/ building.

6 The __ /kėr´nəl/ is getting good __ /koun´səl/ from the general.

7 A __ /kan´vəs/ of voters showed that the tax __ /lev´ē/ would fail.

8 We paid her a __ /kom´plə mənt/ on her beautiful __ /stā´shən ər ē/.

9 At the clash of the __ /sim´bəlz/, a __ /dü´əl/ to the death will begin.

10 We must __ /kom´plə mənt/ her contribution in order to __ /ə fekt´/ the campaign results.

11 Washington, our __ /kap´ə təl/, appeared __ /də zėrt´əd/ in the winter.

12 The storm had only a __ /mī´nər/ __ /ə fekt´/ on the ships in the harbor.

13 We threw the birds a few __ /kėr´nəlz/ of corn for their __ /də zėrt´/.

14 It is a sound __ /prin´sə pəl/ not to __ /wāv/ your rights.

15 The dove and the olive branch are __ /dü´əl/ __ /sim´bəlz/ of peace.

1 wave, levee
2 miner, callus
3 canvas, stationary
4 principal, callous
5 council, capitol
6 colonel, counsel
7 canvass, levy
8 compliment, stationery
9 cymbals, duel
10 complement, affect
11 capital, deserted
12 minor, effect
13 kernels, dessert
14 principle, waive
15 dual, symbols

145

Part A Answers

1 tomato, tomatoes
2 echo, echoes
3 memento, mementos
4 taboo, taboos
5 company, companies
6 menu, menus
7 dwarf, dwarfs
8 lasso, lassos *or* lassoes
9 moose, moose
10 medium, media
   or mediums
11 alibi, alibis
12 studio, studios
13 taxi, taxis
14 loaf, loaves
15 sheep, sheep
16 formula, formulae
   or formulas
17 oasis, oases
18 ox, oxen
19 tooth, teeth
20 crisis, crises
21 pimento, pimentos
22 swine, swine
23 turkey, turkeys
24 soprano, sopranos
25 mimicking
26 occurring
27 admitting
28 revealing
29 managing
30 guiding
31 canvassed
32 levied
33 deserted

Mastery Test 5

A Write the singular and plural form or forms of each word for which the sound-spelling is shown.

1 /tə mā′tō/
2 /ek′ō/
3 /mə men′tō/
4 /tə bü′/
5 /kum′pə nē/
6 /men′ū/
7 /dwärf/
8 /las′ō/
9 /müs/
10 /mē′dē əm/
11 /al′ə bī′/
12 /stü′dē ō/
13 /tak′sē/
14 /lōf/
15 /shēp/
16 /fôrm′ū lə/
17 /ō ā′səs/
18 /oks/
19 /tüth/
20 /krī′səs/
21 /pə men′tō/
22 /swīn/
23 /tėr′kē/
24 /sə pran′ō/

Write the *ing* form of each verb for which the sound-spelling is shown.

25 /mim′ik/
26 /ə kėr′/
27 /ad mit′/
28 /rē vēl′/
29 /man′ij/
30 /gīd/

Write the *ed* form of each verb for which the sound-spelling is shown.

31 /kan′vəs/
32 /lev′ē/
33 /də zėrt′/
34 /koun′səl/
35 /dü′əl/
36 /wāv/

Write the *able* adjective form of each word for which the sound-spelling is shown.

37 /kən trōl′/
38 /chānj/
39 /ə vāl′/
40 /nō′tis/
41 /trān/
42 /ek sīt′/
43 /prof′it/
44 /bē lēv′/
45 /sėr′vis/

146

B

Write the regular spelling of each phrase.

1 /āt/ /sōl′jərz/
2 /pā′shənt/ /frend/
3 /bāzh/ /vāl/
4 /pôr′sə lən/ /sô′sər/
5 /ə fish′ənt/ /kash ir′/
6 /prin′sə pəl/ /sôrs/
7 /pēs/ /uv/ /sē′dər/
8 /nes′ə ser′ē/ /sak′rə fīs/
9 /tə rif′ik/ /hèr′ə kān′/
10 /kə los′əl/ /wāt/
11 /an′ū əl/ /ə kā′zhən/
12 /ə gres′iv/ /sher′if/
13 /suk ses′fəl/ /chal′ənj/
14 /ān′shənt/ /shēld/
15 /də sēt′fəl/ /vil′ən/
16 /ir′ə gā′təd/ /fēldz/
17 /fôr′ən/ /frāt/
18 /nīs/ /nēs/
19 /kal′əs/ /at′ə tüd′/
20 /em bar′əst/ /bùk′kēp′ər/

147

Skill Drill 1   1 accommodate   2 corridor   3 address
4 tariff   5 missile   6 announce   7 collide   8 villain
9 embarrass   10 suppress   11 access   12 terrace
13 immigrant   14 dissatisfy   15 committee

Skill Drill 2   1 molasses   2 opossum   3 tobacco
4 parallel   5 satellite   6 moccasin   7 paraffin   8 colossal
9 appetite   10 terrific   11 threshold   12 welfare

Skill Drill 3   1 pierce   2 niece   3 kerosene   4 scissors
5 scepter   6 mercy   7 adversity   8 eclipse   9 ascent
10 rinse

Skill Drill 4   1 civil   2 lettuce   3 parcel   4 cyclone
5 abscess   6 nuisance   7 sincere   8 discipline   9 recipe
10 circuit   11 cease   12 citrus   13 adolescent   14 incense
15 licorice   16 census   17 celery   18 cylinder   19 faucet
20 icicle   21 precipice   22 miscellaneous

Skill Drill 5   1 weigh   2 rein *or* reign   3 eight   4 foreign
5 neighbor   6 quotient   7 their   8 species   9 sufficient

Skill Drill 6   1 glacier   2 soldier   3 yield   4 fierce
5 fiend   6 niece   7 grieve   8 hygiene   9 sheik   10 either
11 protein   12 leisure   13 friend   14 forfeit   15 counterfeit

Skill Drill 7   1 receive   2 seize   3 conceit   4 siege
5 view   6 shriek   7 weird   8 pierce   9 ancient   10 achieve
11 ceiling   12 receipt   13 sieve   14 patient

Skill Drill 8   1 journeys   2 silos   3 studios   4 potatoes
5 daisies   6 solos   7 dynamos   8 halos   9 alibis
10 burros   11 heroes   12 tattoos   13 radios
14 broncos   15 volcanoes   16 mottoes   17 zeros
18 sopranos

Skill Drill 9 1 mice 2 knives 3 moose 4 scarfs
5 children 6 thieves 7 women 8 halves 9 sheep

Skill Drill 10 1 larvae 2 crises 3 alumni 4 diagnoses
5 stimuli 6 analyses 7 oases 8 parentheses 9 emphases

Skill Drill 11 1 stadia 2 appendices 3 formulae
4 curricula 5 media 6 nuclei 7 fungi 8 pupae 9 data

Skill Drill 12 1 announcement 2 unhappiness
3 regardless 4 forgetful 5 merriment 6 unkindness
7 relentless 8 regretful 9 government 10 plentiful
11 gloominess 12 dutiful

Skill Drill 13 1 omitting 2 leveling 3 auditing
4 suffering 5 compelling 6 committing 7 shivering
8 equaling 9 permitting 10 referring 11 editing
12 propelling 13 covering 14 profiting 15 remitting
16 enrolling 17 conferring 18 labeling 19 rivaling
20 repelling 21 programing 22 focusing 23 kidnaping
24 canceling 25 picnicking 26 mimicking 27 appealing

Skill Drill 14 1 diving 2 bathing 3 lying 4 escaping
5 consuming 6 operating 7 guiding 8 hiding 9 hoping
10 imposing 11 racing 12 plunging 13 relating 14 tying
15 obligating 16 participating 17 shaving 18 preparing

Skill Drill 15 1 livable 2 lovable 3 enforceable
4 pronounceable 5 noticeable 6 movable 7 admirable
8 serviceable 9 manageable 10 usable 11 blamable
12 imaginable 13 salable 14 likable 15 exchangeable
16 advisable 17 embraceable 18 excitable

Skill Drill 16 1 wave, levee 2 miner, callus 3 canvas,
stationary 4 principal, callous 5 council, capitol
6 colonel, counsel 7 canvass, levy 8 compliment,
stationery 9 cymbals, duel 10 complement, affect
11 capital, deserted 12 minor, effect 13 kernels, dessert
14 principle, waive 15 dual, symbols

6 Proofreading for Spelling and Meaning

Many spelling errors are made as the result of carelessness rather than through inability to spell correctly. Hurried writers may *know* which spelling option to use in a word, but they reverse, add, or omit letters without realizing it. Preoccupied writers may not take time to "hear" the sounds in a word, think discriminatingly about the word part, or remember an unexpected spelling. Inattentive writers may confuse words with similar meanings, but recognize mistakes upon thoughtful rereading of what they have written.

Regular and meticulous proofreading of your own written work will strengthen your spelling skills by forcing you to look analytically at written words, noting word parts, spelling options, and the meanings of words in sentences.

This chapter provides practice in proofreading by giving sentences in which words are misspelled or used incorrectly. Each Skill Drill follows a summary of the spelling skills discussed in preceding chapters or chapter sections.

Prefixes

You learned that a prefix is a word part placed at the beginning of a word or word root to change the meaning of the word or root. Prefixes like *un* ("not–opposite"), *pre* ("before"), *super* ("over"), *trans* ("across"), and *inter* ("between") are easy to understand because each has one general meaning. Spelling is no problem since each prefix has one spelling.

Other prefixes like *com* ("with") have single meanings, but these prefixes have spellings that depend upon the first letter of the words or roots to which they are affixed.

150

CHAPTER 6

The purpose of this chapter is to summarize and review the spelling skills of the five preceding chapters in a proofreading context. First the basic spelling generalizations are briefly restated. This is followed by exercises in identifying and correcting errors.

Section A

In this first section, attention is given to the prefixes used with familiar English words which were studied in Chapter 1. Since the explanatory material is quite detailed, it is usually helpful to go through the introductory material with pupils.

Remember that you affix the *com* form to words that begin with *b, p,* or *m,* as in *combat, complain,* and *commingle.* The *com* prefix appears as *cor* before *r* as in *correlate,* as *col* before *l* as in *collect,* and as *co* before a vowel as in *cooperate.* You may affix *co* to the names of people as in *copilot.* The *con* form of *com* appears often in words that you know such as *contest, consent, conform,* and *condense.* The *sub* prefix ("under") appears as *sup* or *sus* before *p* and sometimes *t* as in *suppress* and *sustain.* You see other *sub* forms like *suc, suf,* and *sug* in words like *success, suffix,* and *suggest.*

Some prefixes have several distinctly different meanings. You learned that the *im* prefix means "in" in *impress,* but "not-opposite" in *improper.* The *im* prefix form comes before words that begin with *p, m,* and *b* as in *impossible, immature,* and *imbed.* You change the *im* spelling to *ir* before *r* as in *irregular, il* before *l* as in *illegal,* and *ig* before *n* as in *ignoble.* The *in* spelling form is most frequently used and appears in words such as *incorrect, insane, inform,* and *income.* You use the *dis* prefix to mean "not-opposite" in *discomfort,* but "down" in *dismount.* The *de* prefix means "away" in *deport* and "down" in *depress.* You know the *re* prefix means "back" in *repay* and "again" in *reread; en* means "in" in *encase* but "make" in *enlarge; pro* means "for" in *pronoun* but "onward" in *proceed; ex* means "out" in *extract* but "former" in *ex-champion.*

Skill Drill 1 These sentences have errors involving prefixed English words. Some prefixes and word roots are misspelled; some prefixes are misused. Proofread each sentence and correct the mistakes by writing the correct spellings. Check the meaning of any unfamiliar word. Answers appear at the end of Chapter 6.

1 Unreliable and uncompetent workers caused innumerable delays when we remodeled our house.

2 The audience subpressed dissappointment when the unexperienced magician was unable to make the rabbits disappear.

151

After reading through the prefix material with pupils, and supplementing it with additional explanations when necessary, review the prefix chart on pages 12–13 with pupils. In assigning Skill Drill 1, be sure pupils are aware of the fact that they are to proofread the sentences for prefixes that are misspelled or misused and to correct the mistakes. You may want to do this first Skill Drill as an oral group activity.

3 preoccupied, enriching, compassion

4 incomplete, impatient

5 discredit, dethroned

6 irresponsible, ignobly, supplant

7 prefabricated, suburban

8 dissatisfied, substandard, replaced

9 displaced, encamped

10 discourtesy, uncomfortable

11 prolonged, transcontinental

12 impressive, replanted

13 discontinued, disinterested

14 preexisting, international, unlikely

15 transformed

---

3 The miser was so prooccupied with plans for inriching himself that he had no conpassion for others.

4 "I disapprove of work that is inaccurate and uncomplete,' said the inpatient teacher.

5 A dishonest scheme to descredit the government caused such contention and disunity in the country that the king was exthroned.

6 The iresponsible young prince plotted ilnobly to suplant his father and proclaim himself king.

7 Hundreds of profabricated houses are found in supurban communities that have rebuilt along the superhighways near cities.

8 The disatisfied tenant would not renew her lease until the supstandard furnace had been displaced.

9 Through the cooperation of many people, persons displaced by the flood were removed from their homes and are now incamped on higher ground.

10 You wouldn't react with such descourtesy to the discomfort of others if you had ever been in the same kind of discomfortable position.

11 We had a prelonged discussion about the first intercontinental railroad linking cities on the east and west coasts.

12 It's inpressive to see acres of deforested land being transplanted with small trees.

13 The contest was decontinued until uninterested persons could be found to serve as impartial judges.

14 The prexisting conditions made intranational trade agreements inlikely between some superpowers.

15 The children enjoyed the tale of an impoverished youth informed into a prince by a fairy godmother.

Throughout the final chapter you may, of course, prefer to have pupils rewrite the entire sentence instead of the particular words which are in error. Be sure pupils understand the meaning of each word.

As in previous chapters, the answers to the Skill Drill appear at the conclusion of the chapter. Pupils should check their answers. Or if you prefer, the Skill Drill can be an oral group activity.

Prefixes and Roots

Prefixes are often added to roots which are taken from Latin words. You learned that prefixes change the meanings of Latin roots like *pose* ("put–place"), *pel* ("push"), *tract* ("pull–draw"), *press* ("press–squeeze"), *scribe* ("write"), *port* ("carry"), and *cede–ceed* ("go"), just as they change the meanings of English words. The *re* prefix, for example, which is used in *recall* ("call back") and *resound* ("sound back"), appears in *repel* ("push back"), *report* ("carry back"), *retract* ("pull back"), and *recede* ("go back"). The *de* prefix, which is used in *degrade* ("grade down") and *devalue* ("value down"), appears in *detract* ("pull down"), *depose* ("put down"), and *depress* ("squeeze down, press down").

Prefixes change spellings before certain Latin roots in the same way they change spellings before certain English words. For example, the prefix *com* becomes *con* when affixing it to *tract (contract)* and to *cede (concede);* the *sub* prefix becomes *sup* before roots beginning with *p (support, suppress);* and so on.

Skill Drill 2   Some of the following sentences have errors involving words formed with prefixes added to Latin roots. Some of the prefixed words are misspelled and some are used incorrectly. Proofread the sentences and correct the errors by writing the correct spellings. Check the meaning of any unfamiliar word in your Spelling Dictionary or in the classroom dictionary. Compare your work with the answers at the end of Chapter 6.

1 We expect the floodwaters to receed soon, leaving damage which will excede a million dollars.

2 The followers of the disposed king were immediately deported although many people interceeded in their behalf.

3 The old woman enscribed her name on a will disposing of her property as her lawyer preposed.

4 Careful reading of a contract should always proceed the signing of it.

153

Section B

This section concentrates on prefixes which are combined with Latin roots. These Latin roots are usually not recognizable as English words and therefore the meaning may not be readily understood.

The series of charts which appears between pages 14 and 21 of the text may be useful in reviewing the various prefix-root combinations. Assign the Skill Drill or go through it orally with the class.

Skill Drill 2 Answers (cont'd)

5 compressed, transported,
   exported
6 dispel, proceed, described
7 no errors
8 compel, prescribed
9 repels
10 suppose, succeeded,
   conceded
11 no errors
12 suppressed

5 Cotton was conpressed into huge bales, transposed by rai
to the ship, and imported to foreign countries.

6 It was hard to dispell our fear and precede to an old house
that some people discribed as haunted.

7 "Retract these statements unless you have express proo
to support them," cried the angry man.

8 "No one can compell you to take the medicine I have pro
scribed," the doctor said.

9 "The thought of using heavy oars to propel our boat up
stream repells me," murmured the lazy boy who reposed o
the dock.

10 "I suppoze a few of my pupils have not suceeded in learnin
how to subtract," the teacher conceded.

11 Unfortunately, several words were transposed when th
senator's speech was transcribed in the newspaper.

12 I supressed a yawn often during the protracted lecture.

Roots and Root Words with Suffixes
You learned that a suffix is an addition made at the end o
a word to change the word from one part of speech to anothe
Suffixes like *ness (kindness), ment (treatment), ance–ence (to*
erance, absence), and *ion–sion–tion (fashion, mission, positio*
form nouns. Suffixes like *ful (careful), less (careless), able–ib*
(breakable, flexible), and *ous (porous)* form adjectives. The *an*
ent suffix changes verbs to nouns *(serve-servant, ascen*
ascent) and nouns to adjectives *(tolerance-tolerant, absenc*
absent). You can change many adjectives to adverbs—word
that say something about verbs or adjectives—by affixing th
familiar *ly* suffix *(pleasantly).*

The consonant suffixes like *ment, ful, less, ness,* and *ly* ar
usually added without changing the spelling of root word

Section C
The brief summary of the root-suffix pattern may be supplemented by turning back and reviewing selected parts of Chapter 2. Since certain suffixes such as *ance-ence, ion-sion-tion,* and *able-ible* do not have clear cues t their spelling, it may be desirable to review th appropriate word lists in Chapter 2 to allo pupils to see the spellings.

unless the root word ends in *y* or vowel-*e.* You change *y* to *i* before the consonant suffixes *(merry-merriment, pity-pitiful, penny-penniless, happy-happiness,* and *pretty-prettily).* In words ending in vowel-*e,* you drop the final *e (argue-argument).*

When vowel suffixes like *able–ible* and *ance–ence* are added to roots that end in *e,* you drop the *e (guide-guidance, force-forcible).* Final *e* is also dropped before *ion–tion (rotate-rotation);* an *a* may need to be inserted *(imagine-imagination).* You do not drop the silent *e* before the *able* suffix form in words ending in *ge* or *ce (manageable, traceable).*

Because suffixes are soft syllables with vowel sounds that are hard to *hear,* words ending in /shən/, /əns/, /ənt/, and /ə bəl/ must be *seen* and the suffix spellings remembered.

The *ing* and *ed* endings do not change words from one part of speech to another. These endings are used to change verbs from one form to another. Most verbs that end in silent *e* drop the *e* before adding *ed* or *ing (bake-baked-baking).* Verbs that have a final stressed syllable ending in one vowel and one consonant double the final consonant before adding *ed* or *ing (prefer-preferred-preferring).*

Skill Drill 3 These sentences have errors involving words with suffixes. Some suffixes are misspelled and some words affixed with suffixes are misspelled. Some suffixed words are used incorrectly. Proofread the sentences and correct the errors by writing the correct spellings. Check the meaning of any unfamiliar word in your Spelling Dictionary or in the classroom dictionary. Compare your work with the answers at the end of Chapter 6.

1 "Frequent absence will cause serious problems even for studeous pupils," the principal declared.

2 "This precious vase is not replacable," the woman cried furiously.

3 The owner of this elegent department store was cautous in the appointment of an assistent manager

155

Before assigning the Skill Drill be certain that pupils understand that they are to proofread the sentences for misspelled words, and suffixes that are used incorrectly. Be sure pupils check the meaning of any unknown words they read in the Skill Drill.

4 noticeable
5 spacious, bountiful
6 careful
7 glorious, compelling
8 lovable, permitted
9 careless, appliances
10 awful
11 shivered
12 truly, triumphantly

4 "Changeable weather has a noticable effect upon my health," murmured the pleasant old woman.

5 That spaceous market has a bountyful supply of fruit and every vegetable imaginable.

6 "Yes, an applicant for this position should have a carefull legible handwriting," replied the employer.

7 The pageant commenced with a gloreous scene compeling attention from the audience.

8 The loveable old king is dying of a grievous illness and no one is permited to see him.

9 The servants were carless in operating various valuable appliences in the mansion.

10 An aweful plague of rodents threatened the entire continent with possible illness.

11 We shiverred nervously as mysterious noises broke the silence of the night.

12 "I have cooked a truely delicious dinner," the father cried triumphently.

Prefix-Root-Suffix Words

Hundreds of words are formed by adding suffixes to prefixed words or Latin roots to change the parts of speech or to change the verb forms. Some prefixed words or roots require no spelling changes when the suffix is added *(retract-retraction, suppress-suppressing, resist-resistance, resent-resentment).* You know that spelling changes do occur, however, in many prefixed words or roots. Rules for dropping the final silent *e* and for doubling the final consonant letter apply to prefixed words and roots just as they apply to other words *(recede-receding, but involve-involvement; expel-expelled,* but *deport-deportment.*

156

Section D

The brief summary of the words composed of a *prefix,* a *root,* and a *suffix* is meant to serve as a reminder of the material covered in Chapter 3. It is suggested that specific roots be reviewed as needed using the explanations and word char... in Chapter 3. Emphasize the eye-syllables.

The prefix-root-suffix chart on page 53 useful in summarizing the content of this se...

The final silent *e* changes to *i* in /pōz/ words *(expose-exposition, dispose-disposition)* to make the words easier to pronounce. For the same reason an *a* sometimes is inserted between the root and the suffix *(inform-information, dispense-dispensation)*.

Some prefixed Latin roots change spellings before certain suffixes. The *pel* root becomes *pul (expel-expulsion, repel-repulsive)*. The *cede–ceed* root becomes *ces (intercede-intercession, proceed-procession)*. The *mit* root becomes *miss (permit-permissible, admit-admission)*. In these and other words where the root changes, the pronunciation is made smoother.

The number of changes in root spellings and the vowel sounds that are hard to hear in many suffixes complicate the spelling of prefix-root-suffix words. These long words are easier to spell if you think of the prefix, root, and suffix as eye-syllables which may be spelled as you spell separate words. Knowing the meanings of the prefixes and roots makes the words easier to understand and to use correctly.

Skill Drill 4   Some of the following sentences have errors involving prefix-root-suffix words. Proofread the sentences and correct the mistakes by writing the correct spellings. Check the meaning of any unfamiliar word in your Spelling Dictionary or in the classroom dictionary. Compare your work with the answers at the end of Chapter 6.

1 There was no resistence to having prizes as inducements for acceptible work.

2 "If I had fewer distractions I could finish my work without assistence," exclaimed the secretary.

3 My attention was fixed on a continuous line of visitors passing the display respectfully.

4 The city council unpredictibly revoked permision for use of the park and proclaimed the decision unreversible.

157

n. Section D also offers a good context for viewing the 35 Latin roots introduced in the t. The chart on page 78 will be useful for that rpose.

Be sure pupils understand the directions, then assign Skill Drill 4.

5 perspiring
6 submitted, suppression,
   provoking
7 deference, digressive
8 no errors
9 corruption, impossible
10 impulsively

5 The prespiring men and women showed little inclination fo
continuing their explorations in the jungle heat.

6 The peasants submited abjectly to compression for fear o
provokeing their tyrannical ruler.

7 The senator's message was received with diference al
though his speech was disgressive and uninspiring.

8 These papers are expendable because I have duplicate
copies.

9 There was such corrupsion in the city government that refor
mation seemed imposible.

10 Without reflecting on the consequences, the small child im
pulsivly consumed all the cookies on the plate.

Greek Word Parts

You remember, of course, that many English words are forme
by joining two or more Greek words or word parts. The Gree
mono ("one"), for example, with the Greek *logue* ("speech"
forms *monologue* ("a speech by one"). The same *mono* wor
part joins with the Greek word part *graph* ("writing") to for
monograph ("writing on one subject".) The *graph* word part wi
tele ("far") forms *telegraph* ("far writing"); *tele* with *scop*
("viewer") forms *telescope* ("far viewer"); *scope* with *pe*
("around") forms *periscope* ("around viewer"); and so on.

Certain spellings, like the *ph* spelling of /f/ in the *grap*
word part, appear frequently in words borrowed from Gree
You know to watch for these Greek spellings: *ch* for the /k
sound as in *chorus*, the use of *y* instead of *i* as in *cymbal* ar
cyclone, *rh* as in *rhyme*, *pn* as in *pneumonia*, *ps* as in *psal*
and the final *mn* as in *hymn*.

Skill Drill 5 Some of the following sentences have errors ir
volving words borrowed from Greek or formed by joinir
Greek word parts. Proofread the sentences and correct th

158

Section E
The review of Greek word parts can be facili-
tated somewhat by referring to the study chart
on pages 104 and 105. If necessary, troublesome elements in this section can be reviewed

in greater depth by using applicable parts
Chapter 4.

Skill Drill 5 follows the same pattern a
previous exercises in this chapter. As usual, yc

mistakes by writing the correct spellings. Check the meaning of any unfamiliar word in your Spelling Dictionary or in the classroom dictionary. Answers appear at the end of Chapter 6.

1 "The parameter of a circle is greater than its diameter," the geometry teacher explained.

2 "I've written a splendid autobiography of my mother, the famous arcitect," said the young scholar.

3 In an alfabetic system of writing, letters are symbols that stand for sounds.

4 The word *chord,* meaning "three or more musical notes in harmony," is a synonym of *cord,* meaning "a thick string."

5 "Your heart beat is strong and regular," the doctor announced as she adjusted her periscope.

6 Some perigraphs in our geography book are illustrated with photographs and some with colorful diograms.

7 The atmosphere in the room was tense after an anonomous caller telephoned a threatening message.

8 The conductor of the symphony orchestra complained that the symbol player completely lacked a sense of rythm.

Words from French

Many of the words we use in English have come from French and have retained French spellings. These consonant-sound spellings, for example, are found in words from French: *ch* spelling /sh/ as in *chef* and *machine, gn* spelling /n/ as in *design* and *foreign, ge* or *s* spelling /zh/ as in *beige* or *leisure, gue* spelling /g/ as in *tongue,* and *que* spelling /k/ as in *antique.*

You learned that these vowel-sound spellings are found in English words that come from French: *ou* spelling /ü/ or /u̇/ as in *coupon* or *boulevard, eau* spelling /ō/ as in *plateau,*

159

ve the option of doing the exercise orally or signing it as written work. Also, it may be sirable to have pupils rewrite each of the ght sentences in its entirety.

Section F

French spellings are difficult and deserve a thorough, unhurried review. The chart on page 114 may be used to supplement the summary found here.

Skill Drill 6 Answers

1 amateur
2 trousseau
3 repertoire
4 physique
5 unique
6 memoirs, intriguing, foreign
7 croquettes, luncheon
8 no errors

and *et* spelling /ā/ as in *beret*. These spellings are typical French: *ette* spelling /et/ as in *silhouette, eur* spelling /ər/ as in *amateur, oir* or *oire* spelling /wär/ as in *memoir* and *repertoire,* and *eon* spelling /ən/ as in *surgeon*.

Skill Drill 6 Most of these sentences have errors involving words that have come from French. Proofread the sentences and correct the mistakes by writing the correct spellings. Check the meaning of any unfamiliar word in your Spelling Dictionary or in the classroom dictionary. Compare your work with the answers at the end of Chapter 6.

1 Several amatuer artists were cutting out silhouettes of children at the picnic.

2 That lovely chiffon gown in the top drawer of the bureau was part of my mother's trosseau.

3 The star of a ballet company must have more than seven numbers in her repetoir.

4 A person with a fine phisigue should not feel fatigue after slight exercise.

5 This antique desk has a unigue design on the drawers.

6 The general's memoires include intrigueing stories of visits with foriegn sovereigns.

7 The chef prepared his famous croquets for the pleasure of the guests at the buffet lunchon.

8 "I can't manage to get this huge car into such a tiny garage," cried the chauffeur.

Words with Special Spellings
Words with one or more pairs of double consonant letters account for many spelling errors in English. Do you recall why words like *parallel, occur,* and *accommodate* are hard to spell?

160

Assign the Skill Drill as usual. Although this Skill Drill contains fewer sentences, the exercise will require as much time as some longer exercises because of the difficult spellings.

Section G
The explanatory material in this section summarizes three persistent spelling problems: double consonant letters, alternate spellings of /s/, and *ie-ei* spellings. Guide pupils through

Because we cannot *hear* in some cases both consonant letters that are used to spell a single consonant sound. In other cases only one consonant letter is used. Each word is a separate spelling problem in which the consonant spellings must be carefully noted and remembered.

Words with the /s/ sound are also tricky to spell because we cannot *hear* whether to use *s*, *c*, or *sc* to spell the /s/ sound. The /s/ sound is the same in *rinse*, *trace*, and *scent*, for example. Each /s/ spelling in words like these must be seen and remembered.

Some groupings of *ie* and *ei* words will make their spellings easier to remember, but there are so many exceptions and special cases that good spellers will deal with each *ie–ei* word individually and memorize the spelling. It is helpful, however, to remember some clues that you learned: *ei* is used in /ā/ and /ā/ words like *weigh* and *their*, in *gn* words like *reign* and *foreign*, and following a *c* that spells /s/ in words like *receive*. The *ie* is used in /ī/ words like *pie* and in /ē/ words like *chief*, but *ei* spells the /ē/ sound in words like *seize* and *sheik*. The *ie* option is also used in words like *ancient*, *patient*, and *transient* in which *ci*, *ti*, and *si* spell the /sh/ sound.

 Skill Drill 7   Some of the following sentences have spelling errors involving words with double consonants, words with *s*, *c*, and *sc* spelling /s/, and words with *ie–ei* spellings. Proofread the sentences and correct the mistakes by writing the correct spellings. Check the meaning of any unfamiliar word in your Spelling Dictionary or in the classroom dictionary. Compare your work with the answers at the end of Chapter 6.

1 Lettuce, cabbage, and cellery are garden vegetables that cannot be grown without sufficient irrigation.

2 The picnickers are accustomed to watching the assent of balloons in the morning and thier descent in the afternoon.

3 "What is concealed in the parsel you are carrying with such secresy?" demanded the inspector at the immigration desk.

161

Skill Drill 7 Answers
1 celery
2 ascent, their
3 parcel, secrecy

summary. If necessary, supplement the summary by using appropriate word lists.

Assign Skill Drill 7 after going over the sections with pupils.

It is difficult to generalize about spelling certain plurals, words with vowel suffixes, and homonyms. Therefore, rather than summarizing Sections D, E, and F, here, it is recommended

162

Skill Drill 7 Answers (cont'd)
4 vaccination, sheriff
5 shrieked
6 no errors
7 overrated
8 accommodate
9 receipts
10 kerosene, porcelain

4 "An annual vacinnation against rabies is a necessity every dog in this city," announced the sherrif.

5 "I've spilled the molasses!" shreiked the embarrassed coo

6 Neither challenger in the toboggan race proved to be aggressive opponent for the winner.

7 "This colossal statue of a Greek goddess is overated a work of art," murmured the disappointed tourist.

8 Freight and baggage were carried efficiently from the p by soldiers who wished to accomodate the travelers.

9 The impatient cashier was annoyed when customers ask for reciepts.

10 The scientist poured one ounce of acid and one ounce kerocene into the porscelain saucer.

Remember that the plural forms of words, some words w suffixes, and the homonyms cause special spelling problem too. Review Chapter 5, Section D on spelling plurals, Secti E on affixing suffixes, and Section F on homonyms before y do the next Skill Drill.

Skill Drill 8 The following sentences have errors in us homonyms and in spelling plurals, *ie–ei* words, and words w suffixes. Proofread the sentences and correct the errors by w ing the correct spellings. Check the meaning of any unfami word. Answers appear at the end of Chapter 6.

1 The judge refused to accept any of the alibies offerred the thieves.

2 Several sopranos with lovley voices practice thier solos d in studios in this building.

3 The hostess was complemented on the delicious dessert s served on the two adjoining patioes in her backyard.

162

that pupils turn back to page 129 and review these three sections thoroughly before attempting Skill Drill 8.

Because this Chapter reviews previously studied material, no Mastery Test has been

included. However, if an end of year test desired, it is suggested that you select seve sentences from each of the Skill Drills in th chapter and dictate them for pupils to write.

4 Many unfinished canvasses are lying on the floors of desserted art galleries in the large cities of the country.

5 The city council ruled that taxies would not be allowed to park on the levy until the floodwaters had receded.

6 Many oases are found on the principle deserts of Africa.

7 The neighboring wives and husbands gossipped idly while the potatos burned and the steaks became charred on the broiler.

8 Moose, deers, and sheep may be found in some areas, but bisons, buffaloes, and burros are endangered species that are rarely scene.

9 "Callus treatment of a rebellious minor will make him quite unmanagable," the wise mother admitted.

10 "Do you understand the principals by which the dual controls on the plain are operated?" inquired the flying instructor.

11 "It is outragious foolishness to wave your right to an inheritance that will save you from a pennyless future," the dyeing woman said to her neice.

12 Dampness has a bad affect on pianos, but cellos and banjos are not affected by the weather.

163

Skill Drill 1   1 incompetent   2 suppressed, disappointment, inexperienced   3 preoccupied, enriching, compassion
4 incomplete, impatient   5 discredit, dethroned
6 irresponsible, ignobly, supplant   7 prefabricated, suburban
8 dissatisfied, substandard, replaced   9 displaced, encamped   10 discourtesy, uncomfortable   11 prolonged, transcontinental   12 impressive, replanted   13 discontinued, disinterested   14 preexisting, international, unlikely
15 transformed

Skill Drill 2   1 recede, exceed   2 deposed, interceded
3 inscribed, proposed   4 precede   5 compressed, transported, exported   6 dispel, proceed, described
7 no errors   8 compel, prescribed   9 repels   10 suppose, succeeded, conceded   11 no errors   12 suppressed

Skill Drill 3   1 studious   2 replaceable   3 elegant, cautious, assistant   4 noticeable   5 spacious, bountiful
6 careful   7 glorious, compelling   8 lovable, permitted
9 careless, appliances   10 awful   11 shivered   12 truly, triumphantly

Skill Drill 4   1 resistance, acceptable   2 assistance
3 no errors   4 unpredictably, permission, irreversible
5 perspiring   6 submitted, suppression, provoking
7 deference, digressive   8 no errors   9 corruption, impossible   10 impulsively

Skill Drill 5   1 perimeter   2 biography, architect
3 alphabetic   4 homonym   5 stethoscope   6 paragraphs, diagrams   7 anonymous   8 cymbal, rhythm

Skill Drill 6   1 amateur   2 trousseau   3 repertoire
4 physique   5 unique   6 memoirs, intriguing, foreign
7 croquettes, luncheon   8 no errors

Skill Drill 7   1 celery   2 ascent, their   3 parcel, secrecy
4 vaccination, sheriff   5 shrieked   6 no errors   7 overrated
8 accommodate   9 receipts   10 kerosene, porcelain

Skill Drill 8   1 alibis, offered   2 lovely, their
3 complimented, patios   4 canvases, deserted   5 taxis,
levee   6 principal   7 gossiped, potatoes   8 deer, bison,
seen   9 callous, unmanageable   10 principles, plane
11 outrageous, waive, penniless, dying, niece   12 effect

165

Guide to the Dictionary

The Spelling Dictionary includes 402 of the words used in the Skill Drills of Level 8 and words used as examples in the pupil's text. Guide words are given at the top of each page. A pronunciation key is shown at the bottom of every right-hand page.

An entry word is shown in heavy black type. Pronunciation is shown in sound symbols between slant lines after each entry word.

• **pennant** /pen′ ənt/ *n.* A flag, usually long and narrow, used for signaling on ships; a school banner. [fr L *penne* feather]

Spaces are used to show the ear-syllables in the sound-spelling of an entry word.

• **sufficient** /sə fish′ ənt/ *adj.* As much as is needed; enough; adequate. [fr L *sufficere* put under]

The primary accent is shown by the darker accent mark. The secondary accent is shown by the lighter accent mark.

• **situation** /sich′ ū ā′ shən/ *n.* **1.** Position; place. **2.** Circumstances; case; condition. **3.** Job; place to work. [fr L *situs* place, situation]

The part or parts of speech for an entry word are shown by abbreviations.

• **yield** /yēld/ *v.* **1.** Produce. **2.** Grant; give. **3.** Give up; surrender. *—n.* Amount yielded. [fr OE *gieldan* pay, give, make an offering]

A plural of a noun is shown if it does not form the plural regularly by adding *s* or *es* to the singular.

• **plateau** /pla tō′/ *n.* A large, high plain above sea level. *pl.* **plateaus** or **plateaux** /pla tō′/. [fr F *plat* a flat thing]

The past tense and *ing* verb forms are shown if the spelling of an entry word changes before the endings are added and if the verb is irregular.

• **rely** /rē lī′/ *v.* Depend; trust. **relied, relying.** [fr L *re* back + *legare* bind]

• **crease** /krēs/ *v.* Make or become wrinkled. **creased, creasing.** [fr ME *crest* ridge]

Words with the same spelling and very different meanings are shown as separate entry words.

• **tense**[1] /tens/ *adj.* **1.** Stretched tight. **2.** Keyed up: *tense nerves. —v.* Stiffen. **tensed, tensing.** [fr L *tensus,* fr *tendere* stretch]

• **tense**[2] /tens/ *n.* Form of a verb that shows the time of the action or state expressed by the verb. [fr L *tempus* time]

The origin of an entry word is shown in brackets at the end of the entry. (See next page for abbreviations for word origins.)

• **wield** /wēld/ *v.* Hold and use; manage; control: *The carpenter wielded the hammer confidently.* [fr OE *wieldan* rule < L *valere* be strong]

Spelling Dictionary

Language sources of entry words are abbreviated as listed below.

Am Ind	American Indian	Gk	Greek	ME	Middle English
Ar	Arabic	It	Italian	MF	Middle French
D	Dutch	Jp	Japanese	OE	Old English
E Ind	East Indian	L	Latin	OF	Old French
F	French	MD	Middle Dutch	Sp	Spanish

- **abscess** /ab′ ses/ *n.* A collection of pus in the tissues of some part of the body, that results from an infection. [fr L *ab* away + *cedere* go]
- **absorb** /ab sôrb′/ *or* /ab zôrb′/ *v.* **1.** Take in or suck up: *A blotter absorbs ink.* **2.** Take in and make a part. **3.** Interest very much: *an absorbing book.* [fr L *ab* away + *sorbere* suck]
- **acceptable** /ak sep′ tə bəl/ *adj.* Worth accepting; satisfactory: *Flowers are an acceptable gift to a sick person.* [fr L *ad* to + *capere* take]
- **access** /ak′ ses/ *n.* **1.** Approach; admittance. **2.** A means of approach. [fr L *ad* to + *cedere* approach]
- **accommodate** /ə kom′ ə dāt′/ *v.* **1.** Have room for. **2.** Help out; oblige. **3.** Give lodging and food. **4.** Make fit or suitable; adjust. **accommodated, accommodating.** [fr L *ad* to + *commodare* make fit, help]
- **accurate** /ak′ ū rət/ *adj.* **1.** Making few or no errors: *an accurate observer.* **2.** Without errors. [fr L *ad* to + *cura* care]
- **accustom** /ə kus′ təm/ *v.* Make familiar by use or habit. [fr MF *a* to + *costume* custom]
- **achieve** /ə chēv′/ *v.* **1.** Get done; carry out. **2.** Reach by one's own efforts. **achieved, achieving.** [fr MF *a* to + *chef* end, head < L *caput* head]
- **acid** /as′ id/ *n.* **1.** A chemical compound that reacts with a base to form a salt. **2.** A sour substance. —*adj.* **1.** Having the properties of an acid: *an acid solution.* **2.** Sour. [fr L *acidus* sour]

- **adaptable** /ə dap′ tə bəl/ *adj.* **1.** Easily changed to fit different conditions. **2.** Changing easily to fit different conditions. [fr L *ad* to + *aptare* fit]
- **admission** /ad mish′ ən/ *n.* **1.** Act of allowing entrance: *admission of aliens into a country.* **2.** Power or right to enter. **3.** Acknowledging: *admission of guilt.* [fr L *ad* to + *mittere* let go]
- **affect**[1] /ə fekt′/ *v.* **1.** Produce a result on; have an effect on; influence. **2.** Touch the heart of; stir the feelings of. [fr L *afficere* exert influence on, fr *ad* to + *facere* do]
- **affect**[2] /ə fekt′/ *v.* **1.** Pretend to have or feel: *She affected ignorance of the crime.* **2.** Use because one prefers; choose: *affect an eccentric style.* [fr ME *affecter* strive for < L *ad* to + *fectare* strive]
- **aggressive** /ə gres′ iv/ *adj.* **1.** Taking the first step in an attack or quarrel. **2.** Active; energetic. [fr L *ad* toward + *gradi* step]
- **alibi** /al′ ə bī′/ *n.* **1.** Plea or fact that a person accused of a certain offense was somewhere else when the offense was committed. **2.** *Informal.* An excuse. *pl.* **alibis.** —*v. Informal.* Make an excuse. **alibied, alibiing.** [fr L *alibi* elsewhere]
- **ally** /al′ ī/ *or* /ə lī′/ *n.* **1.** Person or nation united with another for some special purpose. **2.** Helper; supporter. *pl.* **allies.** —*v.* /ə lī′/ **1.** Unite or combine by formal agreement (to *or* with). **2.** Associate; connect. **allied, allying.** [fr L *ad* to + *ligare* bind]
- **alto** /al′ tō/ *n.* **1.** The highest male voice or lowest female voice. **2.** The part sung by that

/a/ ran /ā/ rain /ã/ care /ä/ car /e/ hen /ē/ he /ėr/ her /i/ in /ī/ ice /o/ not /ō/ no /ô/ off
/u/ us /ū/ use /ü/ tool /u̇/ took /ou/ cow /oi/ boy /ch/ church /hw/ when /ng/ sing /sh/ ship
/ᵺ/ this /th/ thin /zh/ vision /ə/ about, taken, pencil, lemon, circus

167

voice. **3.** A singer or instrument having an alto voice or part. *pl.* **altos.** *—adj.* For an alto part; able to sing or play an alto part. [fr It < L *altus* high]

● **alumnus** /ə lum′ nəs/ *n.* Graduate or former student of a school, college, or university. *pl.* **alumni** /ə lum′ nī′/. [fr L *alumnus* foster child]

● **amateur** /am′ ə chər/ *or* /am′ ə tər/ *n.* **1.** Person who does something for pleasure, not for money. **2.** Person who does something rather poorly. **3.** Athlete who is not a professional. *—adj.* **1.** Made or done by amateurs: *an amateur painting.* **2.** Being an amateur: *an amateur pianist.* [fr F < L *amator* lover]

● **ambitious** /am bish′ əs/ *adj.* **1.** Having ambition. **2.** Showing ambition: *an ambitious plan.* **3.** Desiring strongly: *ambitious for power.* **4.** Showy; pretentious: *an ambitious estate.* [fr L *ambi* around + *ire* go]

● **analysis** /ə nal′ ə sis/ *n.* **1.** Separation of a thing into parts for examination of the essential features of each. **2.** Statement giving the results of such an examination. *pl.* **analyses** /ə nal′ ə sēz′/. [fr Gk *analusis* a breaking up]

● **anchor** /ang′ kər/ *n.* **1.** A shaped piece of iron attached to a chain or rope, used to hold a ship in place. **2.** Something that makes a person feel safe and secure: *Her calm manner was an anchor to the worried students.* **3.** Thing for holding something else in place. *—v.* **1.** Stop or stay in place by using an anchor. **2.** Hold in place; fix firmly. [fr L *anchora* anchor < Gk *ankura* anchor]

● **ancient** /ān′ shənt/ *adj.* **1.** Of or belonging to times long past. **2.** Very old. **3.** Old-fashioned. *—n.* **1.** A very old person. **2.** A person who lived in times long past. [fr L *anteanus* going before]

● **annoy** /ə noi′/ *v.* **1.** Make angry; disturb; trouble: *annoy by teasing.* **2.** Hurt; harm; molest: *annoy the enemy by raids.* [fr OF *anoier* make odious < L *in odio* in hatred]

● **annual** /an′ ū əl/ *adj.* **1.** Coming once a year. **2.** In a year; for a year. **3.** Accomplished during a year. **4.** Of a plant living but one year or season. *—n.* **1.** Book or journal published once a year. **2.** Plant that lives one season or a year. [fr L *annus* year]

● **antenna** /an ten′ ə/ *n.* **1.** One of two feelers on the head of an insect or crustacean. **2.** Metal apparatus needed in television or radio for sending or receiving electromagnetic waves; aerial. *pl.* **antennas** *or* **antennae** /an ten′ ē′/. [fr L *antemna,* originally, "sail yard"]

● **antique** /an tēk′/ *adj.* **1.** Old-fashioned: *She wore an antique gown to the costume party.* **2.** Having to do with ancient Greece or Rome. **3.** From long ago: *an antique chair.* **4.** In the style of long ago: *an antique finish on the watch.* *—n.* Something made long ago: *She collects antiques.* [fr F < L *antiquus* ancient, former]

● **appetite** /ap′ ə tīt′/ *n.* **1.** Desire for food. **2.** A craving. [fr L *ad* toward + *petere* seek]

● **applause** /ə plôz′/ *n.* **1.** Approval shown by clapping the hands, by shouting. **2.** Approval; praise. [fr L *applausus* clashing noise, fr *ad* to + *plaudere* clap]

● **apply** /ə plī′/ *v.* **1.** Place in contact; put on. **2.** Put to practical use: *John knows the rule but does not apply it.* **3.** Adapt; fit. **4.** Use for a special purpose. **5.** Make a request. **6.** Devote oneself to work or study. **applied, applying.** [fr L *ad* to + *plicare* fold]

● **appoint** /ə point′/ *v.* **1.** Name to an office or position: *He was appointed postmaster.* **2.** Decide on: *appoint a time to meet.* **3.** Prescribe; fix: *the time appointed for his death.* **4.** Furnish; equip: *Her office is appointed with fine fixtures.* [fr L *ad* to + *pungere* pierce, point]

● **approve** /ə prüv′/ *v.* **1.** Think or speak well of; be pleased with: *She approved the pupil's work.* **2.** Consent to: *Father approved our plans for the picnic; Congress approved the bill.* **approved, approving.** [fr L *ad* to + *probare* admit as good]

● **aquarium** /ə kwãr′ ē əm/ *n.* **1.** Pond or tank or glass bowl in which living fish, water animals, and water plants are kept. **2.** Building used for showing collections of living fish, water animals, and water plants. *pl.* **aquariums** *or* **aquaria** /ə kwãr′ ē ə/. [fr L *aquarius* of water]

● **architect** /är′ kə tekt′/ *n.* Person who makes plans for buildings and sees that these plans are followed by contractors and craftsmen who actually put up the buildings. [fr L *architectus* architect < Gk *arkhi* master + *tekton* builder]

● **arrogant** /ar′ ə gənt/ *adj.* Too proud; haughty. [fr L *ad* to + *rogare* ask]

● **ascend** /ə send′/ *v.* Go up; rise; climb. [fr L *ad* toward + *scandere* climb]

- **ascent** /ə sent'/ *n.* **1.** Act of going up. **2.** A place or way that slopes up: *There was a gradual ascent in the terrace.* [fr L *ascensus* mount, fr *ad* toward + *scandere* climb]
- **asphalt** /as' fôlt/ *or* /as' falt/ *n.* **1.** Dark-colored substance, much like tar. **2.** Mixture of this substance with crushed rock, used for pavements, roofs, etc. [fr Gk *asphaltos* asphalt]
- **assure** /ə shùr'/ *v.* **1.** Make sure or certain. **2.** Tell positively: *He assured his mother that there was no danger.* **3.** Secure; ensure. **4.** Make safe: *Is your life assured?* **assured, assuring.** [fr L *ad* to + *securare* secure]
- **asylum** /ə sī' ləm/ *n.* **1.** Institution for the care of the insane, blind, or other classes of unfortunate persons. **2.** Refuge; shelter: *The hunted man found temporary asylum in the church building.* *pl.* **asylums** *or* **asyla** /ə sī' lə/. [fr L *asylum* sanctuary < Gk *asulon* inviolable place]
- **attitude** /at' ə tüd'/ *or* /at' ə tūd'/ *n.* **1.** Way of thinking, acting, or feeling. **2.** Position of the body appropriate to an action or mannerism revealing emotion: *an attitude of anger.* [fr F < It *attitudine* disposition < L *aptitudo* faculty, fitness]
- **audible** /ô' də bəl/ *adj.* Capable of being heard; loud enough to be heard. [fr L *audire* hear]
- **auspicious** /ô spish' əs/ *adj.* With signs of success; favorable: *an auspicious opening day at the fair.* [fr L *avis* bird + *specere* look]
- **avoid** /ə void'/ *v.* Keep away from; stay out of the way of. [fr OF *esvuidier* leave < L *ex* out + *vocare* be empty]
- **aware** /ə wãr'/ *adj.* Knowing; realizing; conscious: *aware of one's responsibilities; aware of danger.* [fr OE *gewaer* aware]
- **axis** /ak' sis/ *n.* Imaginary or real line that passes through an object and about which that object turns or seems to turn. *pl.* **axes** /ak' sēz'/. [fr L *axis* axle]

b

- **ballet** /bal' ā/ *or* /ba lā'/ *n.* **1.** An elaborate dance by a group on a stage. **2.** The troupe of dancers. [fr F, diminutive of *bal* dance]

- **barrage** /bə räzh'/ *n.* Barrier of artillery fire to check the enemy or to protect one's own soldiers in advance. —*v.* Fire at with artillery: *subject to a barrage.* **barraged, barraging.** [fr F, fr *barrer* bar]
- **basis** /bā' sis/ *n.* **1.** The main part; base; foundation. **2.** A fundamental principle. **3.** Principal ingredient. **4.** Starting point. *pl.* **bases** /bā' sēz'/. [fr L *basis* base < Gk *bema* platform]
- **beige** /bāzh/ *adj.* Pale brown; brownish gray. [fr F, fr OF *bege* undyed wool]
- **belligerent** /bə lij' ər ənt/ *adj.* **1.** At war; fighting. **2.** Fond of fighting; quarrelsome. —*n.* **1.** Nation or state engaged in war. **2.** Person engaged in fighting with another person. [fr L *bellum* war + *gerere* bear]
- **beret** /bə rā'/ *or* /ber' ā/ *n.* A soft, round woolen cap. [fr F < L *birrus* hooded cape]
- **bier** /bir/ *n.* Movable stand on which a coffin or dead body is placed. [fr OE *beran* bear, carry]
- **billion** /bil' yən/ *adj.* **1.** In the United States and France, one thousand millions; 1,000,000,000. **2.** In Great Britain, Germany, and other countries, one million millions; 1,000,000,000,000. [fr L *bis* twice (*i.e.,* to the second power) + *(m)illion* million]
- **bison** /bī' sən/ *or* /bī' zən/ *n.* Wild ox with big, shaggy head and strong front legs; American buffalo. *pl.* **bison.** [fr L *bison* bison]
- **boulevard** /bùl' ə värd/ *n.* A broad street in or around a city, often laid out with trees, grass, plots, etc. [fr F < fr MD *bolwerc* rampart, bulwark]
- **bounteous** /boun' tē əs/ *adj.* **1.** Generous; given freely. **2.** Plentiful: *a bounteous harvest.* [fr L *bonus* good]
- **bouquet** /bō kā'/ *or* /bü kā'/ *n.* **1.** Bunch of flowers. **2.** Fragrance. [fr F, diminutive < OF *bosc* forest]
- **brochure** /brō shùr'/ *n.* Pamphlet. [fr F, fr *brocher* stitch]
- **bronco** /brong' kō/ *n.* A small half-wild horse or pony of the plains of western North America. *pl.* **broncos.** [fr Sp *bronco* rough]
- **brusque** /brusk/ *adj.* Blunt; abrupt in manner. [fr F < It *brusco* coarse]
- **buffet** /bu fā'/ *or* /bù fā'/ *n.* **1.** Piece of dining

/a/ ran /ā/ rain /ã/ care /ä/ car /e/ hen /ē/ he /èr/ her /i/ in /ī/ ice /o/ not /ō/ no /ô/ off
/u/ us /ū/ use /ü/ tool /ù/ took /ou/ cow /oi/ boy /ch/ church /hw/ when /ng/ sing /sh/ ship
/ŦH/ this /th/ thin /zh/ vision /ə/ about, taken, pencil, lemon, circus

room furniture for holding dishes, linens, etc.; sideboard. **2.** Counter where foods and drinks are served. **3.** Restaurant with such a counter. [fr F]

● **bureau** /bū′ rō/ *n.* **1.** In the United States, a chest of drawers for clothes. **2.** In Great Britain, a writing table. **3.** Business office. **4.** Government department. *pl.* **bureaus** or **bureaux** /bū′ rō/. [fr F *bureau* office, desk, woolen covering for desks or tables]

● **burro** /bėr′ ō/ *or* /bür′ ō/ *n.* A donkey, used as a pack animal. *pl.* **burros.** [fr Sp]

c

● **caffein(e)** /kaf ēn′/ *or* /kaf′ ē in/ *n.* A stimulating drug found in coffee and tea. [fr F *cafeine*, fr *cafe* coffee]

● **calico** /kal′ ə kō/ *n.* Cotton cloth that usually has colored patterns printed on one side. *pl.* **calicoes** or **calicos.** —*adj.* **1.** Made of calico. **2.** Spotted in colors: *a calico cat.* [US < E Ind *Calicut* Calcutta]

● **cameo** /kam′ ē ō′/ *n.* A precious or semiprecious stone carved so that there is a raised part on a background. *pl.* **cameos.** [fr It]

● **camouflage** /kam′ ə fläzh′/ *n.* **1.** Disguise, deception: *The white fur of the polar bear is a natural camouflage.* **2.** In warfare, a false appearance of things to deceive the enemy. —*v.* Disguise; give a false appearance to. **camouflaged, camouflaging.** [fr F *camoufler* disguise]

● **camphor** /kam′ fər/ *n.* A white substance with a strong odor and bitter taste, obtained chiefly from laurel trees in the Far East, used to protect clothes from moths and used in medicines, etc. [fr L *camphora* camphor]

● **cancer** /kan′ sər/ *n.* **1.** Malignant tumor. **2.** An evil or harmful thing that tends to spread. [fr L *cancer* crab, tumor]

● **capacity** /kə pas′ ə tē/ *n.* **1.** Amount of space inside; volume. **2.** Power of receiving and holding: *the capacity of a metal for holding heat.* **3.** Ability; power: *a great capacity for learning.* **4.** Position; relation: *A person may act in the capacity of a parent.* *pl.* **capacities.** [fr L *capacitas* able to hold]

● **carcass** /kär′ kəs/ *n.* The dead body of an animal. [fr F < It *carcassa* carcass]

● **cashier** /kash ir′/ *n.* Person who has charge of money in a bank or business. [fr F *caissier* treasurer]

● **caution** /kô′ shən/ *n.* **1.** Act of being very careful; wariness. **2.** A warning. —*v.* Warn; notify of danger or risk. [fr L *cavere* be on one's guard]

● **cautious** /kô′ shəs/ *adj.* Careful to avoid danger or difficulty. [fr L *cavere* be on one's guard]

● **cease** /sēs/ *v.* Come to an end; put an end to; stop. **ceased, ceasing.** [fr OF *cesser* cease < L *cessare* delay]

● **cedar** /sē′ dər/ *n.* **1.** An evergreen tree with wide-spreading branches and fragrant, durable wood. **2.** The wood of these trees. —*adj.* Made of cedar wood. [fr L *cedrus* cedar < Gk *kedros* cedar]

● **celebrate** /sel′ ə brāt′/ *v.* **1.** Observe a special time or day with the proper festivities. **2.** Perform publicly with proper ceremonies: *to celebrate Mass in church.* **3.** Praise; honor: *Her music is celebrated in the musical community.* **4.** *Informal.* Have a gay time. **celebrated, celebrating.** [fr L *celebrare* frequent, celebrate]

● **celebration** /sel′ ə brā′ shən/ *n.* **1.** Act of observing with proper festivities; festivity to honor, praise, or make known publicly. **2.** Whatever is done to observe a special time, person, or event. **3.** Performance of a religious ceremony. [fr L *celebrare* frequent, celebrate]

● **celery** /sel′ ər ē/ *n.* A plant with crisp, whitish stalks, which belongs to the carrot family of vegetables, eaten raw or cooked. [fr Gk *selinon* celery]

● **cello** /chel′ ō/ *n.* Bass violin; instrument much like the violin but much larger; violoncello. *pl.* **cellos.** [fr It *violoncello* violoncello]

● **cellophane** /sel′ ə fān′/ *n.* A transparent substance made from cellulose, used as a wrapping. [fr F *cellule* cell + Gk *phanes* appearing]

● **census** /sen′ səs/ *n.* An official count of the people of a country or district, to find out the number of people, their age, sex, and other facts about them. *pl.* **censuses.** [fr L *censere* value, tax]

● **cereal** /sir′ ē əl/ *n.* **1.** Any grass that produces a grain used as food. **2.** The grain. **3.** Food made from the grain. —*adj.* Having to do with grain. [fr L *Ceres* goddess of growing things]

● **challenge** /chal′ ənj/ *n.* **1.** A summons to a fight. **2.** The message conveying the summons. **3.** Act of calling in question; a dispute.

4. Sudden questioning or calling to answer. —*v.* **1.** Claim as due. **2.** Take exception to; dispute. **3.** Call or invite defiantly to a contest; dare. **4.** Summon to a duel. **5.** Claim a place; assert a right. **challenged, challenging.** [fr L *calumnia* trickery, fr *calumniari* accuse falsely]

• **chaos** /kā′ os/ *n.* Great confusion; complete disorder. [fr Gk *khaos* empty space, chaos]

• **character** /kar′ ik tər/ *n.* **1.** Sum total of all distinguishing qualities of a person or a race of people. **2.** Moral strength or weakness. **3.** Reputation. **4.** A distinguishing quality or feature of a person or thing. **5.** Person in a play or a book. **6.** Letter or sign in writing or printing. **7.** An odd person. [fr Gk *kharakter* engraved mark, fr *kharassein* make sharp, engrave]

• **chasm** /kaz′ əm/ *n.* **1.** Deep opening or crack in the earth; gap; gorge. **2.** Wide difference in feelings or opinions. [fr L *chasma* abyss < Gk *khasma* chasm]

• **chassis** /shas′ ē/ *or* /chas′ ē/ *n.* **1.** Frame, wheels, and machinery of a motor vehicle that supports the body. **2.** Frame on which a gun carriage moves backward and forward. *pl.* **chassis.** [fr L *capsa* box]

• **chauffeur** /shō′ fər/ *or* /shō fèr′/ *n.* Person whose work is driving an automobile. —*v.* Act as a chauffeur to. [fr F *chauffer* heat]

• **chemical** /kem′ ə kəl/ *adj.* **1.** Of chemistry. **2.** Made by or used in chemistry. —*n.* Any substance obtained by or used in a chemical process. [fr L *alchimicus* alchemy < Gk *khymos* molten metal]

• **chiffon** /shi fon′/ *or* /shif′ on/ *n.* A very thin silk or rayon cloth. [fr F *chiffe* rag]

• **choral**[1] /kô′ rəl/ *adj.* **1.** Of a choir or chorus. **2.** Sung by a choir or chorus. [fr L *chorus* chorus]

• **choral**[2] *or* **chorale** /kə ral′/ *or* /kôr′ əl/ *n.* **1.** A hymn tune. **2.** A simple sacred tune, sung in unison. [fr L *choralis* choral]

• **chord**[1] /kôrd/ *n.* **1.** String of a musical instrument. **2.** A particular emotion or feeling. **3.** A straight line connecting two points on a circumference. **4.** A structure in an animal that looks like a string: *The chords in its neck stood out.* [fr L *chorda* string]

• **chord**[2] /kôrd/ *n.* A combination of three or more musical notes sounded together in harmony. [fr ME *cord* agreement]

• **circuit** /sèr′ kət/ *n.* **1.** A trip around. **2.** Way over which a person or group makes repeated journeys at certain times. **3.** Distance around any space. **4.** Path over which an electric current flows. —*v.* Make a circuit of; go in a circuit. [fr L *circuitus* a going around]

• **cistern** /sis′ tərn/ *n.* Tank for storing water. [fr L *cisterna* water tank, fr *cista* box]

• **citrus** /sit′ rəs/ *n.* **1.** Any tree bearing lemons, grapefruit, limes, oranges, or similar fruits. **2.** Fruit of such a tree. *pl.* **citruses.** —*adj.* Of such trees. [fr L *citrus* citron tree]

• **civil** /siv′ əl/ *adj.* **1.** Of a citizen or citizens; having to do with citizens. **2.** Having to do with the government, state, or nation: *civil employees.* **3.** Not military, naval, or connected with the church. **4.** Polite: *a civil answer.* [fr L *civis* citizen]

• **clique** /klēk/ *or* /klik/ *n.* Small exclusive set of snobbish people. [fr F *clique* click]

• **colleague** /kol′ ēg/ *n.* An associate. [fr F < L *com* with + *legere* send as a deputy or substitute]

• **collide** /kə līd′/ *v.* **1.** Come together with force; crash. **2.** Clash; conflict: *Their opinions collided.* **collided, colliding.** [fr L *com* with + *laedere* strike, injure]

• **colossal** /kə los′ əl/ *adj.* Huge; gigantic; vast. [fr Gk *kolossos* colossus, huge statue]

• **combine**[1] /kəm bīn′/ *v.* **1.** Join two or more things. **2.** Unite to form a chemical compound. **combined, combining.** [fr L *com* with + *bini* two by two, double]

• **combine**[2] /kom′ bīn/ *or* /kəm bīn′/ *n.* Informal. Group joined together for business or political purposes. [See **combine**[1].]

• **combine**[3] /kom′ bīn/ *n.* A machine for harvesting and threshing grain. [See **combine**[1].]

• **committee** /kə mit′ ē/ *n.* Group of persons appointed or elected to do certain things. [fr ME *committe* trustee]

• **comply** /kəm plī′/ *v.* Act in agreement with a request or a command: *We complied with the doctor's request for prompt payment.* **complied, complying.** [fr Sp *cumplir* do what is proper < L *com* with + *plere* fill up]

/a/ ran /ā/ rain /ã/ care /ä/ car /e/ hen /ē/ he /èr/ her /i/ in /ī/ ice /o/ not /ō/ no /ô/ off
/u/ us /ū/ use /ü/ tool /u̇/ took /ou/ cow /oi/ boy /ch/ church /hw/ when /ng/ sing /sh/ ship
/ᴛH/ this /th/ thin /zh/ vision /ə/ about, taken, pencil, lemon, circus

- **conceal** /kən sēl'/ *v.* Hide; keep secret. [fr L *com* with + *celare* hide]
- **conceit** /kən sēt'/ *n.* **1.** Too high an opinion of one's worth; vanity. **2.** A witty remark. [fr L *com* with + *capere* take]
- **concerto** /kən cher' tō/ *n.* Long musical composition for one or more principal instruments accompanied by an orchestra. *pl.* **concertos.** [fr It < L *com* together + *canere* sing]
- **concurrent** /kən kėr' ənt/ *adj.* **1.** Happening at the same time. **2.** Agreeing; harmonious. **3.** Working together. **4.** Coming together; meeting at a point. [fr L *com* with + *currere* run]
- **condemn** /kən dem'/ *v.* **1.** Express strong disapproval of; criticize. **2.** Pronounce guilty of crime or wrong. **3.** Declare not sound or suitable for use: *The house was condemned after the fire.* **4.** Take for public use: *The houses were condemned to make room for a highway.* [fr L *com* together + *damnare* condemn]
- **confide** /kən fīd'/ *v.* **1.** Tell as a secret: *He confided the problem to her.* **2.** Show trust by telling secrets. **3.** Put trust. **4.** Give to another to be kept safe; hand over: *She confides her children to the competent babysitter.* **confided, confiding.** [fr L *com* with + *fidere* trust]
- **confident** /kon' fə dənt/ *adj.* Having confidence; firmly believing; certain; sure. [fr L *com* with + *fidere* trust]
- **conscience** /kon' shəns/ *n.* The ideas and feelings within, which tell one what is right and what is wrong and guide one to do the right and avoid the wrong. [fr L *com* with + *scire* know]
- **consequent** /kon' sə kwent/ *adj.* Following as an effect; resulting: *Her hard work and consequent exhaustion caused her to become ill.* [fr L *com* with + *sequi* follow]
- **consist** /kən sist'/ *v.* **1.** Be made up; be formed. **2.** Agree; be in harmony. [fr L *com* with + *sistere* cause to stand]
- **consonant** /kon' sə nənt/ *n.* **1.** A speech sound formed by completely or partially stopping the breath. **2.** Any letter or combination of letters that stands for such a sound: *b, c, d, and f are consonants.* —*adj.* In agreement: *Her beliefs are consonant with her mother's.* [fr L *com* with + *sonare* sound]
- **continue** /kən tin' ū/ *v.* **1.** Keep up; keep on; go on; go on with. **2.** Go on after stopping; take up; carry on. **3.** Last: *The job continued* for ten more years. **4.** Stay: *She must continue to go to classes until August.* **5.** Cause to say; maintain. **6.** Put off until a later time; postpone: *The case will be continued next session.* **continued, continuing.** [fr L *continuare* connect]
- **contradict** /kon' trə dikt'/ *v.* **1.** Say that a statement is not true; deny. **2.** Say the opposite of what someone has said. **3.** Be contrary to; disagree with. [fr L *contra* against + *dicere* speak]
- **correspondent** /kôr' ə spon' dənt/ *n.* **1.** Person who exchanges letters with another. **2.** Person employed by a newspaper, magazine, etc., to send news from a particular place or region. **3.** Person or company that has regular business with another in a distant place. —*adj.* In agreement; corresponding. [fr L *com* with + *respondere* respond]
- **corridor** /kôr' ə dôr, kôr' ə dər/ *or* /kōr' ə dôr, kōr' ə dər/ *n.* **1.** A long hallway. **2.** A narrow strip of land connecting two parts of a country. [fr L *currere* run]
- **corsage** /kôr säzh'/ *n.* Bouquet to be worn at a woman's waist, on her shoulder, pinned on apparel. [fr F < *cors* body]
- **counterfeit** /koun' tər fit/ *adj.* Not genuine; made to deceive or defraud: *counterfeit money.* —*n.* Copy made to deceive and passed as genuine: *That antique is a counterfeit.* —*v.* **1.** Copy in order to defraud. **2.** Pretend. [fr F *contrefait* imitated]
- **coupon** /kü' pon/ *or* /kū' pon/ *n.* **1.** A printed statement of interest due on a bond which can be cut from the bond and be presented for payment. **2.** Part of a ticket, package, etc., that gives the holder certain rights. [fr F < OF *couper* cut]
- **courteous** /kėr' tē əs/ *adj.* Polite, civil. [fr ME *corteis* having manners < L *cohors* enclosure, court, crowd]
- **crease** /krēs/ *n.* Line or mark made by folding; wrinkle. —*v.* Make or become wrinkled. **creased, creasing.** [fr ME *crest* ridge]
- **crevice** /krev' əs/ *n.* A narrow split or crack. [fr L *crepare* crack]
- **crisis** /krī' sis/ *n.* **1.** Turning point in a disease toward recovery or death. **2.** A decisive event in history. **3.** Time of danger or anxiety. *pl.* **crises** /krī' sēz'/. [fr Gk *krisis* decision, fr *krinein* decide]
- **crochet** /krō shā'/ *v.* Knit with a single needle having a hook on one end. **crocheted**

/krō shād′/, **crocheting** /krō shā′ ing/. —n. Knitting done in this way. [fr F, diminutive of *croc* hook]

- **croquet** /krō kā′/ n. An outdoor game played by knocking wooden balls through small wire arches with mallets. [fr F]
- **croquette** /krō ket′/ n. A small mass of chopped cooked meat, fish, vegetables, spices, coated with bread crumbs and fried. [fr F, fr *croquer* crunch]
- **current** /kėr′ ənt/ n. 1. A flow; a stream. 2. Flow of electricity along a wire. 3. Movement; course: *the current of public opinion.* —adj. 1. Of the present time: *current fashions.* 2. Generally used or accepted: *a current opinion.* 3. Passing around: *A rumor is current that prices are going up.* [fr L *currere* run]
- **curriculum** /kə rik′ ū ləm/ n. 1. The whole range of studies offered in a school. 2. Program of studies leading to a particular degree: *the curriculum of the medical school.* pl. **curriculums** or **curricula** /kə rik′ ū lə/. [fr L *curriculum* race course]
- **cyclone** /sī′ klōn/ n. 1. A very violent windstorm; tornado. 2. Storm moving around a calm center, or low pressure, which also moves. [fr Gk *kyklon* movement around in a circle]
- **cylinder** /sil′ ən dər/ n. 1. A hollow or solid body shaped like a roller. 2. Any body in the form of a cylinder. 3. The piston chamber of an engine. [fr Gk *kylindein roll*]
- **cymbal** /sim′ bəl/ n. One of a pair of brass plates used as a musical instrument to make a loud ringing sound. [fr L *cymbalum* cymbal]

d

- **deceit** /dē sēt′/ n. 1. Cheating; lying; making a person believe what is false. 2. A dishonest trick. [fr L *de* from + *capere* take]
- **decimal** /des′ ə məl/ adj. Based upon ten or tenths; increasing or decreasing by multiples of ten: *The metric system is a decimal system of measurement.* —n. 1. A decimal fraction like 0.04 (⁴/₁₀₀). 2. A number like 6.47. [fr L *decimus* tenth]
- **decorate** /dek′ ə rāt′/ v. 1. Make beautiful; adorn; trim. 2. Paint or paper a room, etc. 3.

Give a medal, ribbon, or badge to a person as an honor: *decorate the brave scouts.* **decorated, decorating.** [fr L *decorare* adorn]
- **decoration** /dek′ ə rā′ shən/ n. 1. Ornament; things used to decorate. 2. Metal, ribbon, etc., given as an honor. [fr L *decus* adornment]
- **decoy**[1] /də koi′/ v. 1. Lure wild birds, animals, etc., into a hidden trap or into gunshot range. 2. Lead or tempt into danger. [fr D *de* the + *kooi* cage < L *cavea* cave]
- **decoy**[2] /dē′ koi/ or /də koi′/ n. 1. An imitation bird used to lure wild birds, etc. 2. A trained bird or other animal used for the same purpose. 3. The place into which wild birds or animals are lured. 4. Any person or thing used to tempt into danger. [See **decoy**[1].]
- **dedicate** /ded′ ə kāt′/ v. 1. Set apart for a purpose; devote: *They dedicated the skating rink to the mayor of the city.* 2. Address a book, poem, etc., to a friend or patron. **dedicated, dedicating.** [fr L *de* away + *dicare* proclaim]
- **dedication** /ded′ ə kā′ shən/ n. 1. A setting apart for a sacred or solemn purpose. 2. Giving up wholly or earnestly to some purpose or person. [fr L *dedicus* tiding]
- **deface** /dē fās′/ v. Spoil the appearance of; mar: *She may deface the table if she cuts the meat on top of it.* [fr OF *desfacier* undo, ruin]
- **deficient** /dē fish′ ənt/ adj. 1. Incomplete; defective: *deficient supply of food; deficient motor.* 2. Lacking in power or strength: *The wrestler was deficient in the final match.* [fr L *de* down + *facere* do]
- **defy** /dē fī′/ v. 1. Resist openly and boldly: *The boy thought that he could defy all authority.* 2. Withstand; resist: *This scene defies description.* 3. Challenge to do something that is considered impossible; dare: *I defy you to show that you can jump that far.* **defied, defying.** [fr L *dis* away + *fidere* trust]
- **deign** /dān/ v. 1. Condescend; think fit: *So great a person would not deign to notice petty criticism.* 2. Condescend to give: *He did not deign to answer the letter.* [fr OF *deignier* deign < L *dignus* worthy]
- **delicious** /də lish′ əs/ adj. Very pleasing to taste or smell. [fr L *delicatus* dainty, fr *de* down + *lacere* allure]

/a/ ran /ā/ rain /ã/ care /ä/ car /e/ hen /ē/ he /ėr/ her /i/ in /ī/ ice /o/ not /ō/ no /ô/ off /u/ us /ū/ use /ü/ tool /ù/ took /ou/ cow /oi/ boy /ch/ church /hw/ when /ng/ sing /sh/ ship /ᴛH/ this /th/ thin /zh/ vision /ə/ about, taken, pencil, lemon, circus

- **descent** /dē sent'/ *n.* **1.** Changing from a higher to a lower place. **2.** A downward slope. **3.** Way or passage down. **4.** Ancestry; birth; pedigree. **5.** Decline; sinking to a lower condition. **6.** A sudden attack. [fr L *descensus,* fr *de* down + *scandere* climb]
- **design** /də zīn'/ *n.* **1.** A drawing or plan made to serve as a pattern from which to work. **2.** Arrangement of detail, color, and form in painting, building, etc. **3.** A plan in mind to be carried out. **4.** Scheme of attack; evil plan. **5.** Purpose; aim; intention: *Whether by accident or design, he broke the picture.* —*v.* **1.** Plan out; draw in outline: *She designed the new model.* **2.** Set apart; intend; plan. [fr L *de* down + *signare* mark]
- **detour** /dē' tur/ *n.* **1.** A road used when the main road cannot be traveled. **2.** A roundabout way. —*v.* **1.** Use a detour. **2.** Cause to use a detour: *The traffic was detoured because of the accident.* [fr OF *destorner* turn aside]
- **diagnosis** /dī' əg nō' sis/ *n.* **1.** Process or act of finding out what disease a person or animal has. **2.** A careful study of facts to find out essential features of something. *pl.* **diagnoses** /dī' əg nō' sēz/. [fr Gk *dia* apart + *gignoskein* learn to know]
- **diesel** /dē' zəl/ *or* /dē' səl/ *n.* A diesel engine; engine that burns oil with heat caused by the compression of air. [Named after *R. Diesel,* 1858–1913, its inventor.]
- **digestion** /də jes' chən/ *n.* The changing of food in the stomach so that the body can use it. [fr L *dis* apart + *gerere* carry]
- **diligent** /dil' ə jənt/ *adj.* **1.** Hard-working; industrious. **2.** Careful and steady. [fr L *dis* apart + *legere* choose]
- **diphtheria** /dif thir' ē ə/ *or* /dip thir' ē ə/ *n.* A dangerous disease of the throat, usually accompanied by a high fever and inflamation that hinders breathing. [fr F *diphtherie* diphtheria < Gk *diphthera* leather]
- **disapprove** /dis' ə prüv'/ *v.* **1.** Show dislike of. **2.** Reject: *The plans were disapproved by the committee.* **disapproved, disapproving.** [fr L *dis* apart + *approbare* approve]
- **dismantle** /dis man' təl/ *v.* **1.** Strip of clothing, furniture, equipment, etc. **2.** Pull down; take apart: *We had to dismantle the book cases in order to move out.* **dismantled, dismantling.** [fr L *dis* apart + *mantel* mantle]
- **dissolve** /də zolv'/ *v.* **1.** Make or become liquid by putting or being put into a liquid; cause to pass into solution. **2.** Break up; end: *dissolve a partnership.* **3.** Fade away; lose power. **4.** Solve; explain; clear up. **5.** Separate into parts. **dissolved, dissolving.** [fr L *dis* apart + *solvere* loosen, free]
- **distaste** /dis tāst'/ *n.* Dislike. [fr L *dis* not + OF *taster,* originally, ''feel'']
- **disturb** /dis tėrb'/ *v.* **1.** Destroy the peace, quiet, or rest of. **2.** Break in upon with noise. **3.** Put out of order: *She always disturbed her brother's books.* **4.** Make uneasy; trouble. **5.** Inconvenience. [fr L *dis* apart + *turbare* trouble]
- **ditto** /dit' ō/ *n.* **1.** The same; exactly the same as was said or appeared before. **2.** Mark (") that stands for ditto. **3.** A copy. *pl.* **dittos.** —*v* Copy; duplicate. **dittoed, dittoing.** —*adv.* Likewise. [fr It *ditto* said]
- **dolphin** /dol' fən/ *n.* A sea mammal, related to the whale, but smaller. [fr Gk *delphis* dolphin]
- **dominate** /dom' ə nāt'/ *v.* **1.** Control or rule by strength or power. **2.** Hold a commanding position over: *The mountain dominates the harbor.* **dominated, dominating.** [fr L *dominari* be master]
- **domino** /dom' ə nō'/ *n.* **1.** A masquerade costume consisting of a hooded robe and a half mask. **2.** A kind of mask, or the half mask; originally, a hood worn by certain clergymen. **3.** A person wearing a domino. **4.** One of a set of small pieces of bone or wood dotted like dice. **5.** *pl.* The game played with them. *pl.* **dominoes, dominos.** [fr L *dominus* master]
- **dynamite** /dī' nə mīt'/ *n.* Powerful explosive made of nitroglycerin mixed with an absorbent material and pressed into sticks. —*v.* Blow up or destroy with dynamite. **dynamited, dynamiting.** [fr Gk *dunamis* power]
- **dynamo** /dī' nə mō'/ *n.* Machine that changes mechanical energy into electrical energy and produces electric current (short for *dynamoelectric* machine). *pl.* **dynamos.** [fr Gk *dunamis* power]

e

- **eclipse** /i klips'/ *n.* **1.** A darkening of the sun or moon when some other heavenly body is in a position that partly or completely cuts off its light. **2.** Loss of importance for a time. —*v.*

1. Darken; cut off the light from. **2.** Surpass; outshine. **eclipsed, eclipsing.** [fr Gk *ex* out + *leipein* leave]

● **effervescent** /ef′ ər ves′ ənt/ *adj.* **1.** Giving off bubbles of gas; bubbling: *effervescent ginger ale.* **2.** Lively and gay: *He has an effervescent personality.* [fr L *ex* out + *fervescere* begin to boil]

● **efficient** /ə fish′ ənt/ *adj.* Highly capable or productive; effective in operation: *The workers were efficient.* [fr L *efficere* bring about]

● **ego** /ē′ gō/ *n.* **1.** The individual in his capacity to think, feel, and act; self. **2.** *Informal.* Conceit. [fr L *ego* I]

● **eligible** /el′ ə jə bəl/ *adj.* Fit to be chosen; desirable; qualified: *players eligible for the team.* −*n.* An eligible person. [fr L *eligere* choose]

● **eloquent** /el′ ə kwənt/ *adj.* **1.** Having a flow of graceful and forceful speech; fluent: *an eloquent speaker.* **2.** Very expressive: *an eloquent speech.* [fr L *ex* out + *loqui* speak]

● **embarrass** /em bar′ əs/ *v.* **1.** Disturb a person; make self-conscious: *Meeting strangers embarrassed the shy boy.* **2.** Burden with debt. [fr F *embarrasser* put in bars]

● **emergent** /i mer′ jənt/ *adj.* Coming into existence, view, or attention. [fr L *ex* out + *mergere* plunge]

● **emphasis** /em′ fə sis/ *n.* **1.** Special force; importance: *My school puts emphasis on studies that prepare students for college.* **2.** Special stress, or force, on words, phrases, or syllables: *A speaker puts emphasis on certain words in sentences.* *pl.* **emphases** /em′ fə sēz′/. [fr Gk *en* in + *phainein* show]

● **endure** /en dür′/ *or* /en dūr′/ *v.* **1.** Keep on; last: *Their friendship has endured for a long time.* **2.** Put up with; bear; stand. **endured, enduring.** [fr L *im* in + *durare* harden]

● **envy** /en′ vē/ *n.* **1.** Feeling of discontent or dislike because another has what one wants. **2.** The object of such feeling; person or thing envied. *pl.* **envies.** −*v.* **1.** Feel envy toward. **2.** Feel envy because of: *He envied her success.* **envied, envying.** [fr L *im* in + *videre* see]

● **epitaph** /ep′ ə taf′/ *n.* A short statement in memory of a dead person, usually put on his tombstone. [fr Gk *epi* at + *taphos* tomb]

● **etiquette** /et′ ə kət/ *or* /et′ ə ket′/ *n.* Conventional rules for behavior in polite society. [fr F *etiquette* prescribed routine]

● **evident** /ev′ ə dənt/ *adj.* Easy to see and understand; plain; apparent. [fr L *ex* out + *videns* seeing]

● **exhibit** /eg zib′ it/ *v.* **1.** Show; display: *He exhibits concern for her welfare.* **2.** Show publicly; put on display: *She exhibits her paintings in Chicago.* −*n.* **1.** A public showing: *an art exhibit.* **2.** Things shown publicly. **3.** Thing shown in court as evidence: *The book was displayed as Exhibit A.* [fr L *ex* out + *habere* have]

f

● **fatigue** /fə tēg′/ *n.* **1.** Weariness; exhaustion. **2.** Weakness of structural materials caused by long-continued use or strain. −*v.* Cause weariness; tire: *He was fatigued by the long drive.* **fatigued, fatiguing.** −*adj.* Having to do with fatigue, or weariness: *a fatigue stop on a long journey.* [fr F *fatiguer* tire]

● **faucet** /fô′ sət/ *n.* Device containing a valve for controlling the flow of water or other liquid from a pipe, tank, barrel, etc., by opening or closing. [fr F *fausset* faucet]

● **feasible** /fē′ zə bəl/ *adj.* **1.** That can be done easily; possible without difficulty or damage: *Her plan was the most feasible of all.* **2.** Likely; probable. **3.** Suitable; convenient. [fr L *facere* do]

● **feign**/fān/ *v.* **1.** Pretend: *Some animals feign death when in danger.* **2.** Invent falsely: *feign an excuse.* [fr OF *faindre* feign < L *fingere* form]

● **feint** /fānt/ *n.* **1.** False appearance; pretense. **2.** Pretended blow; movement intended to deceive. −*v.* Make a pretended blow or false attack: *The boxer feinted with his right hand and struck with his left.* [fr F *feinte* feint]

● **fictitious** /fik tish′ əs/ *adj.* **1.** Not real; imaginary: *Characters in novels are usually fictitious.* **2.** Assumed in order to deceive; false: *The criminal used a fictitious name.* [fr L *ficticius* artificial]

● **fiend** /fēnd/ *n.* **1.** An evil spirit. **2.** A very wicked or cruel person. **3.** *Informal.* A person

/a/ ran /ā/ rain /ã/ care /ä/ car /e/ hen /ē/ he /ėr/ her /i/ in /ī/ ice /o/ not /ō/ no /ô/ off
/u/ us /ū/ use /ü/ tool /u̇/ took /ou/ cow /oi/ boy /ch/ church /hw/ when /ng/ sing /sh/ ship
/ŦH/ this /th/ thin /zh/ vision /ə/ about, taken, pencil, lemon, circus

who gives himself up to some habit, practice, or game: *a sports fiend who attends every baseball game.* [fr OE *feond* enemy]

- **flamingo** /flə ming' gō/ *n.* A tropical wading bird with very long legs and neck and feathers that vary from pink to scarlet. *pl.* **flamingos, flamingoes.** [fr L *flamma* flame]
- **fleece** /flēs/ *n.* **1.** Wool that covers a sheep or similar animal. **2.** Something remindful of fleece: *the fleece of newly fallen snow.* —*v.* **1.** Cut the wool from. **2.** Rob; cheat. **fleeced, fleecing.** [fr OE *fleos* fleece]
- **fluorescent** /flü' ə res' ənt/ *adj.* Having or showing light by means of electromagnetic radiation. [fr L *fluere* flow + *escent* continuing state]
- **focus** /fō' kəs/ *n.* **1.** Point at which rays of light, heat, etc., meet or appear to meet after being bent by a lens or other means. **2.** Distance of this point from the lens. **3.** Correct adjustment of a lens to make a clear image. **4.** The central point of attention. *pl.* **focuses** or **foci** /fō' sī'/. —*v.* **1.** Bring rays of light to a point. **2.** Adjust a lens, etc., to make a clear image. **3.** Concentrate: *focus your mind on a lesson.* [fr L *focus* hearth]
- **forcible** /fôr' sə bəl/ *or* /fōr' sə bəl/ *adj.* **1.** Made or done by force: *forcible entry into a house.* **2.** Strong; convincing: *a forcible argument; a forcible speaker.* [fr L *fortis* strong]
- **forfeit** /fôr' fit/ *v.* Lose or have to give up as a penalty: *He forfeited his life by careless driving.* —*n.* **1.** Loss of something as a penalty. **2.** Thing lost as a penalty. [fr F *forfaire* transgress]
- **formula** /fôrm' ū lə/ *n.* **1.** Rule for doing something. **2.** Recipe; prescription: *a formula for making soap.* **3.** Expression showing by symbols the composition of a compound: *The chemical formula for water is* H_2O. **4.** Expression showing by symbols a rule: $(a + b)^2 = a^2 + 2ab + b^2$ *is an algebraic formula. pl.* **formulas** *or* **formulae** /fôrm' ū lē'/. [fr L *formula*, diminutive of *forma* form]
- **frequent** /frē' kwənt/ *adj.* Happening often, near together, or every little while. —*v.* /frē kwent'/ *or* /frē' kwənt/ Go to often; be often in: *Frogs frequent the marshes.* [fr L *frequens* crowded]
- **frolic** /frol' ik/ *n.* **1.** Gay prank; fun. **2.** Merry game. —*v.* Have fun; make merry. **frolicked, frolicking.** [fr D *vrolijk* frolic]
- **frontier** /frun tir'/ *or* /frun' tir, fron' tir/ *n.* **1.**

The farthest part of a settled country. **2.** Part of a country next to another country; border. **3.** Uncertain or underdeveloped region: *the frontiers of science.* [fr F *front* front < L *frons* forehead]

- **fungo** /fung' gō/ *n.* A fly ball hit especially for practice fielding by a player who tosses a ball in the air and hits it as it comes down. *pl.* **fungoes.** [Origin uncertain.]
- **fungus** /fung' gəs/ *n.* Any of a group of plants without flowers, leaves, or green coloring matter: *Mushrooms and molds are funguses. pl.* **funguses** or **fungi** /fun' jī'/. [fr L *fungus* fungus]
- **fury** /fūr' ē/ *n.* **1.** Rage; wild, fierce anger. **2.** A raging violent person. *pl.* **furies.** [fr L *furia* rage]
- **fuselage** /fū' sə läzh'/ *or* /fū' zə lij'/ *n.* Framework of the body of an airplane to which the wings and tail are attached. [fr F, fr *fuseler* shape like a spindle]

g

- **generate** /jen' ə rāt'/ *v.* Cause to be; bring into being; produce: *to generate electricity.* **generated, generating.** [fr L *generare* borne, be of a kind]
- **genius** /jēn' yəs/ *or* /jē' nē əs/ *n.* **1.** Very great natural power of mind. **2.** Person having such power. **3.** Great natural ability: *a genius at the piano. pl.* **geniuses** or **genii** /jē' nē ī'/. [fr L *genius* guardian spirit]
- **ghetto** /get' ō/ *n.* **1.** Formerly, part of a city where Jews were required to live. **2.** Part of the city where many poor people live, usually in very crowded conditions. *pl.* **ghettos.** [fr It]
- **glacier** /glā' shər/ *n.* A large mass of ice, which is formed where snowfall exceeds melting and which moves slowly down a mountain or valley: *There are glaciers in the Alps and in parts of Greenland.* [fr L *glacies* ice]
- **goddess** /god' əs/ *n.* **1.** A female god. **2.** A very beautiful or charming woman. [fr OE *god* deity]
- **gracious** /grā' shəs/ *adj.* **1.** Pleasant; kindly: *a gracious manner.* **2.** Merciful. —*interj.* Exclamation of surprise. [fr L *gratiosus* gracious]
- **grandeur** /gran' jər/ *or* /gran' jür'/ *n.* Majesty; nobility; splendor. [fr F, fr *grand* grand]
- **grieve** /grēv/ *v.* **1.** Feel deep sadness: *He*

grieved over his father's death. **2.** Cause to feel deep sadness; afflict: *The wicked sons grieved their parents.* **grieved, grieving.** [fr L *gravis* heavy]

• **grouse**[1] /grous/ *n.* A game bird with feathered legs; prairie chicken. *pl.* **grouse.** [Origin uncertain.]

• **grouse**[2] /grous/ *v. Slang.* Grumble; complain. **groused, grousing.** −*n.* Complaint. [fr OF *groucer* grumble]

h

• **halo** /hā′ lō/ *n.* **1.** A circle of light which appears to surround a shining body such as the sun or the moon. **2.** A golden circle of light around the head of a saint, etc., in pictures. **3.** The glamour or glory that surrounds anything that has been idealized: *A halo of romance surrounds the age of chivalry.* *pl.* **halos, haloes.** −*v.* To surround with a halo. **haloed, haloing.** [fr Gk *halos* threshing floor, disk of the sun or moon]

• **harmony** /här′ mə nē/ *n.* **1.** A getting along well together; agreement in opinions, interests, facts, etc. **2.** An orderly and pleasing arrangement of parts, giving unity of effect. **3.** The sounding together of musical notes in a chord. **4.** Sweet or musical sound. *pl.* **harmonies.** [fr Gk *harmos* joint]

• **hazard** /haz′ ərd/ *n.* **1.** Risk; danger; peril. **2.** Chance. **3.** Any obstruction on a golf course. −*v.* **1.** Take a chance. **2.** Expose to risk. [fr OF *hasard* hazard]

• **heir** /ār/ *n.* Person who inherits anything; person who receives or has something from someone before him. [fr L *heres* heir]

• **hesitate** /hez′ ə tāt′/ *v.* **1.** Fail to act promptly. **2.** Feel that perhaps one should not; be unwilling. **3.** Stop for an instant; pause. **4.** Speak with short stops or pauses; stammer. **hesitated, hesitating.** [fr L *haesitare* hesitate, stick fast]

• **hiccup** /hik′ up/ *n.* An involuntary catching of the breath. −*v.* Catch the breath involuntarily. Also spelled **hiccough.** [Probably imitative.]

• **hideous** /hid′ ē əs/ *adj.* Very ugly; horrible: *hideous monster.* [fr OF *hide* fear, horror]

• **honorable** /on′ ər ə bəl/ *adj.* **1.** Honest; upright: *an honorable man.* **2.** Causing honor: *an honorable position.* **3.** Worthy of honor; noble. [fr L *honos* honor]

• **hurricane** /hèr′ ə kān′/ *n.* A tropical cyclone; violent windstorm with winds blowing from 70 to 100 miles per hour. [fr Sp *huracan* hurricane]

• **hydrant** /hī′ drənt/ *n.* An upright cylinder or street fixture with a valve for drawing water directly from a main. [fr Gk *hydor* water]

• **hygiene** /hī′ jēn′/ *n.* Rules of health; science of keeping well. [fr Gk *hugies* healthy]

• **hymn** /him/ *n.* **1.** Song in praise of God. **2.** Any song of praise. [fr Gk *hymnos* hymn]

• **hyphen** /hī′ fən/ *n.* Mark (-) used to connect the parts of some compound words or the parts of a word divided at the end of a line: *We use two hyphens in the word "merry-go-round."* [fr Gk *upo* under + *hen* one]

i

• **ignore** /ig nôr′/ *v.* Refuse to take notice of; disregard. **ignored, ignoring.** [fr L *ignorare* know not]

• **immigrant** /im′ ə grənt/ *n.* A person who comes into a foreign country to make his home. −*adj.* Migrating: *the immigrant family.* [fr L *im* in + *migrate* migrate]

• **incident** /in′ sə dənt/ *n.* **1.** A happening; occurrence; event. **2.** A slight matter. −*adj.* Liable to happen; belonging: *Hardships are incident to the life of a missionary.* [fr L *incidens* happening, fr *im* in + *cadere* fall]

• **incline**[1] /in klīn′/ *v.* **1.** Be favorable; tend: *Dogs incline to eat meat as food.* **2.** Make favorable: *Incline your heart to obey the law.* **3.** Slope: *The land inclines to the west.* **4.** Lean: *The ladder inclined on the house.* **inclined, inclining.** [fr L *inclinare* bend toward]

• **incline**[2] /in′ klīn/ *or* /in klīn′/ *n.* **1.** Slope: *a steep incline.* **2.** Sloping surface: *He slid down the incline.* [See **incline**[1].]

• **indorse** /in dôrs′/ *v.* **1.** Support; approve. **2.** Write one's name, comment, etc., on the back of a check or other document. **indorsed, indorsing.** [fr OF *endosser* put on back]

• **inflate** /in flāt′/ *v.* **1.** Force air or gas into a

/a/ ran /ā/ rain /ã/ care /ä/ car /e/ hen /ē/ he /èr/ her /i/ in /ī/ ice /o/ not /ō/ no /ô/ off
/u/ us /ū/ use /ü/ tool /ù/ took /ou/ cow /oi/ boy /ch/ <u>ch</u>ur<u>ch</u> /hw/ <u>wh</u>en /ng/ si<u>ng</u> /sh/ <u>sh</u>ip
/ᴛʜ/ <u>th</u>is /th/ <u>th</u>in /zh/ vi<u>si</u>on /ə/ <u>a</u>bout, tak<u>e</u>n, penc<u>i</u>l, lem<u>o</u>n, circ<u>u</u>s

balloon, tire, etc., causing it to swell. **2.** Swell or puff out: *He was inflated with pride.* **3.** Increase prices beyond past amounts. **inflated, inflating.** [fr L *im* in + *flare* blow]

- **inherit** /in her' it/ *v.* **1.** Get or have after someone dies; receive as an heir: *She inherited all her father's treasures.* **2.** Receive physical or mental characteristics from one's parents or ancestors through heredity. **3.** Receive from one who came before: *I inherited the books from the man who lived in the house before us.* [fr L *im* in + *hereditare* inherit]
- **irrigate** /ir' ə gāt'/ *v.* **1.** Supply with water by using ditches. **2.** Supply with a continuous flow of some liquid. **irrigated, irrigating.** [fr L *im* in + *rigare* wet]
- **issue** /ish' ü/ *v.* **1.** Send out. **2.** Come out; go out; proceed. **issued, issuing.** —*n.* **1.** Something sent out. **2.** A sending out; a putting forth: *the issue of stamps.* **3.** A coming forth; a discharge: *the issue of blood.* **4.** Way out; outlet; exit. **5.** Result; outcome. **6.** Point to be debated; problem. **7.** Child or children; offspring. [fr L *ex* out + *ire* go]

j

- **judicious** /jü dish' əs/ *adj.* Having, using, or showing good judgment; wise; sensible. [fr L *judicium* judgment]

k

- **kerosene** /ker' ə sēn/ *or* /ker' ə sēn'/ *n.* Coal oil used in lamps and stoves. [US < Gk *keros* wax]
- **kimono** /kə mō' nə/ *or* /kə mō' nō/ *n.* A loose outer garment held in place by a sash, worn by Japanese persons. *pl.* **kimonos.** [fr Jp]

l

- **laborious** /lə bôr' ē əs/ *adj.* **1.** Requiring much work: *Climbing a mountain is laborious.* **2.** Hard-working; industrious: *Bees and ants are laborious insects.* **3.** Not easy. [fr L *labor* labor]
- **larva** /lär' və/ *n.* **1.** The early form of an insect: *A caterpillar is the larva of a butterfly.* **2.** An immature form of a certain animal that is different in structure from the adult form. *pl.* **larvae** /lär' vē'/. [fr L *larva* ghost]

- **league** /lēg/ *n.* **1.** Association of persons, parties, or countries formed to help one another. **2.** An association of baseball clubs, football clubs, hockey clubs, etc. **3.** Persons or parties associated in a league. —*v.* Form a league. **leagued, leaguing.** [fr OF *ligue* bind]
- **legible** /lej' ə bəl/ *adj.* Easy to read; plain and clear: *Her handwriting is both beautiful and legible.* [fr L *legere* read]
- **leisure** /lē' zhər/ *n.* Time free from required work or employment; convenience. —*adj.* Free; not busy: *The boys devoted most of their leisure time to sports.* [fr L *licere* be permitted]
- **libel** /lī' bəl/ *n.* **1.** Written statements tending to damage a person's reputation. **2.** Crime of writing or printing a libel. **3.** Any false or damaging statement about a person. —*v.* Make or write false or damaging statements about. [fr L *libellus,* diminutive of *liber* book]
- **licorice** /lik' ə ris, lik' ə rish/ *or* /lik' ris, lik' rish/ *n.* **1.** Sweet, black gummy extract used as a flavoring. **2.** Candy flavored with this extract. [fr Gk *glykys* sweet + *rhiza* root]
- **ligament** /lig' ə mənt/ *n.* Band of strong tissue which connects bones or holds organs of the body in place. [fr L *ligare* bind]
- **logical** /loj' ə kəl/ *adj.* **1.** Having to do with logic; according to the principles of logic. **2.** Reasonable; reasonably expected. **3.** Reasoning correctly: *a logical person.* [fr Gk *logos* reason]

m

- **magnificent** /mag nif' ə sənt/ *adj.* **1.** Richly colored or decorated. **2.** Splendid; noble. [fr L *magnificus* noble in character, fr *magnus* great]
- **malicious** /mə lish' əs/ *adj.* Showing active ill will; spiteful. [fr L *malus* evil]
- **malign** /mə līn'/ *v.* Speak evil of: *They malign him with their constant gossip.* —*adj.* **1.** Evil; injurious. **2.** Hateful. [fr L *malus* bad + *genus* kind]
- **massage** /mə säzh'/ *n.* A rubbing and kneading of the muscles and joints to make them work better and to increase the circulation of the blood. —*v.* Give a massage to. **massaged, massaging.** [fr F, fr *masse* mass]
- **mature** /ma tür'/ *or* /mə tür'/ *adj.* **1.** Ripe; full-grown: *The apples reached a mature stage.* **2.** Fully developed; well thought out:

Her mature plans led to success. — v. **1.** Work out or develop carefully. **2.** Due or payable. **matured, maturing.** [fr L *maturus* mature]

● **maximum** /mak' sə məm/ n. The largest or highest amount. pl. **maximums** or **maxima** /mak' sə mə/. — adj. Largest; highest; greatest possible: *The maximum score on the test is 100.* [fr L *maximum* greatest]

● **mechanic** /mə kan' ik/ n. **1.** Worker skilled with tools. **2.** Worker who repairs machinery. [fr L *mechanicus* mechanic < Gk *mechane* machine]

● **medieval** /mē' dē ē' vəl/ adj. Having to do with the Middle Ages (the years from about 500 to 1500 A.D.). Also spelled **mediaeval.** [fr L *medium* middle + *aevum* age]

● **medium** /mē' dē əm/ adj. Having a middle position, quality, or condition. — n. **1.** That which is in the middle. **2.** Subject or agent through which anything acts; a means: *The telephone is a medium of communication.* **3.** Substance in which something can live. **4.** Liquid with which paints are mixed. **5.** Person through whom supposed messages from the spirit world are sent. pl. **mediums** or **media** /mē' dē ə/. [fr L *medius* middle]

● **memento** /mə men' tō/ n. Thing serving as remembrance, warning, or reminder: *These post cards are mementos of our trip.* pl. **mementos, mementoes.** [fr L *memento* I remember]

● **memo**/mem' ō/ n. Memorandum. pl **memos.** [fr L *memorandum* thing to be remembered]

● **memoir** /mem' wär/ or /mem' wôr/ n. **1.** Autobiography: *Her memoirs are a personal account of her life.* **2.** A record of a person's own experiences. **3.** Biography. [fr F < L *memor* mindful]

● **migrate** /mī' grāt/ v. **1.** Move from one place to settle in another. **2.** Go from one region to another with the change of seasons: *Birds may migrate to warmer countries in the winter.* **migrated, migrating.** [fr L *migrare* migrate]

● **mimic** /mim' ik/ v. **1.** Make fun of by imitating. **2.** Copy closely: *A parrot can mimic a person's voice.* **mimicked, mimicking.** — n. Person that imitates. — adj. **1.** Imitative. **2.** Not real, but pretended. [fr L *mimicus* mimic]

● **minimum** /min' ə mum/ n. The least; smallest amount: *The minimum is ten dollars.* — adj. The smallest: *The minimum amount you may pay on the bill is ten dollars.* pl. **minimums** or **minima** /min' ə mə/. [fr L *minimum* smallest thing]

● **mirage** /mə räzh'/ n. **1.** Misleading appearance, usually in the desert or at sea. **2.** Illusion; thing that does not exist. [fr F, fr *mirer* look at carefully, *se mirer* see reflected in a mirror]

● **miscellaneous** /mis' ə lā' nē əs/ adj. Not all of one kind or nature: *a miscellaneous collection of trinkets.* [fr L *miscere* mix]

● **missile** /mis' əl/ n. Object that is thrown or shot such as a stone, bullet, rocket, arrow, etc. [fr L *missilis,* fr *mittere* send]

● **moccasin** /mok' ə sən/ n. **1.** A soft-leather heelless shoe or sandal. **2.** A poisonous snake found in the southern part of the United States. [fr Am Ind (Algonquian)]

● **molasses** /mə las' əs/ n. A sweet syrup obtained in making sugar from sugar cane. [fr L *mel* honey]

● **morgue** /môrg/ n. **1.** Place in which the bodies of unknown dead persons are kept until identified. **2.** In a newspaper office, the reference library. [fr F]

● **morphine** /môr' fēn'/ n. Drug made from opium, used to dull pain and cause sleep. [fr Gk *Morpheus* Morpheus, the god of sleep]

● **mortal** /môr' təl/ adj. **1.** Sure to die sometime. **2.** Of humans. **3.** Of death. **4.** Causing death: *a mortal wound.* **5.** Causing death of the soul: *a mortal sin.* **6.** Deadly: *mortal fear.* — n. **1.** A being that is sure to die sometime. **2.** A human being. [fr L *mors* death]

● **mosque** /mosk/ n. A Moslem place of worship. [fr F < Ar *masjid* mosque]

● **motto** /mot' ō/ n. **1.** A brief sentence adapted as a rule of conduct: *"Think before you speak,"* is a good motto. **2.** Sentence, word, or phrase written or engraved on some object. pl. **mottoes, mottos.** [fr L *muttum* grunt, word]

● **myth** /mith/ n. **1.** Legend or story, usually attempting to account for something in nature: *The myth of Persephone is an attempt to explain the seasons.* **2.** An imaginary person

---

/a/ ran   /ā/ rain   /ã/ care   /ä/ car   /e/ hen   /ē/ he   /ėr/ her   /i/ in   /ī/ ice   /o/ not   /ō/ no   /ô/ off
/u/ us   /ū/ use   /ü/ tool   /ů/ took   /ou/ cow   /oi/ boy   /ch/ church   /hw/ when   /ng/ sing   /sh/ ship
/ŦH/ this   /th/ thin   /zh/ vision   /ə/ about, taken, pencil, lemon, circus

or thing: *Her rich uncle was only a myth.* [fr Gk *mythos* story]

n

- **necessity** /nə ses′ ə tē/ *n.* **1.** Fact or quality of being necessary. **2.** That which cannot be done without: *Food is a necessity.* **3.** That which forces people to act in a certain way. **4.** That which is inevitable: *the necessity of death.* **5.** Need; poverty. *pl.* **necessities.** [fr L *necesse* necessary, fr *ne* not + *cedere* withdraw]
- **negligent** /neg′ lə jənt/ *adj.* **1.** Neglectful. **2.** careless; indifferent. [fr L *neglectus* neglect]
- **neigh** /nā/ *n.* Sound that a horse makes. —*v.* Make the sound that a horse makes. [fr OE *hnaegan* neigh]
- **nominate** /nom′ ə nāt′/ *v.* **1.** Name as candidate for an office. **2.** Appoint to an office or duty. **nominated, nominating.** [fr L *nomere* name]
- **nomination** /nom′ ə nā′ shən/ *n.* **1.** A naming as a candidate for office. **2.** Selection or appointment for office or duty. **3.** A being nominated. [fr L *nomen* name]
- **notorious** /nō tô′ rē əs/ *or* /nō tō′ rē əs/ *adj.* **1.** Well-known because of something bad; having a bad reputation: *a notorious thief.* **2.** Well-known: *a notorious book.* [fr L *notus* known]
- **nucleus** /nü′ klē əs/ *or* /nū′ klē əs/ *n.* **1.** A beginning to which additions are made. **2.** Central part of an atom. **3.** Central part around which other parts are collected. **4.** In biology, an active body in the protoplasm of a cell, without which the cell cannot grow and divide. *pl.* **nucleuses** *or* **nuclei** /nü′ klē ī, nū′ klē ī/. [fr L *nucleus* fr *nux* nut]
- **nutritious** /nü trish′ əs/ *or* /nū trish′ əs/ *adj.* Valuable as food; nourishing. [fr L *nutrix* nurse]

o

- **oasis** /ō ā′ sis/ *n.* A fertile or green spot in a desert. *pl.* **oases** /ō ā′ sēz′/. [fr Gk]
- **oblique** /ō blēk′/ *adj.* **1.** Not straight; slanting: *oblique lines.* **2.** Not straightforward; indirect: *an oblique answer.* —*v.* Advance in an oblique manner; slant. **obliqued, obliquing.** [fr F < L *obliquus* oblique]
- **observe** /əb zėrv′/ *v.* **1.** See and note; notice.

2. Study; examine for a specific purpose. **3.** Remark: *"Bad weather," she observed.* **4.** Keep: *observe silence; observe a rule.* **5.** Celebrate: *observe a holiday.* **observed, observing.** [fr L *ob* over + *servare* keep watch]
- **obvious** /ob′ vē əs/ *adj.* Easily seen and understood; plain: *It is obvious that two and two make four.* [fr L *ob* in the way of + *via* way]
- **occasion** /ə kā′ zhən/ *n.* **1.** A particular time. **2.** A special event. **3.** A good chance; opportunity. **4.** Cause; reason: *The boy who was the occasion of the quarrel ran away.* —*v.* Cause; bring about. [fr L *ob* in the way of + *cadere* fall]
- **occupation** /ok′ ū pā′ shən/ *n.* **1.** Business; employment. **2.** Being occupied. [fr L *occupatio* a taking possession, fr *occupare* take into possession]
- **occupy** /ok′ ū pī′/ *v.* **1.** Take up; fill. **2.** Keep busy; engage. **3.** Take possession of. **4.** Hold; have in use; live in; keep possession of. **occupied, occupying.** [fr L *occupare* take into possession]
- **occur** /ə kėr′/ *v.* **1.** Take place; happen: *Storms occur in the winter.* **2.** Come to mind: *What answer occurs to you?* **occurred, occurring.** [fr L *ob* in the way of + *currere* run]
- **offense** /ə fens′/ *n.* **1.** A breaking of the law. **2.** Cause of wrongdoing. **3.** Condition of being offended; hurt feelings. **4.** Act of offending. **5.** Attack; assault: *A gun was the weapon of offense.* [fr L *ob* in the way of + *fendere* strike]
- **opinion** /ə pin′ yən/ *n.* **1.** Belief not so strong as knowledge; judgment. **2.** Impression. **3.** A formal judgment by an expert; professional advice. [fr L *opinio* opinion, belief]
- **opossum** /ə pos′ əm/ *n.* A small mammal that lives mostly in trees, common in the United States. [fr Am Ind word meaning "white animal"]
- **opponent** /ə pō′ nənt/ *adj.* Opposing; opposite. —*n.* Person who is on the other side in a game, fight, discussion, etc.: *The tennis player faced her opponent.* [fr L *ob* in the way of + *ponere* place]
- **oppose** /ə pōz′/ *v.* **1.** Be against; be in the way of; try to hinder; resist. **2.** Set up against; place in the way of. **3.** Put in contrast: *Night is opposed to day.* **opposed, opposing.** [fr L *ob* in the way of + *ponere* place]
- **oppress** /ə pres′/ *v.* **1.** Govern harshly: *The*

wicked ruler oppressed the poor. **2.** Burden; weigh down: *oppressed by debts.* [fr L *ob* in the way of + *premere* press]

● **orchid** /ôr′ kid/ *n.* **1.** Plant with beautiful, queerly shaped flowers. **2.** Flowers of this plant. **3.** A light purple color. —*adj.* Light-purple. [fr L *orchideae* orchid]

● **orphan** /or′ fən/ *n.* Child whose parents are dead. —*adj.* **1.** Of or for such a child or children: *an orphan home.* **2.** Without a father or mother or both. —*v.* Make an orphan of: *She was orphaned at an early age.* [fr Gk *orphanos* orphan]

p

● **pageant** /paj′ ənt/ *n.* **1.** An elaborate spectacle; procession in costume; pomp; display. **2.** A public entertainment that represents scenes from history or legend. [fr ME *pagen* a movable stage]

● **paraffin** /par′ ə fin/ *n.* A white or colorless, tasteless substance, obtained from crude petroleum and used for making candles, sealing jars, etc. —*v.* Treat or test with a paraffin substance. [fr L *parum* too little + *affinis* bordering on]

● **parallel** /par′ ə lel′/ *adj.* **1.** At or being the same distance apart everywhere. **2.** Similar. —*n.* **1.** A parallel line or surface. **2.** In geography, lines parallel to the equator, marking degrees of latitude. **3.** Thing like another. **4.** Comparison: *draw a parallel between two men.* —*v.* **1.** Be at the same distance from: *This street parallels the river.* **2.** Be like to: *Her story parallels his.* **3.** Find a case similar to: *Can you parallel this story?* **4.** Compare in order to show likeness. [fr Gk *para* beside + *allelois* one another]

● **parcel** /pär′ səl/ *n.* **1.** Package; bundle. **2.** Piece: *a parcel of land.* **3.** A collection. —*v.* **1.** To divide and distribute by parts: *to parcel out supplies.* **2.** To make up into a parcel. [fr L *particula* small part]

● **parenthesis** /pə ren′ thə sis′/ *n.* **1.** Word, phrase, sentence, etc., inserted within a sentence to explain or qualify something. **2.** Either or both of two curved lines [( )] used to set off such an expression. *pl.* **parenthe-**

ses /pə ren′ thə sēz′/. [fr Gk *para* beside + *en* in + *thesis* a placing]

● **patient** /pā′ shənt/ *adj.* **1.** Enduring pain, trouble, etc., calmly. **2.** Long-suffering. **3.** With steady effort or hard work. —*n.* Person being treated by a doctor. [fr L *pati* suffer]

● **penitent** /pen′ ə tənt/ *adj.* Sorry for doing wrong. —*n.* Person who is sorry for wrong-doing. [fr L *paenitere* repent]

● **pennant** /pen′ ənt/ *n.* A flag, usually long and narrow, used for signaling on ships; a school banner. [fr L *penne* feather]

● **perceive** /pər sēv′/ *v.* **1.** Be aware of through the senses; hear, feel, see, taste, or smell. **2.** Take in with the mind; observe: *I perceived that she would not change her mind.* **perceived, perceiving.** [fr L *per* through + *capere* grasp]

● **peril** /per′ əl/ *n.* Danger. —*v.* Put in danger. [fr F < L *periculum* danger]

● **permanent** /per′ mə nənt/ *adj.* Intended to last; not for a short time only. —*n. informal.* Permanent wave. [fr L *per* through + *manere* remain]

● **persistent** /pər sis′ tənt/ *adj.* **1.** Not giving up, especially in the face of difficulties. **2.** Going on; continuing; lasting: *a persistent headache.* [fr L *per* through + *sistere* stand firm]

● **perspire** /pər spīr′/ *v.* Sweat. **perspired, perspiring.** [fr L *per* through + *spirare* breathe]

● **pheasant** /fez′ ənt/ *n.* A game bird with a long tail and brilliant feathers, found in many parts of Europe and America. [fr Gk *phasianos* Phasian, a reference to the River Phasis in Colchis]

● **physique** /fə zēk′/ *v.* Body; bodily structure: *a person of strong physique.* [fr F *physique* physical]

● **pier** /pir/ *n.* **1.** A support for a bridge span. **2.** A breakwater; a structure supported on columns extending into the water and used as a walk or a landing place. **3.** Solid part of a wall between windows, doors, etc. [fr ME *pere* a support < OF *puiere* a support]

● **pimento** /pə men′ tō/ *n.* Kind of pepper used as vegetable, relish, etc. *pl.* **pimentos.** [fr Sp]

● **pinto** /pin′ tō/ *n.* A pinto horse. *pl.* **pintos.** —*adj.* Spotted in two colors: *a pinto pony.* [US < Sp *pintado* painted]

/a/ ran /ā/ rain /ā/ care /ä/ car /e/ hen /ē/ he /ėr/ her /i/ in /ī/ ice /o/ not /ō/ no /ô/ off /u/ us /ū/ use /ü/ tool /u/ took /ou/ cow /oi/ boy /ch/ church /hw/ when /ng/ sing /sh/ ship /ᵺ/ this /th/ thin /zh/ vision /ə/ about, taken, pencil, lemon, circus

- **pique** /pēk/ *n.* Feeling of wounded pride: *She left the party in a pique after the argument.* —*v.* **1.** Wound the pride of. **2.** Stir up: *Their curiosity was piqued by the locked trunk.* **piqued, piquing.** [fr F *piquer* prick, sting]

- **piteous** /pit' ē əs/ *adj.* To be pitied; moving the heart: *a piteous child begging for food.* [fr OF *pitos* pity < L *pietosus* pitiful]

- **plague** /plāg/ *n.* **1.** Dangerous disease that spreads rapidly and often causes death. **2.** Thing or person that vexes, offends, annoys, or troubles. —*v.* Annoy; vex; bother. **plagued, plaguing.** [fr L *plaga* pestilence]

- **planetarium** /plan' ə tãr' ē əm/ *n.* **1.** Apparatus that shows the movement of the sun, moon, stars, and planets. **2.** Room or building with such an apparatus. *pl.* **planetariums** or **planetaria** /plan' ə tãr' ē ə/. [fr Gk *planetes* planet + *aer* air]

- **plaque** /plak/ *n.* An ornamental tablet of metal, porcelain, etc. [fr F < D *plak* flat board]

- **plateau** /pla tō'/ *n.* A large, high plain above sea level; tableland. *pl.* **plateaus** or **plateaux** /pla tō'/. [fr F *plat* a flat thing]

- **pneumatic** /nü mat' ik/ *or* /nū mat' ik/ *adj.* **1.** Containing air: *a pneumatic tire.* **2.** Worked by air: *a pneumatic drill.* **3.** Having to do with air and other gases. [fr Gk *pneuma* wind]

- **pneumonia** /nü mōn' yə/ *or* /nū mōn' yə/ *n.* Disease in which the lungs are inflamed. [fr Gk *pneumon* lung]

- **porcelain** /pôr' səl ən/ *or* /pôrs' lən/ *n.* Very fine earthenware; china. [fr F < It *porcellana* a kind of shell]

- **pore**[1] /pôr/ *or* /pōr/ *n.* A very small opening: *Sweat comes through pores in the skin.* [fr Gk *poros* passage]

- **pore**[2] /pôr/ *or* /pōr/ *v.* **1.** Gaze earnestly or steadily: *He pored in wonder at the beautiful scenery.* **2.** Study long and steadily: *The student pored over his books.* **pored, poring.** [Origin uncertain.]

- **possess** /pə zes'/ *v.* **1.** Own; have: *Washington possessed great wisdom.* **2.** Hold as property. **3.** Control; influence strongly. **4.** Control by an evil spirit: *He fought like one possessed.* [fr L *possidere* possess]

- **prance** /prans/ *v.* **1.** Spring about on the hind legs: *horses prancing in a parade.* **2.** Ride on a horse doing this. **3.** Move proudly; swagger. **4.** Caper; dance. **pranced, prancing.** —*n.* Riding or moving proudly. [Origin uncertain.]

- **precious** /presh' əs/ *adj.* **1.** Valuable; costly. **2.** Much loved; dear. **3.** Too nice; overrefined. —*adv. Informal.* Very: *He had precious little money.* [fr L *pretium* price, value]

- **precipice** /pres' ə pis/ *n.* A very steep cliff. [fr L *praeceps* steep, fr *prae* first + *caput* head]

- **premier**[1] /prə mir'/ *or* /prē' mē ər/ *n.* Prime minister. [fr L *primus* first]

- **premier**[2] /prē' mē ər/ *or* /prēm' yər/ *adj.* **1.** Chief: *a premier commander.* **2.** Earliest: *the premier performance of a play.* [See **premier**[1].]

- **preside** /prē zīd'/ *v.* **1.** Hold the place of authority; have charge of a meeting. **2.** Have authority; have control: *The owner presides over the office of the company.* **presided, presiding.** [fr L *praesedere* sit before]

- **prestige** /pres tēzh'/ *or* /pres' tij/ *n.* Reputation or distinction based on what is known of one's abilities, achievements, etc. [fr F *prestige* magic spell]

- **privacy** /prī' və sē/ *n.* **1.** Condition of being away from others. **2.** Absence of publicity; secrecy: *He told his secret in strict privacy.* [fr L *privatus* apart from the State]

- **proficient** /prō fish' ənt/ *adj.* Skilled; expert: *proficient in music.* [fr L *pro* onward + *facere* make]

- **prominent** /prom' ə nənt/ *adj.* **1.** Well-known; important. **2.** Easy to see; conspicuous; noticeable. **3.** Standing out; projecting: *The beautiful Ozark Mountains were prominent on the horizon.* [fr L *prominere* jut out, project]

- **prophet** /prof' ət/ *n.* **1.** Person who foretells what will happen. **2.** Person who preaches what he thinks has been revealed to him. [fr Gk *pro* before + *phanai* speak]

- **protein** /prō' tēn/ *n.* A complex compound which contains nitrogen and which is a necessary part of the cells of animals and plants. [fr Gk *proteios* primary, fr *protos* first]

- **psalm** /säm/ *or* /sälm/ *n.* A sacred song or poem. [fr Gk *psalmos* performance on a stringed instrument]

- **psychiatrist** /sī kī' ə trist/ *or* /si kī' ə trist/ *n.* Doctor who treats mental diseases. [fr Gk *psyche* mind + *iatreia* cure]

- **psychology** /sī kol' ə jē/ *n.* **1.** The science of the mind. **2.** The mental state and processes of a person or persons; mental nature and behavior: *She understood her son's psychol-*

ogy. *pl.* **psychologies.** [fr Gk *psyche* soul + *logos* teaching]

- **pueblo** /pweb′ lō/ *n.* An American Indian village built of adobe and stone. *pl.* **pueblos.** [fr Sp < fr L *populus* people]
- **pupa** /pū′ pə/ *n.* **1.** Stage between the larva and the adult in the development of many insects. **2.** Form of the insect in this stage. *pl.* **pupas** or **pupae** /pū′ pē′/. [fr L *pupa,* originally, "doll"]
- **pygmy** /pig′ mē/ *n.* A very small person; dwarf. *pl.* **pygmies.** —*adj.* Very small. Also spelled **pigmy.** [fr Gk *pygmaioi* dwarfish]
- **pyramid** /pir′ ə mid/ *n.* **1.** A solid having triangular sides meeting in a point. **2.** Thing having the shape of a pyramid. —*v.* **1.** Be or put in the form of a pyramid; heap up. **2.** Raise or increase costs, etc., gradually. [probably fr Egyptian *pi-mar* the pyramid]
- **python** /pī′ thon/ or /pī′ thən/ *n.* **1.** Any of several large snakes of the Eastern Hemisphere that are related to the boas and kill their prey by crushing. **2.** Any large boa. [fr Gk *python* python]

q

- **quartette** /kwôr tet′/ *n.* **1.** Group of four singers or players performing together. **2.** Piece of music for four voices or instruments. **3.** Any group of four. [fr L *quartus* fourth]
- **quotient** /kwō′ shənt/ *n.* Number obtained by dividing one number by another. [fr L *quotiens* how many times]

r

- **rabbi** /rab′ ī/ *n.* Pastor or teacher of the Jewish religion. *pl.* **rabbis, rabbies.** [fr Hebrew *rabbi* my master]
- **radius** /rā′ dē əs/ *n.* **1.** Any line going straight from the center to the outside of a circle or sphere. **2.** A circular area measured by the length of its radius: *The explosion could be heard within a radius of ten miles. pl.* **radiuses** or **radii** /rā′ dē ī′/. [fr L *radius* ray, spoke of a wheel]
- **reasonable** /rē′ zən ə bəl/ *adj.* **1.** Sensible; not foolish. **2.** Not asking too much; fair. **3.** Not costing too much; inexpensive. **4.** Able to reason. [fr L *ratio* reason]
- **receipt** /rē sēt′/ *n.* **1.** A writing that acknowledges the receiving of goods, letters, or money. **2.** A receiving. **3.** Recipe. —*v.* Mark as paid or received. [fr L *recipere* receive, fr *re* back + *capere* take]
- **recess** /rē′ ses/ or /rə ses′/ *n.* **1.** Time during which work stops: *a short recess before the next meeting.* **2.** Alcove; niche. **3.** Inner place or part: *the dark recesses of the cave.* —*v.* **1.** Take a recess: *The class recessed for lunch.* **2.** Set back; put in a recess. [fr L *re* back + *cedere* go]
- **recipe** /res′ ə pē/ *n.* **1.** Set of directions for preparing food. **2.** Set of directions for preparing anything. [fr L *receptus* a receiving]
- **recite** /rē sīt′/ *v.* **1.** Say over; repeat: *recite a lesson.* **2.** Give an account of in detail: *recite one's experiences.* **3.** Repeat a poem, speech, etc., in order to entertain. **recited, reciting.** [fr L *re* again + *citere* appeal to]
- **regulate** /reg′ ū lāt′/ *v.* **1.** Control by rule, principle, or system: *The school strongly regulates the students' behavior at recess.* **2.** Put in condition to work properly. **3.** Keep at some standard: *The dial regulates the volume of the music.* **regulated, regulating.** [fr L *regula* rule]
- **reign** /rān/ *n.* **1.** The time during which a ruler is in power: *The king's reign lasted twenty years.* **2.** Royal power; rule: *The reign of an unwise king ruins his country.* **3.** Prevalence. —*v.* **1.** Be a ruler. **2.** Prevail. [fr L *regere* guide, rule, fr *regnare* reign, fr *rex* king]
- **rein** /rān/ *n.* **1.** Long, narrow strap fastened to a bridle or bit, by which to guide and control an animal. **2.** A means of control: *the reins of government.* —*v.* **1.** Check or pull with reins. **2.** Guide and control: *Rein your tongue.* [fr OF *rene* rein < L *retinere* hold back]
- **rely** /rē lī′/ *v.* Depend; trust: *Rely on your own efforts.* **relied, relying.** [fr L *re* back + *legare* bind]
- **repent** /rē pent′/ *v.* **1.** Feel sorry for having done wrong and seek forgiveness. **2.** Feel sorry for; regret: *They repented their choice.* [fr L *re* again + *poenitere* make repent]

/a/ ran /ā/ rain /ā/ care /ä/ car /e/ hen /ē/ he /ėr/ her /i/ in /ī/ ice /o/ not /ō/ no /ô/ off
/u/ us /ū/ use /ü/ tool /u̇/ took /ou/ cow /oi/ boy /ch/ church /hw/ when /ng/ sing /sh/ ship
/ᵺ/ this /th/ thin /zh/ vision /ə/ about, taken, pencil, lemon, circus

- **repertoire** /rep′ ər twär/ *n.* List of plays, operas, parts, pieces, etc., that a company, artist, or performer is prepared to perform. [fr F *repertoire* catalogue or list, repertoire]
- **reprieve** /rē prēv′/ *v.* 1. Delay the execution of (a person condemned to death). 2. Give relief from evil or trouble. **reprieved, reprieving.** —*n.* 1. Delay in carrying out punishment, especially of the death penalty. 2. Temporary relief. [fr L *re* back + *prehendere* grasp]
- **reserve** /rē zėrv′/ *v.* 1. Keep or hold back. 2. Set apart; save for later use. **reserved, reserving.** —*n.* 1. Anything kept back for future use; extra supply. 2. Public land set apart for a special purpose. 3. Self-restraint in action or speech. 4. Soldiers kept ready to help the main army in battle when needed. 5. Actual cash in a bank or assets that can be turned into cash. [fr L *re* back + *servare* keep]
- **reservoir** /rez′ ər vwär/ *n.* 1. Place where water is collected and stored for use. 2. Anything to hold a liquid. 3. Place where anything is collected and stored. 4. A great supply. [fr F, fr *reserver* keep in store]
- **resident** /rez′ ə dənt/ *n.* Person living in a place permanently; dweller. —*adj.* 1. Staying; dwelling in a place: *a resident owner.* 2. Living in a place while on duty or doing active work: *She is a resident physician at the clinic.* [fr L *residere* sit back, remain]
- **resistible** /rē zis′ tə bəl/ *adj.* Capable of being resisted. [fr L *re* again + *sistere* take a stand]
- **responsible** /rē spon′ sə bəl/ *adj.* 1. Obliged or expected to account for; accountable; answerable: *You are responsible for your own schedule.* 2. Deserving credit or blame: *The snow was responsible for three accidents on the street.* 3. Trustworthy; reliable. 4. Involving obligation or duties. [fr L *respondere* reply]
- **retrieve** /rē trēv′/ *v.* 1. Get again; recover. 2. Restore: *retrieve one's fortune.* 3. Make amends for: *retrieve a mistake; retrieve a loss.* 4. Find and bring to a person: *The hunting dog retrieved game for his master.* **retrieved, retrieving.** [fr OF *re* again + *trouver* find]
- **reverent** /rev′ ər ənt/ *adj.* Feeling respect; showing awe. [fr L *re* again + *vereri* fear]
- **rhetoric** /ret′ ə rik/ *n.* 1. Art of using words in speaking or writing. 2. Mere display of language. [fr Gk *rhetor* orator]

- **rheumatism** /rü′ mə tiz′ əm/ *n.* Disease with inflammation, swelling, and stiffness of the joints. [fr Gk *rheuma* a flux]
- **rhubarb** /rü′ bärb/ *n.* A garden plant with very large leaves, whose sour stalks are used for sauce, in pies, etc. [fr Gk *rha* rhubarb]
- **rhythm** /riŦH′ əm/ *n.* 1. Movement with a regular beat, accent, rise, and fall. 2. The repetition of an accent; pattern of beats in a line of poetry. 3. Regular grouping by accents or beats. [fr Gk *rhythmos* measured motion, measure, proportion]
- **rinse** /rins/ *v.* 1. Wash with clean water. 2. Wash lightly. **rinsed, rinsing.** —*n.* A rinsing. [fr L *recens* fresh]
- **rodeo** /rō′ dē ō′/ *or* /rō dā′ ō/ *n.* 1. A public performance showing skill in roping cattle, riding horses, etc. 2. In western North America, a roundup of cattle. *pl.* **rodeos.** [fr Sp *rodear* surround]
- **rouge** /rüzh/ *n.* 1. Red powder, paste, or liquid for coloring the cheeks or lips. 2. Red powder used for polishing metals, jewels, etc. —*v.* Color with rouge. **rouged, rouging.** [fr F *rouge* red]
- **route** /rüt/ *or* /rout/ *n.* The way to go; road. —*v.* Arrange the route for; send by a certain route. **routed, routing.** [fr OF *rupta* a way]

s

- **satellite** /sat′ əl īt′/ *n.* 1. A small planet that revolves around a larger planet. 2. A sphere or other object launched into orbit around the earth. 3. Follower or attendant upon a person of importance. 4. Country actually controlled by a more powerful country. [fr L *satelles* attendant]
- **scandal** /skan′ dəl/ *n.* 1. A shameful action that brings disgrace. 2. Disgrace; damage to reputation. 3. Evil gossip; slander. [fr Gk *skandalon* trap]
- **scent** /sent/ *n.* 1. Smell: *the scent of roses.* 2. Sense of smell: *a keen scent.* 3. Smell left in passing: *The dogs followed the fox by scent.* 4. Perfume. —*v.* 1. Smell: *The dogs scented the rabbit.* 2. Fill with odor. 3. Be aware of; have suspicion of: *He scented the man's fear.* [fr OF *sentir* smell]
- **scepter** /sep′ tər/ *n.* 1. The rod or staff carried by a ruler as a symbol of royal power. 2. Royal power or authority. [fr Gk *skeptron* staff]

- **schedule** /skej′ ŭl/ *n.* **1.** A written or printed statement of details; a list. **2.** A timetable. —*v.* **1.** Make a schedule of. **2.** *Informal.* Plan or arrange something for a future date. **scheduled, scheduling.** [fr L *schedula* slip of paper]
- **scheme** /skēm/ *n.* **1.** A plan; program of action. **2.** A plot. **3.** System of connected things, parts, thoughts, etc.: *The color scheme of the room was beautiful.* —*v.* Plan; plot. **schemed, scheming.** [fr Gk *schema* shape, outline]
- **scholar** /skol′ ər/ *n.* **1.** A learned person. **2.** A pupil at school; a learner. [fr L *schola* school]
- **scorpion** /skôr′ pē ən/ *n.* **1.** A small animal belonging to the same family as the spider and having a poisonous sting in its tail. **2.** A whip. [fr L *scorpio* scorpion]
- **scythe** /sīᴛʜ/ *n.* Long, slightly curved blade on a long handle, used for cutting grass, etc. [fr OF *sithe* scythe]
- **seize** /sēz/ *v.* **1.** Take hold of suddenly; clutch; grab: *She seized his arm.* **2.** Grasp with the mind: *seized the idea.* **3.** Take possession of by force: *seize the fortress.* **4.** Come upon suddenly: *Fear seized him.* **seized, seizing.** [fr OF *seisir* seize]
- **seizure** /sē′ zhər/ *n.* **1.** Act of clutching; grasping; taking possession of; act of seizing. **2.** Condition of being seized. **3.** Sudden attack of illness: *a seizure of influenza.* [fr OF *seisir* seize]
- **serious** /sir′ ē əs/ *adj.* **1.** Thoughtful; grave. **2.** Not joking; sincere; in earnest. **3.** Important; needing thought. **4.** Important because it may do much harm; dangerous. [fr L *serius* grave, earnest]
- **serum** /sir′ əm/ *n.* **1.** A clear, pale-yellow part of the blood. **2.** Liquid used to prevent or cure a disease. **3.** Whey. *pl.* **serums** or **sera** /sir′ ə/. [fr L *serum whey*]
- **sheaf** /shēf/ *n.* Bundle of things of the same kind bound together or arranged so that they can be bound together: *a sheaf of wheat.* *pl.* **sheaves.** [fr OE *sceaf* sheaf]
- **sheik** /shēk/ *n.* An Arab chief or head of a tribe or village. [fr Ar *shaikh,* originally, "old man"]
- **sheriff** /sher′ if/ *n.* The chief law enforcement officer of a county or other community. [fr OE *scir* shire + *gerefa* reeve]
- **shriek** /shrēk/ *n.* **1.** A loud, shrill sound: *The engine whistle shrieked in the night.* **2.** A loud shrill laugh. —*v.* **1.** Make a loud, sharp, shrill sound because of terror, pain, anger, amusement, etc. **2.** Utter loudly and shrilly. [akin to Scandinavian *skraekja* shriek, scream]
- **siege** /sēj/ *n.* **1.** The surrounding of a fortified place by the army trying to capture it. **2.** Any long and persistent effort to overcome resistance; a long-continuing attack: *a siege of illness.* —*v.* Besiege; attempt to get by long and persistent effort. **sieged, sieging.** [fr OF *siege* seat]
- **sieve** /siv/ *n.* Utensil having holes that let liquids and smaller pieces pass through, but not the larger pieces: *Shake the flour through the sieve to remove the lumps.* —*v.* Put through a sieve. **sieved, sieving.** [fr OE *sife* sieve]
- **silhouette** /sil′ ü et′/ *n.* **1.** An outline portrait cut out of black paper or filled in with some single color. **2.** A dark image outlined against a lighter background. —*v.* Show in outline: *The mountain was silhouetted against the sky.* **silhouetted, silhouetting.** [Named after E. de Silhouette (1709–1767), French politician.]
- **silo** /sī′ lō/ *n.* An airtight building or pit in which green food for farm animals is stored. *pl.* **silos.** [fr Gk *siros* graincellar]
- **similar** /sim′ ə lər/ *adj.* **1.** Much the same; alike: *A crayon and a pencil are similar.* **2.** In geometry, having the same shape: *similar triangles.* [fr L *similis* like, similar]
- **situate** /sich′ ü āt′/ *v.* Place or locate. **situated, situating.** [fr L *situs* place]
- **situation** /sich′ ū ā′ shən/ *n.* **1.** Position; place. **2.** Circumstances; case; condition. **3.** Job; place to work. [fr L *situs* place, situation]
- **sleigh** /slā/ *n.* Carriage or cart mounted on runners for use on ice or snow. —*v.* Travel by sleigh; ride in a sleigh. [fr D *slee* sled]
- **sombrero** /som brâr′ ō/ *n.* Broad-brimmed hat worn in the Southwest, Mexico, and South America. *pl.* **sombreros.** [fr Sp < L *sub* under + *umbra* shade]
- **soprano** /sə pran′ ō/ *n.* **1.** Highest singing voice in women or boys. **2.** Singer with such a

/a/ ran /ā/ rain /ã/ care /ä/ car /e/ hen /ē/ he /ėr/ her /i/ in /ī/ ice /o/ not /ō/ no /ô/ off
/u/ us /ū/ use /ü/ tool /u̇/ took /ou/ cow /oi/ boy /ch/ church /hw/ when /ng/ sing /sh/ ship
/ᴛʜ/ this /th/ thin /zh/ vision /ə/ about, taken, pencil, lemon, circus

voice. **3.** Part sung by soprano voice. *pl.* **sopranos.** —*adj.* Of or having to do with a soprano. [fr L *supra* on the top, above]

- **source** /sôrs/ *or* /sōrs/ *n.* **1.** Beginning of a brook or river. **2.** Place from which anything comes or is obtained. **3.** Person, book, statement, etc., that supplies information. [fr L *surgere* rise or surge]

- **souvenir** /sü′ və nir′/ *or* /sü′ və nir′/ *n.* Something to remind one of a place, person, or thing; keepsake; remembrance. [fr F *souvenir* memory < L *subvenire* to come up, come to mind]

- **sovereign** /sov′ rən/ *n.* Monarch; supreme ruler; king or queen. —*adj.* **1.** Greatest in importance: *of sovereign value.* **2.** Independent: *a sovereign state; a sovereign nation.* [fr OF *soverain* sovereign < L *super* over]

- **spacious** /spā′ shəs/ *adj.* Vast; having much room; extensive. [fr L *spatium* space]

- **species** /spē′ shēz/ *n.* **1.** Group of plants or animals that have certain characteristics in common. **2.** Distinct sort of kind. *pl.* **species.** [fr L *species* a sight, outward appearance, sort, fr *specere* look at]

- **stagnant** /stag′ nənt/ *adj.* **1.** Not running or flowing: *stagnant water.* **2.** Foul from standing still. **3.** Not active; sluggish; dull: *Business is stagnant during this season.* [fr L *stagnum* a piece of standing water]

- **statuette** /stach′ ū et′/ *n.* A small statue. [fr F, diminutive of *statue* statue]

- **stimulate** /stim′ ū lāt′/ *v.* **1.** Spur on; stir up: *Praise stimulated her to work harder.* **2.** Increase temporarily the functional activity (of a part of the body, etc.). **stimulated, stimulating.** [fr L *stimulus* goad]

- **stimulus** /stim′ ū ləs/ *n.* **1.** Something that stirs to action or effort: *Ambition is a stimulus to work.* **2.** Something that excites some part of the body to activity. *pl.* **stimuli** /stim′ ū lī′/. [fr L *stimulus* goad]

- **stirrup** /stèr′ əp/ *or* /stir′ əp/ *n.* **1.** Support for a rider's foot, hung from a saddle. **2.** Piece somewhat like a stirrup used as a support or clamp. [fr OE *stige* climbing + *rap* rope]

- **sufficient** /sə fish′ ənt/ *adj.* As much as is needed; enough; adequate. [fr L *sufficere* put under]

- **sulphur** /sul′ fər/ *n.* A light-yellow, nonmetallic chemical element that burns with a blue flame and a stifling odor. Also spelled **sulfur.** [fr L *sulfur, sulpur, sulphur* brimstone]

- **suppress** /sə pres′/ *v.* **1.** Put an end to; stop; put down: *suppress the rebellion.* **2.** Hold back: *suppress a yawn.* **3.** Check the flow of: *suppress the bleeding.* [fr L *sub* under + *premere* press]

- **suspicious** /səs pish′ əs/ *adj.* **1.** Causing one to suspect: *The man walked into the bank in a suspicious manner.* **2.** Feeling suspicion; suspecting: *He was always suspicious of strangers.* **3.** Showing suspicion: *She saw the suspicious glance.* [fr L *sub* under + *specere* look]

- **symphony** /sim′ fə nē/ *n.* **1.** An elaborate musical composition for an orchestra: *Mozart's Fourth Symphony was the main work on the concert program.* **2.** Harmony of sound. **3.** Harmony of colors: *The autumn leaves are a symphony in brown, red, and yellow. pl.* **symphonies.** [fr Gk *sym* together + *phone* sound]

- **synopsis** /sə nop′ sis/ *n.* A brief statement giving a general view of some subject, book, etc.; summary. *pl.* **synopses** /sə nop′ sēz′/. [fr Gk *sym* together + *opsis* a view]

- **system** /sis′ təm/ *n.* **1.** Set of things or parts making a whole. **2.** Ordered group of facts, principles, beliefs, etc.: *system of education.* **3.** Plan; scheme; method. **4.** Orderly way of getting things done. **5.** The body as a whole. [fr Gk *sym* along with + *histanai* place]

t

- **tariff** /tar′ if/ *n.* **1.** List of duties or taxes on imports and exports. **2.** System of duties or taxes on imports and exports. **3.** Any duty or tax on such a list or system: *There is a high tariff on jewelry.* **4.** A table or scale of prices. [fr Ar *tarif* information, explanation]

- **technique** /tek nēk′/ *n.* **1.** Method of performing the mechanical details of an art: *the pianist's technique; the pitcher's technique.* **2.** Special system used to accomplish something: *the teacher's technique of teaching arithmetic.* [fr F]

- **tenant** /ten′ ənt/ *n.* **1.** Person paying rent for the use of property. **2.** Person or things that occupy: *Birds are tenants of the trees.* [fr F < L *tenere* hold]

- **tense**[1] /tens/ *adj.* **1.** Stretched tight; strained to stiffness: *a tense rope.* **2.** Keyed up: *tense nerves.* —*v.* Stiffen: *He tensed his muscles for the jump.* **tensed, tensing.** [fr L *tensus,* fr *tendere* stretch]

● **tense**[2] /tens/ *n.* Form of a verb that shows the time of the action or state expressed by the verb. [fr L *tempus* time]

● **terrace** /ter' əs/ *n.* **1.** A flat, raised piece of land; a raised level. **2.** A flat roof of a house. **3.** Street along the top or side of a flat, raised piece of land. **4.** Row of houses along such a street. **5.** Mall; a strip of park in the middle of a street. —*v.* Make or form into small parklike levels. **terraced, terracing.** [fr L *terra* earth, land, country]

● **terrific** /tə rif' ik/ *adj.* **1.** Causing great fear; terrifying. **2.** *Informal.* Very great, severe, etc. [fr L *terrificus* terrific]

● **thesis** /thē' sis/ *n.* **1.** Proposition or statement to be proved or maintained against objections. **2.** Essay. *pl.* **theses** /thē' sēz'/. [fr Gk *thesis,* originally, "a setting down"]

● **threshold** /thresh' ōld/ *or* /thresh' hōld/ *n.* **1.** Piece of wood under a door. **2.** Doorway. **3.** Beginning point: *The scientist is on the threshold of a discovery.* [fr OE *threscwald* threshold]

● **tier** /tir/ *n.* One of a series of rows arranged one above another: *tiers of seats in an arena.* —*v.* Arrange in tiers. [fr F *tirer* order]

● **toboggan** /tə bog' ən/ *n.* A long, narrow flat sled without runners. —*v.* **1.** Slide downhill on a toboggan. **2.** Decline rapidly in value. [fr Canadian French *tabagane* toboggan]

● **tourist** /tùr' ist/ *n.* One who tours or travels for pleasure or culture. [fr OF *tour* lathe, circuit, turn]

● **transient** /tran' shənt/ *adj.* **1.** Passing through and not staying long: *transient guests in a hotel.* **2.** Not lasting long; fleeting: *the transient days of summer.* —*n.* Visitor who stays only a short time. [fr L *trans* through + *ire* go]

● **triumph** /trī' umf/ *n.* **1.** Victory; success. **2.** Joy because of victory or success. —*v.* **1.** Gain victory; win success: *Their team triumphed over ours again.* **2.** Rejoice because of victory or success. [fr L *triumphus* gain]

● **trophy** /trō' phē/ *n.* **1.** Memorial of victory: *The hunter kept the lion's skin as a trophy.* **2.** Prize. **3.** Anything serving as a remembrance. *pl.* **trophies.** [fr F *trophee* trophy]

● **trousseau** /trü sō'/ *or* /trü' sō/ *n.* A bride's outfit of clothes, linen, etc. *pl.* **trousseaus** /trü sōz', trü' sōz/ *or* **trousseaux** /trü sō'/. [fr F *trousseau* bundle]

● **truant** /trü' ənt/ *n.* **1.** Student who stays away from school without permission. **2.** Person who neglects duty. —*adj.* **1.** Staying away from school without permission. **2.** Guilty of neglecting duty: *The truant worker always forgot to lock his file drawer.* **3.** Lazy. **4.** Wandering. **5.** Of or having to do with a truant or truants. [fr OF *trugant* a vagrant]

● **tuxedo** /tuk sē' dō/ *n.* A man's coat for evening wear, made without tails. *pl.* **tuxedos, tuxedoes.** [Named after Tuxedo Park, New York.]

● **typhoon** /tī fün'/ *n.* **1.** Violent storm or tempest occuring in India. **2.** Violent hurricane in the West Pacific. [fr Chinese *tai fung* big wind; influenced by Gk *typhon* whirlwind]

● **tyrant** /tī' rənt/ *n.* **1.** Person who uses his power cruelly or unjustly. **2.** Cruel ruler; cruel master. [fr L *tyrannus* tyrant]

u

● **unique** /ū nēk'/ *adj.* Having no like or equal; being the only one of a kind. [fr L *unicus* sole]

● **unworthy** /un wėr' ᴛнē/ *adj.* Not worthy; not deserving; shameful. [fr L *un* not + OE *weorth* worth]

● **utter**[1] /ut' ər/ *adj.* Complete; total; absolute: *utter surprise.* [fr OE *uterra* outer]

● **utter**[2] /ut' ər/ *v.* **1.** Make known; speak: *utter your thoughts.* **2.** Give forth; give out: *utter a cry of joy.* [See **utter**[1].]

v

● **vacant** /vā' kənt/ *adj.* **1.** Not occupied: *a vacant chair.* **2.** Empty; not filled: *a vacant space.* **3.** Empty of thought or intelligence. **4.** Free from work, business, etc.: *vacant time.* [fr L *vacare* be empty]

● **vaccinate** /vak' sə nāt'/ *v.* **1.** Inoculate with cowpox vaccine to prevent smallpox. **2.** Take similar measures against other diseases. **vaccinated, vaccinating.** [fr L *vacca* cow]

● **vague** /vāg/ *adj.* Not clear, exact, definite, or distinct. [fr L *vagus* wandering]

/a/ ran /ā/ rain /ã/ care /ä/ car /e/ hen /ē/ he /ėr/ her /i/ in /ī/ ice /o/ not /ō/ no /ô/ off /u/ us /ū/ use /ü/ tool /ù/ took /ou/ cow /oi/ boy /ch/ church /hw/ when /ng/ sing /sh/ ship /ᴛн/ this /th/ thin /zh/ vision /ə/ about, taken, pencil, lemon, circus

- **vary** /vãr′ ē/ *v.* **1.** Alter or change. **2.** In music, repeat a tune or theme with variations and ornament. **3.** Differ. **4.** Give variety; make of different kinds. **varied, varying.** [fr L *variare* vary, fr *varius* various]
- **venom** /ven′ əm/ *n.* **1.** The poison of snakes, spiders, etc. **2.** Spite; malice: *Her enemies dreaded the venom of her tongue.* [fr L *venenum* poison]
- **verse** /vėrs/ *n.* **1.** Poetry. **2.** Single line of poetry. **3.** Group of lines or short portion in poetry: *the first verse of the poem.* **4.** Short division of a chapter in the Bible. [fr L *versus,* originally, "row"]
- **vertebra** /vėr′ tə brə/ *n.* One of the bones of the backbone. *pl.* **vertebras** *or* **vertebrae** /vėr′ tə brē′/. [fr L *vertere* turn]
- **veto** /vē′ tō/ *n.* **1.** Power or right to prevent action. **2.** Refusal of consent; prohibition. *pl.* **vetoes.** —*v.* **1.** Reject by a veto. **2.** Refuse to consent to: *His parents vetoed his plan to buy a bicycle.* **vetoed, vetoing.** [fr L *veto* I forbid, fr *vetare* forbid]
- **vibrate** /vī′ brāt/ *v.* **1.** Move rapidly to and fro: *The guitar strings vibrate.* **2.** Cause to swing to and fro; set in motion. **3.** Be moved; quiver. **4.** Thrill: *Their hearts vibrated with joy.* **5.** Resound. **vibrated, vibrating.** [fr L *vibrare* shake]
- **vicious** /vish′ əs/ *adj.* **1.** Wicked; evil. **2.** Having a bad disposition or bad habits; not tamed. **3.** Having faults; defective. **4.** Malicious: *The loser made a vicious attempt to ruin the celebration.* **5.** *Informal.* Unpleasantly severe. [fr L *vitiosus* wicked, fr *vitium* vice]
- **vigor** /vig′ ər/ *n.* **1.** Active strength or force. **2.** Energy or power. [fr OF *vigor* strength < L *vigere* be lively or strong]

- **villain** /vil′ ən/ *n.* **1.** A very wicked person. **2.** Playful name for a mischievous person. [fr L *villa* country house]
- **violent** /vī′ ə lənt/ *adj.* **1.** Done with strong, rough force: *a violent blow.* **2.** Caused by strong, rough force: *a violent death.* **3.** Showing very strong feeling: *violent language.* **4.** Severe; very great: *violent pain.* [fr L *violentus* force]
- **visible** /viz′ ə bəl/ *adj.* **1.** Capable of being seen. **2.** Exposed to view; apparent. [fr L *visus* seen, fr *videre* see]
- **vogue** /vōg/ *n.* **1.** The fashion: *Hoop skirts were in vogue many years ago.* **2.** Popularity: *That song once had a great vogue.* [fr F *vogue* a rowing, course, success]

w

- **weird** /wird/ *adj.* **1.** Relating to witchcraft; mysterious; unearthly. **2.** Having to do with fate or destiny. **3.** *Informal.* Odd; fantastic; queer. [fr OE *wyrd* fate]
- **wield** /wēld/ *v.* Hold and use; manage; control: *The carpenter wielded the hammer confidently.* [fr OE *wieldan* rule < L *valere* be strong]
- **wince** /wins/ *v.* Draw back suddenly; flinch slightly: *He winced at the sight of the dentist's drill.* **winced, wincing.** —*n.* Act of flinching. [fr OF *guencir* wince]

y

- **yield** /yēld/ *v.* **1.** Produce. **2.** Grant; give. **3.** Give up; surrender. **4.** Give away. **5.** Give place. —*n.* Amount yielded. [fr OE *gieldan* pay, give, make an offering]